THE ESSENCE OF

COMPILERS

THE ESSENCE OF COMPUTING SERIES

Published titles

The Essence of Artificial Intelligence
The Essence of Databases
The Essence of Discrete Mathematics
The Essence of Human-Computer Interaction
The Essence of Logic
The Essence of Program Design
The Essence of Professional Issues in Computing
The Essence of Programming Using C++
The Essence of Systems Analysis and Design

Forthcoming titles

The Essence of Z

THE ESSENCE OF

COMPILERS

Robin Hunter

Prentice Hall

LONDON NEW YORK TORONTO SYDNEY TOKYO
SINGAPORE MADRID MEXICO CITY MUNICH

First published 1999 by
Prentice Hall Europe
Campus 400, Maylands Avenue
Hemel Hempstead
Hertfordshire, HP2 7EZ
A division of
Simon & Schuster International Group

Typeset in 10 on 12 pt Times
by Mathematical Composition Setters Ltd, Salisbury

Printed and bound in Great Britain by
Biddles Ltd, Guildford and King's Lynn

Library of Congress Cataloging-in-Publication Data

Available from the publisher

British Library Cataloguing in Publication Data

A catalogue record for this book is available from
the British Library

ISBN 0–13–727835–7

1 2 3 4 5   03 02 01 00 99

Contents

Preface

The study of compilers is a central aspect of computer science and, to some at least, one of the most satisfying. Compiler writing requires knowledge of both source language and object machine, and provides the link between the two. It is, nowadays, well supported by tools, relieving the compiler writer of many of the tedious and error-prone aspects of producing compilers.

My first acquaintance with compilers was through attending a course by Peter Naur, originator of the early ALGOL 60 compilers, at the University of Newcastle upon Tyne in 1967, and this was followed by another memorable experience when I was privileged to attend an Advanced Course in Compiler Construction in the Technical University of Munich (in F.L. Bauer's Department) in 1974. I have been involved with compilers and related tools, on and off, ever since.

Much of the theory and many of the methods used in compiler construction have been around since the 1970s and, in some cases, even earlier. However, developments in programming languages have presented a constant challenge to compiler writers, from the definition of ALGOL 60, which led to the early work of Naur in Denmark and Randell and Russell in the UK, to the more recent demands of Ada and object oriented languages. To come right up to date, the requirements of Java for security over networks as well as for efficiency and portability, have presented compiler writers with new challenges. The emergence of the Java Virtual Machine has, at the same time, provided an excellent example of an intermediate language to illustrate aspects of code generation and storage allocation.

A constant theme throughout these developments has been the issue of tool support. Compiler construction is at the same time creative and mundane, and requires good tool support. Many compiler development tool kits are available, some free of charge over the Internet, but by far the most used, and most popular, set of tools are the Unix tools Lex and YACC, now available on other platforms as well. There are also free versions of Lex and YACC, known as Flex and Bison, available over the Internet. Originally C-based, turbo Pascal versions of the tools can now also be obtained.

Many compiler texts describe Lex and YACC and give examples of their use, but very few include enough information about the tools to allow the reader to make use of them to solve their own problems. One of the aims of this book, from the start, was to provide comprehensive (though not complete, given the space available) coverage of Lex and YACC, and their use is illustrated, not only through examples concerned with compiler construction, but also through examples concerned with other syntax-directed tools, such as simple measurement tools to evaluate source-code metrics.

The use of Lex and YACC suggests the use of C as the main language in which to express the various algorithms described in the book. Also, since the book is primarily about the compilation of imperative languages, C is also assumed to be the source language in many of the examples describing aspects of compilation. However, many of the language features whose compilation we wish to discuss are not relevant to C, and other languages such as FORTRAN, Pascal, Ada, ALGOL 68, C++ and Java are used to illustrate particular points, as appropriate.

The first part of the book is about the analysis stage of compilation and, after an introduction to the compilation process (chapter 1), there are chapters on language definition, lexical analysis, top-down parsing, bottom-up parsing and semantic analysis (chapters 2–6). The shorter second part of the book, on the synthesis stage of compilation, consists of two chapters: one on storage allocation and one on code generation (chapters 7 and 8). Each chapter has a set of exercises associated with it, to which solutions are provided, and some further reading and bibliographical notes. A glossary provides, in a single place, definitions of most of the technical terms used.

The book is intended to support a one-semester course on compilers and related tools, and the material in it is used as such in the University of Strathclyde. The course at Strathclyde also has a practical aspect in which students undertake simple programming exercises using Lex and YACC. As with other texts in the Essence Series, the book aims to bring out all the essential aspects of the compilation process without attempting in any way to provide comprehensive coverage of the area.

Acknowledgements

It is a pleasure to acknowledge the help and support of Prentice Hall in producing this book; for persuading me to write it in the first place and for encouraging and supporting me throughout its production. I have to thank Boris Cogan and Tamara Matveeva for their helpful comments on the manuscript. I also have to thank my wife Kate for her encouragement and forbearance throughout, as well as for proof checking the entire manuscript, which she so willingly performed. Thanks also to the publisher's reviewers and the series editor, Ray Welland, for their constructive comments at various stages of the work.

Robin Hunter
Glasgow
May 1998

CHAPTER 1

The compilation process

1.1 **Introduction**

In this chapter we introduce the idea of a language compiler, its function, its structure, and how it is produced. In particular we will:

- discuss the relationship between the various languages involved in a typical compiler;
- explain how a compiler is typically structured;
- describe the functions of the main phases of compilation;
- discuss the design aims of typical compiler projects;
- explain the role of tools in compiler development and discuss the extent to which compiler development may be automated.

1.2 **Basic ideas**

Software may be written in a wide variety of languages: traditional imperative languages such as COBOL, FORTRAN, Pascal or C; object oriented languages such as C++, Smalltalk or Java; functional or logical languages such as LISP or Prolog; fourth generation languages or visual languages such as Visual C++, Visual BASIC or Delphi. The function of compilers is to transform these user-oriented representations of the software into machine-oriented representations for their eventual execution on an actual computer. Compilers are basically sophisticated text processing systems and have much in common with other tools that process text written either in programming or natural languages. The text that they process may be produced manually, as in the case of conventional languages, or semi-automatically, as in the case of Visual or fourth generation languages.

The task of the compiler is usually thought of as consisting of two *stages*:

1. The *analysis stage* in which the input text is analysed.
2. The *synthesis stage* during which the machine-oriented representation is generated.

The input to the analysis stage is referred to as *source text* or *source code*, and the output from the synthesis stage as *object text* or *object code*. The transformation of source code to object code is usually referred to as the *compilation process* and is the process performed by the compiler. A language compiler may also be referred to as an *implementation* of the language. The object code produced by a compiler may be in the form of machine code for some machine (computer) or assembly code, or possibly some intermediate code, to be further transformed (by other tools) into assembly code or machine code for some machine. Alternatively, the intermediate code may be directly executed by means of an *interpreter*.

This text is principally about the compilation process, but the opportunity will be taken to discuss other applications of textual analysis as well. As far as compilation is concerned, we will spend more time on analysis than on synthesis, because of the greater generality and applicability of the ideas involved in the analysis stage of compilation, compared with the relatively *ad hoc* and machine-dependent issues involved in synthesis.

Compiler technology has advanced considerably since the early days of computers and it is now possible to automate the production of compilers to a large extent using widely available tools to produce analysers, at least, though the automatic production of code generators is less well advanced. A common theme in the chapters to come will be the extent to which compiler production can be automated, and we will make considerable use of the analyser generator tools Lex and YACC.

Since the language normally used to implement compilers using Lex and YACC is C, we will normally think of C as the *implementation language* (the language in which the compiler is written) and describe algorithms in C. In order to avoid having to switch from one language to another too often, we will also tend to think of the language being implemented as C. However, we will also use other languages to illustrate specific points, as appropriate.

1.3 **The compilation process**

The compilation process is essentially a transformation from one language to another, from the *source code* in which the programmer writes, or is generated automatically from some higher-level representation, to the *object code*, which is executed on the machine, possibly after some further transformation. The situation is shown diagrammatically in Figure 1.1.

As has been mentioned, the compiler will also involve a third language, the *implementation* language. This may be the same language as the source code or the object code, but need not be. If possible, the compiler should be

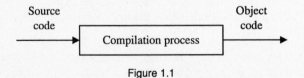

Figure 1.1

written in a language that is good for writing compilers in, either because of the language's intrinsic merits, such as lack of error-proneness, or its availability and compatibility with development tools.

It is convenient, as we will see, to represent the three languages involved in an implementation, by means of a T-diagram showing each of the languages in a different arm of the T. Figure 1.2 represents a compiler that is written in C and translates Java into Bytecode (the language interpreted by the Java Virtual Machine).

Figure 1.3, on the other hand, represents a Pascal compiler written in M-code and producing M-code. This example illustrates the fact that an operational compiler will normally be written in, and produce code for, the machine on which it will run. In some circumstances, however, a piece of software, perhaps for an embedded system, will be compiled on a different machine from the one on which it is intended to run. In this case there are two machine codes involved, the one for the machine on which the compiler is run (the language in which the compiler will be written), and the one for the machine on which the software will run (the language which will be generated by the compiler). For example, Figure 1.4 might represent the compiler used for compiling software for embedded systems.

While an executable compiler has to be in the code of the machine on which it is being run, this code will very often not be a suitable one for compiler writing, since it is likely to be at a very low level. The normal way to obtain a program in a low-level language, of course, is to compile it from a high-level language, and compilers themselves are usually written in high-level languages, and then

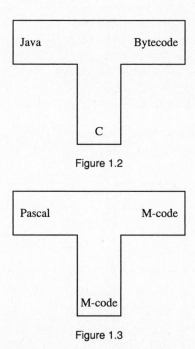

Figure 1.2

Figure 1.3

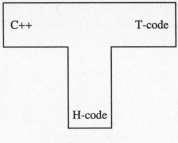

Figure 1.4

compiled by means of a pre-existing compiler in to their executable form. Here we have an example of a compiler, the pre-existing one, having compilers both as its input and its output. This can be represented by three adjacent T-diagrams, as shown in Figure 1.5.

The top left compiler is the compiler as it was originally written in its own language, C++, and the top right compiler is the executable compiler, obtained after it has been compiled by the bottom compiler. T-diagrams may be joined together in this way to show how one compiler may be obtained from another, as long as certain consistency rules are observed. For example, the two languages in the corresponding top two positions in the uppermost compilers must be the same, and the two adjacent occurrences of C++ and M-code must each refer to the same language. The bottom occurrence of M-code could in fact be any language, but would dictate the machine on which the compiler is compiled.

T-diagrams may be used to illustrate how a compiler may be ported from one machine to another. Given a compiler that runs on machine A, the implementation language at least will need to be changed in order for it to run on machine B. Rather than attempting to translate the machine code of one machine into the machine code of another, it will probably be simpler to go back to the original version of the compiler written in a high-level language and compile this into machine code for B.

In many cases it will also be necessary to change the code output by the compiler – presumably to be the code of machine B. This is another matter, and

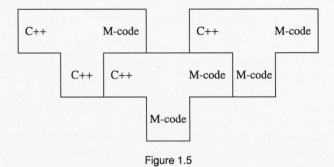

Figure 1.5

may or may not be simple, depending, among other things, on how self-contained the code production aspects of the compiler are.

1.4 **Stages, phases and passes**

A well-written compiler is highly modular in design, and should present a good example of a well-structured program. Logically, the compilation process is divided into *stages*, which are in turn divided into *phases*. Physically, the compiler is divided into *passes*. We will describe these terms in more detail.

As we have seen, the principal (and often the only) stages that are represented in a compiler are *analysis*, in which the source code is analysed to determine its structure and meaning, and *synthesis* in which the object code is built or synthesised. In addition, however, there may be a pre-processor stage in which source files are included, macros expanded and so on. This stage is usually fairly straightforward and is mainly relevant to the languages C and C++. We will not consider it in detail.

Figure 1.6 shows the typical phases of the compilation process.

The analysis stage is usually assumed to consist of three distinct phases:

1. Lexical analysis.
2. Syntax analysis.
3. Semantic analysis.

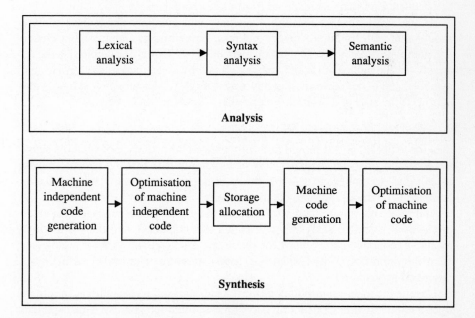

Figure 1.6

The synthesis stage consists of some or all of:

- machine independent code generation;
- optimisation of machine independent code;
- storage allocation;
- machine code generation;
- optimisation of machine code.

Lexical analysis is a relatively simple phase in which the *symbols* (or *tokens*) of the language are formed. It is convenient to think of language words such as

```
for     do     while
```

and user-defined identifiers such as

```
name     salary
```

as well as certain sequences of characters such as

```
++     ==
```

as single symbols, as far as the later phases of analysis are concerned. It is the role of the lexical analysis phase or the *lexical analyser*, as it is otherwise known, to read sequences of characters and to replace them by language symbols for input to the syntax and semantic analysers. In so doing the lexical analyser mimics what the human reader would do in reading a piece of program. After all, the human reader would not be expected to see the program as a sequence of characters, but as a sequence of symbols made up from these characters.

At the same time as forming characters into symbols the lexical analyser should deal with (multiple) spaces and remove comments and any other characters not relevant to the later stages of analysis. It is important to emphasise the relatively simple nature of lexical analysis. It is *only* concerned in the formation of symbols, and is not concerned in any way with the order in which symbols may appear. If the start of a program, supposed to be written in C, was

```
; number int return do == ++
```

then the lexical analyser should faithfully pass on the sequence of symbols shown to the syntax analyser. Another way of looking at it is that the lexical analyser usually has no context to work with. As it is processing one symbol it has no knowledge of any of the symbols that preceded or will follow this symbol.

The relatively simple and well-defined nature of lexical analysis makes the production of lexical analysers well suited to automation, and there are widely available tools that can be used for producing a lexical analyser for a language, from the definition of its lexical (i.e. local) structure. The use of such tools is described in chapter 3.

Despite the relative simplicity of the lexical analyser, its execution can turn out to be a relatively time-consuming part of the compilation process. This is perhaps not as surprising as it may seem at first, when account is taken of the fact that lexical analysis is the only phase of compilation that deals with characters, of which there are relatively many, rather than symbols, of which there are relatively few. Indeed if, for some compiler, lexical analysis did not account for a large proportion of the compilation time, one might begin to ask questions concerning the efficiency of the other phases of the process!

Syntax analysis is the phase in which the overall structure of a program is identified, and involves an understanding of the order in which the symbols in a program may appear. This implies that the *syntax analyser* or *parser* (as it is sometimes called) needs to know something about the context in which it is operating, in terms of symbols that have been already read. The output from the parser is often a tree-like structure representing the program known as the *syntax tree*. For example, an expression such as

$$(a + b) * (c + d)$$

occurring in a program might be represented as shown in Figure 1.7.

This representation is known as the *abstract syntax tree*. Notice that there is no need to show the brackets in the original expression since the structuring implied by the brackets is represented in the tree structure. Complete programs can be represented by abstract syntax trees in this way.

As the syntax analyser reads the symbols in a program from left to right (normally) it should be capable of indicating whether the sequence of symbols read so far is the start of some program in the compiler source language, or not. For example, the first ten symbols in the input stream may be the start of some program, though the first eleven may not be. What the syntax analyser should do then depends on what type of *error recovery* is to be performed. At the very least, it should point to symbol number eleven, and indicate that at this point the input then becomes invalid. Many compilers do more than this and give some

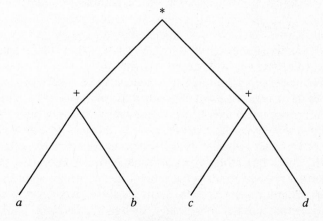

Figure 1.7

(supposedly helpful) message such as:

```
semi-colon missing?
```

though occasionally such messages may be more confusing than helpful!

The fact that the input becomes invalid at the eleventh symbol may well be due to the fact that the eleventh symbol is incorrect in some sense. However, it is also possible that the situation could arise from some earlier error on the part of the programmer, and this is one reason why compiler diagnostics are often unhelpful. This does not mean that compilers are liable to indicate faults when none exists, just that the apparent position of the fault may be in error, and the error message may be misleading. The production of good error diagnostics and error recovery strategies, important as it undoubtedly is, is not covered in detail in the text as it seemed more appropriate to give greater priority to more central issues in an Essence Series text.

Syntax analysers to check the syntax of the input can usually be built from a definition of the language being implemented automatically (by using tools), though code will normally have to be written to form the abstract syntax tree. The use of such tools is discussed in chapters 4 and 5.

Syntax analysis is not only the key phase of the analysis stage of compilation but provides the framework for the compiler as a whole. It drives the lexical analysis phase and builds the structure upon which semantic analysis is performed. It is by traversing this same structure that code is generated during the synthesis stage. Syntax analysis also provides a framework for a whole range of source code analysis tools, including measuring tools of various sorts, cross-referencers, layout tools and so on. All these types of analysis are examples of *static analysis*, analysis that can be performed on source code without executing it. Code analysis, which is dependent on code execution, is referred to as *dynamic analysis*.

Methods of syntax analysis have, not surprisingly, been the subject of extensive study. Some methods are more general than others, in that they can be applied to a wider class of languages; some are more easily automated than others, and some are more efficient than others. We will describe two of the principal methods in chapters 4 and 5, one of which (*recursive descent*) is very intuitive and easy to code, and the other of which (*SLR(1) parsing*) is readily automated and applicable to an extremely wide range of languages.

Some features of programming languages cannot be checked in a single left to right scan of the source code without setting up arbitrary sized tables, to provide access to information that may be an arbitrary distance away (in terms of source code symbols) when it is required. For example, information concerning the type and scope of variables falls into this category. As far as the compilation process is concerned, checking of these types of features, which are usually referred to as *static semantics*, is *not* normally performed in the syntax analysis phase, but in a separate *semantic analysis* phase. Thus the parser, as such, will normally not notice if types are used inconsistently, though this will be checked by the semantic analysis phase.

Semantic analysis is usually performed by code actions called by the parser to set up and access appropriate tables. The fact that semantic analysis may not be performed automatically by the parser has the advantage that static semantic program errors (such as the inconsistent use of types) should have clear diagnostics associated with them, and should be relatively easy to recover from.

As has been seen, the *synthesis stage* of compilation consists of the following main phases:

- Machine independent code generation.
- Optimisation of machine independent code.
- Storage allocation.
- Machine code generation.
- Optimisation of machine code.

Some of the phases may be absent in particular cases. For example, if a compiler compiles directly to machine code, the first two phases would be missing. Code optimisation may occur at the machine independent code level, the machine code level, at both levels, or at neither level. Storage allocation is a key phase that is driven by one of the code generation phases.

There are good reasons for producing machine independent code in the first instance. It provides an aid to portability (of the compiler) and serves to separate the language dependencies and the machine dependencies in the compiler. Many compilers produce some type of intermediate code, which may be source language independent, machine independent or even independent of both the source language and the machine.

Considerable research has gone into the definition of a so-called Universal Intermediate Language (UIL), suitable to be used as an intermediate language for compiling all, or at least a wide range of, languages on to all machines, but this desirable goal has proved elusive. However, there do exist well-established intermediate languages for compiling particular source languages, such as P-code for Pascal, Diana for Ada and Bytecode for Java, and there also exist intermediate languages for compiling on to particular machines, such as CTL for the Manchester MU5 machine. If a suitable UIL was available, the problem of implementing m languages on n machines would consist of producing m *front ends*, each consisting of an analyser for one of the m languages and a UIL generator, together with n *back ends* each consisting of a translator from UIL to one of the machine languages. The idea is illustrated in Figure 1.8. On the other hand, to implement each compiler independently would require the construction of $m * n$ pieces of software, one for mapping *each* language on to *each* machine.

One of the difficulties of finding a suitable UIL is of designing it at the right level. It is liable to be at too high a level for some of the languages or at too low a level for some of the machines. Nonetheless, there are a number of examples of families of compilers written for the same language and operating on several machines and equally for a number of languages implemented on the same machine.

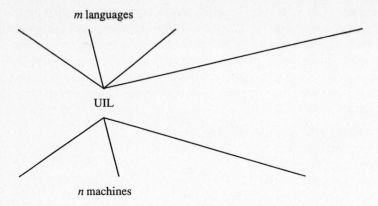

m languages

UIL

n machines

Figure 1.8

As far as code optimisation is concerned, the need for it is varied. If very efficient code is required, then extensive optimisation will be performed by the compiler. However, in many environments, the execution speed of the software is not critical and little optimisation will be required. It turns out that some optimisations are cheap to perform and are often included in compilers, whereas others, especially global as opposed to local forms of optimisation, are expensive in terms of both time and space at compile time, and are rarely performed. Many compilers provide a flag that the user can use to indicate whether extensive (and expensive) optimisation should be performed or not.

Every constant and variable appearing in the program must have storage space allocated for its value during the *storage allocation* phase. This storage space may be one of the following types:

- *Static storage* if its lifetime is the lifetime of the program and the space for its value once allocated cannot later be released.
- *Dynamic storage* if its lifetime is a particular block or function or procedure in which it is allocated so that it may be released when the block or function or procedure in which it is allocated is left.
- *Global storage* if its lifetime is unknown at compile time and it has to be allocated and deallocated at run time. The efficient control of such storage usually implies run-time overheads.

After space is allocated by the storage allocation phase, an *address*, containing as much as is known about its location at compile time, is passed to the code generator for its use.

The synthesis stage of compilation, unlike the analysis stage, is not so well suited to automation, and tools to support its production are not so widely available. The early idea of a *compiler-compiler*, a piece of software whose input was the specification of a language and a machine, and whose output was an implementation of the language on the machine, has been largely realised for the analysis stage of compilation, but only to a lesser extent for the synthesis stage.

While in logical terms a compiler is thought of as consisting of *stages* and *phases*, physically it is made up of *passes*. The compiler has one pass for each time the source code, or a representation of it, is read. Many compilers have just a *single pass* so that the complete compilation process is performed while the code is read once. The various phases described will therefore be executed in parallel, as indeed is often the most convenient arrangement, obviating the need for complex communication between the passes. Early compilers such as the Gier ALGOL 60 developed in Copenhagen had a large number of passes, typically seven or eight, because of the limited memory space available on the machines at the time. Most modern compilers are single pass since memory space is not usually a problem, and most languages can be compiled in a single pass. Some languages, such as ALGOL 68, however, are not capable of being compiled in a single pass and require multiple pass compilers. This is because information required by a particular phase is not available at the point in the source code at which it is used. A multiple pass compiler could well be described as a compiler with a number of preliminary passes to collect information and store it in tables, for use by the main analysis and synthesis pass.

1.5 Integrated Development Environments

Nowadays compilers are less likely to be used as stand-alone tools than to be part of *integrated development environments* (*IDEs*) sometimes known as programming environments. As well as providing compilation facilities, a modern IDE will provide facilities for language oriented editing, debugging, run-time profiling, configuration management, etc. A good example of such an environment is the Borland IDE for C/C++ which provides, in a Windows environment, facilities for each of the following, arranged in distinct menus, as well as a range of other facilities:

- *Editing* with facilities for *cutting*, *pasting*, *undoing*, etc.
- *Searching* with facilities for searching for text, replacing text and locating functions during debugging.
- *Viewing* the various windows containing diagnostic and other information associated with the current project, including information on the calling hierarchy, positions of break points, contents of registers, positions of variables, use of classes and other such information.
- *Project management* including setting up new projects, compiling and linking project components together with controlling separate compilation facilities and *make* files.
- *Debugging* for running programs in normal or debugging modes with

facilities for stepping through code, setting break points, keeping track of the values of expressions, viewing symbol tables, etc.
- *Running* tools associated with the IDE.

The Borland Pascal IDE for windows provides a similar interface, thus making it easy to transfer from one language to the other. The detailed discussion of IDEs, as such, is beyond the scope of this text but we may from time to time mention some of the tools of which they are composed.

1.6 Compiler design

The overall structure of the compiler to a large extent follows from its phase structure, and the structure of its parser. The parser in turn provides a framework for most of the phases and its structure reflects the properties of the source language. The design of the compiler is also likely to be affected by non-functional requirements such as:

- efficient compilation;
- minimal compiler size;
- minimal size of object code;
- production of efficient object code;
- ease of portability;
- ease of maintenance;
- optimal usability including good error diagnostics and error recovery.

It is not usually possible to satisfy all of these desirable aims simultaneously, and priorities have to be set. For example, ease of portability and ease of maintenance may not be consistent with a minimal sized compiler, and the production of efficient object code may not go with efficient compilation.

In a teaching environment, efficient compilation and good diagnostics may be more important than the production of efficient object code, while for embedded systems the size and efficiency of the object code may be all-important. Many compilers have flags that can be set or unset to determine the mode in which the compiler should operate with respect to possible optimisations, performing run-time checks, etc.

1.7 Use of tools

The two main types of tools used in compiler production are

- a *lexical analyser generator*;
- a *syntax analyser generator* (or parser generator).

A lexical analyser generator takes as its input the lexical structure of a language, which defines how its tokens are made up from characters, and produces as output a lexical analyser (a program in C for example) for the language. This is illustrated in Figure 1.9.

A syntax analyser generator takes as its input the syntactical definition of a language, and produces as output a syntax analyser (a program in C for example) for the language. This is illustrated in Figure 1.10.

Parser generators have been developed which support most popular parsing methods, but probably the most widely known is the Unix-based YACC, which is

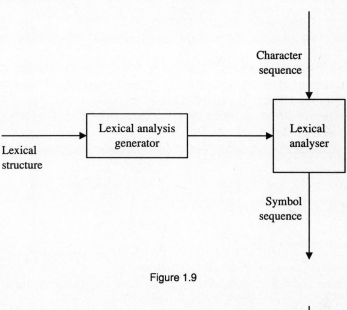

Figure 1.9

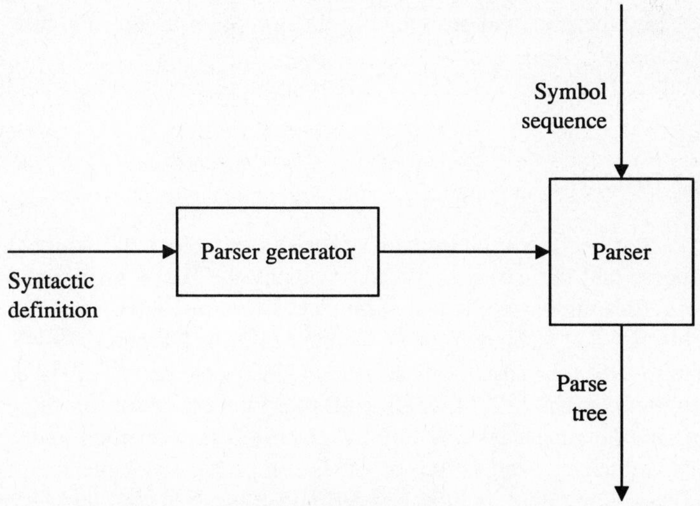

Figure 1.10

normally used in conjunction with the Unix lexical analyser generator Lex. YACC (Yet Another Compiler-Compiler) supports a fairly general type of bottom-up parsing method and allows for the insertion of compiler actions written in C, as well as producing its output in C. It has a close relative, Bison, which is in the public domain and there is also a public domain version of Lex, known as Flex. Object oriented versions of Lex and YACC, Lex ++ and YACC ++ are also available and have actions written in C++. There are a number of reasons for advocating the use of well-established tools in compiler construction including:

- ease of effort in producing the compiler;
- greater confidence in the reliability of the compiler, based on confidence in the tools;
- ease of compiler maintenance, owing in part to understandability of the compiler;
- compatibility within a range of compilers;
- provision of a framework for the complete compilation process, including code generation;
- the possibility of different types of analysis being integrated in to the same tool.

1.8 Summary

In this chapter we have:

- introduced the basic ideas of compilation;
- explained how a compiler is composed of *stages*, *phases* and *passes*;
- described the purposes of the main components;
- discussed the principal design aims of a compiler project, and how they may conflict;
- introduced Lex and YACC as examples of compiler development tools.

Further reading

There are a number of good introductory books available that describe the compilation process and the issues involved. Probably the best known and one of the most useful (despite its age) is Aho, Sethi and Ullman (1985). More recent books include Fischer and Leblanc (1988), Bennett (1990), Ullmann (1994), Wilhelm and Maurer (1995), Loudon (1997), Appel (1997) and Terry (1997). In addition the monograph, Wirth (1996), deals with more general issues in the context of compiling the language Oberon; and Diller (1988) is concerned with compiling functional languages. Watt (1993) provides comprehensive coverage of the area. Early texts on compilers include Randell and Russell (1964) and Gries (1971). The work of Naur on the early ALGOL 60 compilers is described in Naur (1964).

The only text wholly devoted to Lex and YACC is Levine, Mason and Brown (1992). Copies of the public domain versions of Lex and YACC (Flex and Bison) can be obtained through consulting the GNU internet site

```
http://www.gnu.ai.mit.edu/home.html
```

or (for higher educational establishments in the UK)

```
http://micros.hensa.ac.uk/
```

Exercises

1.1 Enumerate the compatibility rules for joining T-diagrams.

1.2 The same identifier x is used to represent two distinct variables in a C program. Would you expect a lexical analyser to distinguish between the two variables? Give a reason for your answer.

1.3 Show an abstract syntax tree for an assignment statement.

1.4 Suggest three ways of measuring the size of a program written in a high-level language.

1.5 In which phase of the compilation process would you expect the type of a literal to be recognised?

1.6 In which phase of the compilation process would you expect type incompatibilities to be identified?

1.7 Which type of variable storage is not well suited to a stack-based approach?

1.8 Suggest aims for a compiler project, other than those mentioned in the chapter.

1.9 Suggest a quantitative definition of compiler reliability.

1.10 Give arguments for and against C as an implementation language.

CHAPTER 2

Language definition

2.1 **Introduction**

In this chapter we introduce methods of defining languages, in general, and programming languages, in particular. As well as defining the strings that constitute a language, we will also be concerned with the meanings of these strings. This will lead us to the consideration of the fundamental problem of the analysis stage of compilation, the *parsing problem*. In this chapter we will:

- introduce methods of defining infinite sets of strings;
- introduce the notion of a grammar for defining programming languages;
- define a hierarchy of grammars, based on their expressive power;
- illustrate how sentences of a language may be derived from a grammar for the language;
- introduce ambiguous grammars;
- introduce the so-called parsing problem – how to find a derivation of a sentence from a grammar;
- introduce methods of defining programming language semantics.

2.2 **Defining the syntax**

A compiler is expected to produce correct object code for all input in the source language for which it was designed, and one or more error messages, for any other (invalid) input. Checking the validity of the input requires a definition of the language in which the source code is written that is

- precise (or formal);
- concise – so as not to make the compiler too large;
- machine readable.

Language textbooks are usually not precise or concise enough for the purpose and a language Standard, if available, is usually more suitable. Use of a Standard should also ensure compatibility with other compilers for the language.

The definition of a language should define all those strings of symbols that belong to the language (its *syntax*) together with the meanings, or intended effects, of those strings (its *semantics*). If a language only contained a finite number of strings this would be straightforward, though possibly tedious, since all the strings in the language could be listed. However, since *all* languages of interest contain an infinite number of strings, some means of representing an infinite number of strings in a finite manner is required.

First we look at some very simple languages, and show a simple method of representing the infinite number of strings of symbols that the language contains. For example, the language consisting of all strings containing an arbitrary number of xs could be expressed using set notation as

$$\{x^n \mid n > 0\}$$

where the '|' may be read as 'where', n is an integer and multiplication is to be interpreted as concatenation.

Another example of a language would be

$$\{x^n y^n \mid n > 0\}$$

where the language consists of all strings containing at least one x followed by the same number of ys. For example, the following strings would be in the language

xy
xxxyyy
xxxxxxxxyyyyyyyy

On the other hand

$$\{x^m y^n \mid m, n > 0\}$$

would represent the language consisting of strings with at least one x at the start followed by at least one y, where the number of xs is not necessarily the same as the number of ys. If, however, the definition had been

$$\{x^m y^n \mid m, n \geq 0\}$$

then the strings

xxx   *(zero ys)*

and

yyyyyyy   *(zero xs)*

would also be in the language, as would

ε

the empty string containing zero *x*s and zero *y*s. We will see, as we go along, that the empty string has an important part to play in the definition of programming languages.

The above language could also be defined as a *regular expression* as follows:

x*y*

where the * (sometimes referred to as the *Kleene star*) denotes zero or more occurrences of that which precedes it. If each string in the language was required to include at least one *x* and at least one *y* then the language could be defined as

xx*yy*

or, alternatively,

x⁺*y*⁺

where the plus means *one* or more occurrences of that which precedes it. Alternation is also possible in regular expressions using the '|' pronounced 'or' in this context. Thus

x* | *y**

denotes the language consisting of zero or more *x*s *or* zero or more *y*s, whereas

(a | b)*

denotes the language consisting of zero or more *a*s or *b*s, or put another way, any string in the language consists of zero or more characters, *each* of which may be either an *a* or a *b*. The brackets are required in this instance to override the relative precedences of the operators * and |, * having higher precedence (i.e. it binds more closely) than |. So the language

a | b*

would contain *only* the strings consisting of a single *a* or zero or more *b*s. Another example of *a* regular expression is

(aab | ab)*

which contains the following strings, among others:

ε
aababaab
ababab
aabaabaabab

The regular expression

(aab | ab)*

illustrates the three operators used in regular expressions, which are

*

concatenate (represented by juxtaposition)

|

in decreasing order of precedence.

In order to define the notion of a regular expression more formally, we first define the notion of an *alphabet*. An alphabet is a finite set of symbols. Examples are

{0, 1}
{α..ω}
{0..9}

If A is an alphabet then the following are regular expressions:

- the empty string denoted by ε;
- any element of A.

Also, if P and Q are regular expressions then so are

PQ	(*P* followed by *Q*)
P|Q	(*P* or *Q*)
P*	(zero or more occurrences of *P*)

introducing the three operators associated with regular expressions. Notice that the + introduced earlier, meaning *one or more occurrences of*, is not strictly a regular expression operator, since it is not required in order to define any regular expression. This is because any expression involving + can be replaced by an equivalent expression using concatenation and the * operator. For example,

(abc)⁺

is equivalent to

(abc)(abc)*

However, since the inclusion of the + operator does not increase the power of the notation in any way, it is often used as if it were a regular expression operator.

As we will see, regular expressions are not very useful for defining complete programming languages, but are often used to define the symbols of a programming language in terms of the characters of which they consist. For example, an identifier in many languages can be represented by the following regular expression

l(l| d)*

where *l* denotes a letter and *d* denotes a digit, while a fixed-point number might be represented by

(d*d.d*)| (d*.dd*)

where *d* represents a digit. Notice that the definition requires a digit *before* or *after* the point.

One of the languages defined earlier in this section

$\{x^n y^n \mid n > 0\}$

cannot be defined by a regular expression since there is no way of specifying, in a regular expression, that the number of *x*s must be the same as the number of *y*s. We need some more powerful mechanism to define this, apparently simple, language. One method is to use *productions* such as

$S \rightarrow xSy$
$S \rightarrow xy$

in which the '$\rightarrow$' is pronounced 'derives' and the productions can be used to generate strings of a language as follows

1. Start with the symbol *S* and replace it with a string on the right of one of the productions.
2. If the string produced no longer contains *S* then it is a string in the language. Otherwise replace *S* in the string using a production and repeat 2.

For example the sequence of strings might be

S
xSy

xxSyy
xxxyyy

which is usually written

$$S \Rightarrow xSy \Rightarrow xxSyy \Rightarrow xxxyyy$$

where '$\Rightarrow$' also is pronounced 'derives' (but used in a different context to $\rightarrow$, which only appears in grammars). The sequence of steps involved in generating a string using the productions of a grammar is referred to as a *derivation* of the string.

It is clear that all strings in the language

$$\{x^n y^n \mid n > 0\}$$

may be generated in this way and, just as important, no other strings can be generated in this way.

We are now ready to define the notion of grammar based on the idea of productions that we have just described.

2.3 Grammars

A grammar is defined to be a quadruple

$$(V_T, V_N, P, S)$$

where

V_T is an alphabet whose symbols are known as *terminal symbols* (or *terminals*),
V_N is an alphabet known as *nonterminal symbols* (or *nonterminals*),
V_T and V_N have no symbols in common (i.e. $V_T \cap V_N = \varnothing$)
(V is defined to be $V_T \cup V_N$),
P is a set of *productions* (or *rules*), each element of which consists of a pair (α, β), where α is known as the left side of the production, β is known as the right side of the production, and a production is written as

$$\alpha \rightarrow \beta$$

where α is in V^+ (strings of one or more symbols of V) and β is in V^* (strings of zero or more symbols of V). S is a member of V_N and is known as the *sentence symbol* (or *axiom*) of the grammar and is the starting point in the generation of any string in the language.

A grammar is used to generate sequences of symbols that make up the strings of a language by starting with the sentence symbol and successively replacing it, or a nonterminal in a string derived from it, using one of the productions of the grammar. At each stage, a production with the nonterminal to be replaced on its left side, is applied by replacing the nonterminal by the sequence of symbols comprising the right side of the production. The process terminates when a string of terminal symbols (i.e. containing no nonterminals) has been generated. Any string of symbols that can be generated in this way (and no other string) is said to belong to the language generated by the grammar.

For example, a grammar generating the language

$$\{x^n y^n \mid n > 0\}$$

would then be G_1 where

$$G_1 = (\{x, y\}, \{S\}, P, S)$$

where

$$P = \{S \rightarrow xSy, S \rightarrow xy\}$$

while a grammar generating

$$\{x^m y^n \mid m, n \geqslant 0\}$$

would be G_2 where

$$G_2 = (\{x, y\}, \{S, B\}, P, S)$$

and P is the set of productions

$$S \rightarrow xS$$
$$S \rightarrow yB$$
$$S \rightarrow x$$
$$S \rightarrow y$$
$$B \rightarrow yB$$
$$B \rightarrow y$$

together with

$$S \rightarrow \varepsilon$$

since the empty string is in the language.

The string

$$xxyyy$$

would be generated as follows

$$S \Rightarrow xS \Rightarrow xxS \Rightarrow xxyB \Rightarrow xxyyB \Rightarrow xxyyy$$

Each of the strings involved in the derivation is known as a *sentential form* and the last string (containing only terminals) is known as a *sentence* of the language. The use of the symbol '$\Rightarrow$' between two sentential forms implies that the string on the right is derived from the string on the left by applying a single production. However we may also write

$$S \overset{*}{\Rightarrow} xyyy$$

meaning that *xyyy* can be derived from S by zero or more applications of productions, or

$$S \overset{+}{\Rightarrow} xxyyy$$

meaning that *xxyyy* can be derived from S by one or more applications of productions.

One further convention, instead of writing

$$B \rightarrow yB$$
$$B \rightarrow y$$

this may be shortened to

$$B \rightarrow yB \,|\, y$$

the '|' symbol again being pronounced 'or'.

As in the above examples, we will normally use lower case letters (or sometimes complete words in lower case letters) to denote terminals in a grammar and upper case letters (or sometimes complete words in upper case letters) to denote nonterminals. The sentence symbol need not be represented by the letter S, but often will be. Greek letters will often be used to stand for strings of terminals and/or nonterminals. We will indicate if we depart from these conventions on any occasions.

Notice that there is normally no unique grammar for generating a particular language. At a trivial level, any nonterminal could be replaced by another symbol, not already used. More significantly the form and number of the productions can also often be changed. Consider the language

$$\{x^m y^n \,|\, m, n \geqslant 0\}$$

which could be generated by the following set of productions:

$$S \rightarrow XY$$
$$X \rightarrow xX$$
$$X \rightarrow \varepsilon$$
$$Y \rightarrow yY$$
$$Y \rightarrow \varepsilon$$

which are different from the ones given earlier for the same language. Two grammars generating the same language are said to be *equivalent* and, as will be seen later, it is often useful, or even necessary, from a compiler writing point of view, to replace a given grammar by another equivalent grammar.

The definition of a grammar given above allows for more general types of grammars than the examples we have seen so far. For example, the left side of a production need not consist of a single symbol, as is shown in the following example:

$$G_3 = (\{a\}, \{S, N, Q, R\}, P, S)$$

where the elements of P are

$$S \rightarrow QNQ$$
$$QN \rightarrow QR$$
$$RN \rightarrow NNR$$
$$RQ \rightarrow NNQ$$
$$N \rightarrow a$$
$$Q \rightarrow \varepsilon$$

in which, according to the second production, N can be replaced by R in a derivation *as long as* it is preceded by Q and, from the fourth production, R can be replaced by NN *as long as* it is followed by Q. The productions are *context sensitive*, a term that will be defined more precisely shortly. A typical derivation using this grammar would be

$$S \Rightarrow QNQ \Rightarrow QRQ \Rightarrow QNNQ \overset{+}{\Rightarrow} aa$$

as would

$$S \Rightarrow QNQ \Rightarrow QRQ \Rightarrow QNNQ \Rightarrow QRNQ \Rightarrow QNNRQ \Rightarrow QNNNNQ \overset{+}{\Rightarrow} aaaa$$

illustrating the fact that we always get a number of as that is a power of two, the exact power of two depending at what stage we choose to replace the sequence of Ns (of length a power of two) by as. The language generated by the grammar is then

$\{a^m \mid m$ is a positive power of 2$\}$

We are now ready to introduce the important *Chomsky hierarchy* of grammars/languages. Chomsky defined four classes of grammars, and called them type-0 through to type-3 grammars. First *type-0* or *recursively enumerable grammars* are defined as all grammars which correspond to the definition given above, without any restriction on the types of productions which may appear. Type-0 is the most general type of grammar and, as we will see, the other types of grammar will be defined by imposing restrictions on the form of productions that may be used.

Type-0 grammars are equivalent to Turing machines in the sense that, given any type-0 grammar, there exists a Turing machine that accepts, and only accepts, all sentences generated by the grammar. Conversely, given a Turing machine, there exists a type-0 grammar that generates *exactly* all the sentences accepted by the Turing machine.

The first restriction on the form of production that may appear in a grammar is to state that for all productions of the form

$\alpha \rightarrow \beta$

the length of the string α must be less than or equal to the length of the string β in terms of the number of symbols it may contain, i.e.

$|\alpha| \leqslant |\beta|$

The class of grammar whose productions are all of this form is known as *type-1* or *context sensitive*. For those familiar with automata theory, type-1 grammars are equivalent to *linearly bound automata* in the same sense that type-0 grammars are equivalent to Turing machines. Notice that the grammar given above for the language

$\{a^m \mid m$ is a non-negative power of 2$\}$

is type-0 rather than type-1 because in the production

$Q \rightarrow \varepsilon$

the left side is longer than the right side.

The class of grammar that has the further restriction that only a single non-terminal may appear on the left side of a production is known as *type-2* or *context free*. With the exception of G_3 all the grammars we have discussed in this chapter are type-2 and, as compiler theory is based almost entirely on type-2 and type-3 grammars, we will hardly mention type-0 or type-1 grammars from here on.

It is convenient to allow the production

$S \rightarrow \varepsilon$

in context-free grammars (even though this is not strictly allowed even in context-sensitive grammars) to allow us to include the empty string in the language. In some grammars we will also see productions in which other nonterminals generate the empty string. Allowing this does not increase the power of context-free grammars at all, but may at times be convenient. Type-2 grammars are equivalent to *push-down automata*.

The final class of grammar in the Chomsky hierarchy is the *type-3* or *regular grammar*. First, however, we define a *right linear grammar* to be one in which *every* production is one of two forms:

$A \rightarrow a$

or

$A \rightarrow bC$

using the usual convention regarding terminal and nonterminals. For example, the grammar with productions

$S \rightarrow xS$
$S \rightarrow yB$
$S \rightarrow x$
$S \rightarrow y$
$B \rightarrow yB$
$B \rightarrow y$

is right linear, and if we wish to include the empty string in the language generated by the grammar we may consider the production

$S \rightarrow \varepsilon$

where S is the *sentence symbol*, to be in the grammar as well. However the equivalent grammar

$S \rightarrow XY$
$X \rightarrow xX$
$X \rightarrow \varepsilon$
$Y \rightarrow yY$
$Y \rightarrow \varepsilon$

is *not* right linear because productions 1, 3 and 5 are not of the required form. Nonterminals, other than the sentence symbol, may not generate the empty string in a right linear grammar.

A grammar that is right linear is said to be *regular*. Also any grammar that is left linear, where left linear is defined in an analogous way to right linear, is also defined to be regular. For example, the grammar with the following productions is left linear, and therefore regular:

$$S \rightarrow Sy$$
$$S \rightarrow Bx$$
$$S \rightarrow x$$
$$S \rightarrow y$$
$$B \rightarrow Bx$$
$$B \rightarrow x$$

and again it is permissible to add

$$S \rightarrow \varepsilon$$

While any grammar, *all* of whose productions are right linear, is defined to be regular, and also any grammar, *all* of whose productions are left linear, is also defined to be regular, a grammar that has some productions which are *right linear* such as

$$A \rightarrow aB$$

together with some which are *left linear* such as

$$P \rightarrow Qr$$

is *not* regular.

Note that the left linear grammar above generates the same language

$$\{x^m y^n \mid m, n \geqslant 0\}$$

as the right linear grammar. In general, *any* language that can be generated by a right linear grammar may also be generated by a left linear grammar.

A language that can be generated by a regular grammar is said to be *regular*. The regular language

$$\{x^m y^n \mid m, n \geqslant 0\}$$

can also be defined by a regular expression

$$x^* y^*$$

and this is the case for all regular languages. Conversely any language defined by any regular expression can be generated by a regular grammar. Hence the name *regular*. Regular languages and regular expressions are equivalent in automata terms to finite automata. We therefore have a three-way equivalence between regular expressions, regular languages and finite automata, as shown in Figure 2.1. For those unfamiliar with the notion of a finite automaton, it is defined in the next chapter.

The Chomsky hierarchy is inclusive, so that all type-3 grammars are type-2 grammars, all type-2 grammars are type-1 grammars and all type-1 grammars are type-0 grammars. This is shown diagrammatically in Figure 2.2.

A type-3 language is defined to be a language that has a type-3 grammar, a type-2 language to be a language with a type-2 grammar and so on. There is therefore an inclusive hierarchy of languages corresponding to the hierarchy of grammars. However, it should not be assumed, because a language has a grammar that is not type-3, that the language itself is not type-3, since the same language may also have a type-3 grammar. An example of a type-3 language that has a type-2 grammar is the one we have already considered

$$\{x^m y^n \mid m, n \geqslant 0\}$$

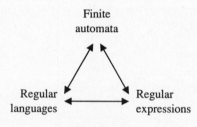

Finite
automata

Regular
languages

Regular
expressions

Figure 2.1

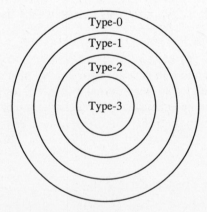

Type-0

Type-1

Type-2

Type-3

Figure 2.2

which can be generated by the following productions;

$$S \rightarrow XY$$
$$X \rightarrow xX$$
$$X \rightarrow \varepsilon$$
$$Y \rightarrow yY$$
$$Y \rightarrow \varepsilon$$

which are not type-3, as well as by the productions

$$S \rightarrow xS$$
$$S \rightarrow yB$$
$$S \rightarrow x$$
$$S \rightarrow y$$
$$B \rightarrow yB$$
$$B \rightarrow y$$
$$S \rightarrow \varepsilon$$

which are type-3.

Although we will have little more to say about type-0 and type-1 grammars and languages, type-2 and type-3 grammars and languages have an important role to play in compiler writing. We will be particularly interested, in the rest of this chapter, in the distinguishing features and limitations, in terms of representational power, of these types of grammars and languages.

2.4 Distinction between regular and context-free languages

Both context-free (type-2) languages and regular (type-3) languages are used extensively in compiler writing. Regular grammars and languages are subsets of context-free grammars and languages, and have advantages over context-free grammars and languages in terms of their simplicity. It makes sense therefore to use regular grammars and languages, where possible, in connection with the analysis stage of compilation. There is therefore a need to recognise situations where regular grammars and languages are adequate for the purpose in hand. There is, fortunately, a simple property of a grammar which may be used to deduce that the language generated is regular, which we will come to shortly. First, however, we will introduce the idea of recursion in a grammar.

Productions such as

$$A \rightarrow Ab$$
$$B \rightarrow cB$$
$$C \rightarrow dCf$$

all contain *direct recursion*, since the single nonterminal on the left side of the production also appears on its right side. In the first case we have *left recursion*, since the nonterminal on the left side appears in the leftmost position on the right side of the production, in the second case *right recursion* for the corresponding reason, and in the third case we have *middle recursion* since the nonterminal on the left side appears on the right side of the production but in neither the leftmost or rightmost position. Almost all grammars contain recursion of some sort since otherwise arbitrarily long sentences could not be generated. The type of recursion, may, however, be significant, and in this section we are particularly interested in *middle recursion*. We should note that recursion is not always *direct* but may also be *indirect* as shown by the following examples:

1. $A \rightarrow Bc$
   $B \rightarrow Cd$
   $C \rightarrow Ae$
2. $P \rightarrow xQz$
   $Q \rightarrow wPy$

In the first case we have *indirect left recursion*, and in the second *indirect middle recursion*. The number of productions involved in indirect recursion may be arbitrarily large. Although indirect recursion seems more complex than direct recursion, the difference is not so significant as it may seem, since there is a simple algorithm, which we need not go into here, to convert indirect recursion to direct recursion. For this reason we need only consider grammars with direct recursion.

To determine if a given grammar generates a regular language, it is first necessary to consider whether it contains any recursion. In the unlikely event that it contains *no* recursion the language is finite, and therefore regular, since we could list all the sentences in the language. Any finite set of strings can be represented by a regular grammar. An extremely useful result, which we do not prove here, then tells us that if a grammar contains no middle recursion (also known as *self-embedding*) then the language generated by the grammar is regular.

Thus the language with the productions

$S \rightarrow XY$
$X \rightarrow xX$
$X \rightarrow x$
$Y \rightarrow yY$
$Y \rightarrow y$
$S \rightarrow x$
$S \rightarrow y$
$S \rightarrow \varepsilon$

is regular, since the productions contain no middle recursion – right recursion, which is present, is not a problem.

For a simple language that is not regular consider

$$\{x^n y^n \mid n > 0\}$$

with productions

$S \rightarrow xSy$
$S \rightarrow xy$

Here the first production contains middle recursion, and therefore the language is not regular. So there are quite simple languages that are not regular!

We now consider the relevance of these ideas to compiler production. The lexical aspects of most languages, such as variable names, numbers, constants and multi-character symbols (for example ++), can almost always be defined by regular expressions, and hence can be generated by regular grammars. However, when it comes to arithmetic expressions or compound statements, there is nearly always an element of bracket matching, which *cannot* be expressed by a regular grammar. For example, the productions for a grammar generating the language consisting of strings of matching brackets would be

$S \rightarrow (S)$
$S \rightarrow SS$
$S \rightarrow \varepsilon$

which contains self-embedding, which cannot be removed.

To sum up, regular (type-3) grammars can almost always be used as a basis for lexical analysis, while context-free (type-2) grammars are generally required for syntax analysis. Strictly speaking, parsers based purely on context-free grammars are not sufficiently general to cover all aspects of syntax analysis, and we will see later how they can be augmented to include those relatively few aspects of syntax analysis that they are unable to represent.

2.5 Derivations

We have already shown how a derivation is used to generate a sentence of a language from a grammar for the language. For example, the language

$$\{x^n y^n \mid n > 0\}$$

is generated by the grammar with productions

$S \rightarrow xSy$
$S \rightarrow xy$

The derivation

$$S \Rightarrow xSy \Rightarrow xxSyy \Rightarrow xxxSyyy \Rightarrow xxxxyyyy$$

generates the sentence

xxxxyyyy

and is the *only* derivation that generates that particular sentence. In general, however, derivations are not unique. Consider the language

$\{x^m y^n \mid m, n > 0\}$

generated by the productions

$$S \rightarrow XY$$
$$X \rightarrow xX$$
$$X \rightarrow x$$
$$Y \rightarrow yY$$
$$Y \rightarrow y$$

The sentence

xxxyy

may be generated by the derivation

$$S \Rightarrow XY \Rightarrow xXY \Rightarrow xxXY \Rightarrow xxxY \Rightarrow xxxyY \Rightarrow xxxyy$$

or by the derivation

$$S \Rightarrow XY \Rightarrow XyY \Rightarrow Xyy \Rightarrow xXyy \Rightarrow xxXyy \Rightarrow xxxyy$$

as well as by a number of other derivations, depending on the order in which the productions for X and Y are used. In the first derivation the leftmost nonterminal in the sentential form was replaced at each stage of the derivation, and such a derivation is known as a *leftmost derivation*. For a similar reason the second derivation is known as a *rightmost derivation*. Some derivations are neither left-most nor rightmost, for example

$$S \Rightarrow XY \Rightarrow xXY \Rightarrow xXyY \Rightarrow xxXyY \Rightarrow xxXyy \Rightarrow xxxyy$$

Notice that each of the derivations of

xxxyy

used each of the productions of the grammar the same number of times, though in a different order.

It is also worth noting that regular grammars (at least those expressed in their simplest form) allow only a single derivation for a given string, basically because there is never more than one nonterminal in a sentential form. For example, using the grammar with productions

$S \rightarrow xA$
$A \rightarrow xA$
$A \rightarrow yB$
$A \rightarrow y$
$B \rightarrow yB$
$B \rightarrow y$

which also generates the language

$\{x^m y^n \mid m, n > 0\}$

the sentence

xxxyy

can only be derived in one way, i.e.

$S \Rightarrow xA \Rightarrow xxA \Rightarrow xxxA \Rightarrow xxxyB \Rightarrow xxxyy$

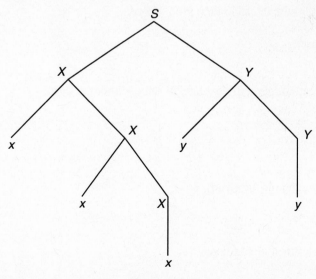

Figure 2.3

Another way of describing a derivation is by mean of a *syntax tree* or *parse tree*. For example, the derivation

$$S \Rightarrow XY \Rightarrow xXY \Rightarrow xXyY \Rightarrow xxXyY \Rightarrow xxXyy \Rightarrow xxxyy$$

corresponds to the parse tree shown in Figure 2.3, as does any other derivation for the sentence. Different derivations correspond to composing the parts of the tree in a *different order*.

2.6 Ambiguous grammars

For many grammars, each sentence that can be generated by the grammar has a unique parse tree as well as a unique leftmost derivation and a unique rightmost derivation. In fact these three conditions are equivalent and any one of the three implies the other two. Put another way, if one of the following statements concerning a grammar is true, then the other two are also true:

- Each sentence generated by the grammar has a unique leftmost derivation.
- Each sentence generated by the grammar has a unique rightmost derivation.
- Each sentence generated by the grammar has a unique parse tree.

This is a well-known result of grammar theory and we do not prove it here. A grammar with the above properties is said to be *unambiguous*. Otherwise it is said to be *ambiguous*. An *ambiguous language* is one for which *all* grammars generating it are ambiguous.

An example will serve to show that some grammars are ambiguous. Consider the grammar with the following productions:

$$S \rightarrow S + S$$
$$S \rightarrow x$$

Clearly the grammar will generate all sentences of the form

$$x$$
$$x + x$$
$$x + x + x$$

Take as an example the string

$$x + x + x$$

It has two leftmost derivations

$$S \Rightarrow S + S \Rightarrow x + S \Rightarrow x + S + S \Rightarrow x + x + S \Rightarrow x + x + x$$

and

$$S \Rightarrow S + S \Rightarrow S + S + S \Rightarrow x + S + S \Rightarrow x + x + S \Rightarrow x + x + x$$

as well as two rightmost derivations. It also has two distinct syntax trees as shown in Figure 2.4.

The grammar is clearly ambiguous and, for that reason, is unsuitable for certain parsing methods we may wish to use. At the very least it may be necessary, if a syntax tree is to be built, to add disambiguating rules to the grammar to specify exactly which tree is to be built. For this reason compiler writers often prefer to use unambiguous grammars as the basis of the parser though, as will be shown later, this is not always strictly necessary. Two questions come to mind:

1. Given an ambiguous grammar, could there exist an unambiguous grammar that generates the same language?
2. Are there algorithms to determine where a given grammar or language is ambiguous?

The answer to the first is yes, and to the second (unfortunately) no. To illustrate the answer to the first question, consider the language defined above, by an ambiguous grammar. It is also defined by the grammar with the following productions:

$$S \rightarrow S + x$$
$$S \rightarrow x$$

The sentence

$$x + x + x$$

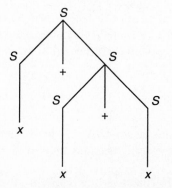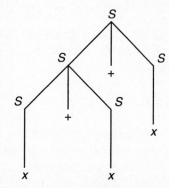

Figure 2.4

has only one *leftmost* derivation using this grammar

$$S \Rightarrow S + x \Rightarrow S + x + x \Rightarrow S \Rightarrow x + x + x$$

and, similarly, only one rightmost derivation and only one syntax tree. The same is true for any sentence generated by the grammar, so the *language* is unambiguous since it may be generated by an unambiguous *grammar* (and this has been shown by finding such a grammar).

Since (as has just been stated in the answer to the second question) there is no algorithm to determine, in general, whether a grammar is ambiguous or not, then it follows that there cannot be an algorithm that will, in all possible cases, produce the unambiguous equivalent of an ambiguous grammar. This must be the case since, otherwise, we could determine from the output of the algorithm whether its input language was ambiguous or not.

Thus the problem of whether a language is ambiguous or not is also unsolvable. That is, it is known from theoretical considerations that no algorithm to solve the problem in general exists. For readers familiar with the relevant theory, the problem of determining whether a language is ambiguous or not is equivalent to determining whether a Turing machine will terminate or not when it reads a particular input. For either problem, it is possible to write an algorithm that will solve the problem for a finite set of instances but not one that will solve it in general. Language theory abounds with such unsolvable (or *undecidable*) problems, which serves to make it interesting, or frustrating, depending on your point of view. At the very least it makes us aware that even computers have their limitations!

So, there are two related unsolvable problems concerning ambiguity in languages, namely

- the problem of whether a grammar is ambiguous;
- the problem of whether a language is ambiguous.

As far as grammars are concerned, while the general problem is unsolvable, there is one particular class of grammar, the members of which are known to be ambiguous, namely grammars containing one or more productions exhibiting both left and right recursion. Therefore the grammar considered above which contained the production

$$S \rightarrow S + S$$

is clearly ambiguous. However, the opposite is not true, i.e. grammars not containing left and right recursion are not necessarily unambiguous – otherwise we would have a test for ambiguity!

The best known ambiguous grammar (fragment) which appears in many programming languages is that used to define the *if-statement* with an optional *else-part*. It is often defined as follows:

statement → **if** *expr* **then** *statement* **else** *statement* |
          if *expr* **then** *statement* |
          other

in which the bold words are terminals in the grammar and 'other' generates statements other than **if**-statements. We have also departed from our usual convention regarding lower and upper case letters representing terminals and nonterminals, respectively, since *statement* is a nonterminal.

None of the productions in the grammar exhibits left and right recursion, though one of them is doubly recursive! It is well known, however, that the productions are ambiguous, which may be illustrated by identifying a string which may have more than one leftmost or rightmost derivation or more than one syntax tree. The simplest such string (there are an infinite number of such strings) is

if *expr* **then if** *expr* **then** *other* **else** *other*

One way of expressing the ambiguity is to point out that the **else** could be paired with either of the two **then**s. Some languages (e.g. COBOL) resolve the ambiguity by saying that, on reading the code from left to right; each **else** is paired with the nearest preceding **then** which has not already been paired with an **else**. The two syntax trees for the sentence are shown in Figures 2.5 and 2.6.

In COBOL, and most other languages exhibiting this feature, the first syntax tree would be the correct one, rather than the second one. However, this could *not* be inferred from the grammar usually given for the language, but is usually stated in rather formal English (in most COBOL texts and manuals at least). This might suggest that it is not possible to resolve this ambiguity by means of the grammar alone. This is not, however, the case since the alternative

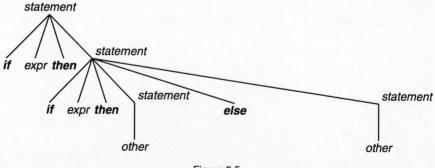

Figure 2.5

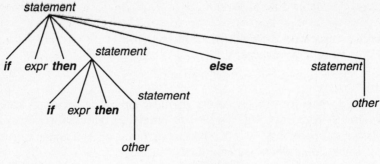

Figure 2.6

productions

> *statement*→   *matched* |
>   *unmatched*
> *matched*→   **if** *expr* **then** *matched* **else** *matched* |
>   *other*
> *unmatched*→ **if** *expr* **then** *statement* |
>   **if** *expr* **then** *matched* **else** *unmatched*

generate the same sentences, but are not ambiguous. However, these productions tend not to be used, presumably because they are much less intuitive. We will also see later, in connection with the YACC parser generator, that there are other, more natural and elegant, ways of resolving the ambiguity.

So ambiguous grammars arise occasionally in compiler development – the above example being by far the best known occurrence – but there are often simple ways of resolving the ambiguities and in practice few problems arise. Ambiguous languages (languages for which there exists no unambiguous grammar) would almost certainly prove difficult for humans to understand, and do not normally arise in programming languages.

2.7 **Limitations of context-free grammars**

It is now time to address the question of how *adequate* context-free grammars are for generating programming languages. We first observe that there are some quite simple languages that cannot be generated by context-free grammars. For example, the one we used earlier (G_3 in section 2.3) to demonstrate the use of a grammar that was not context free since the left-hand sides of some productions did not consist of a single nonterminal. The language generated by G_3 was

> $\{a^m \mid m$ *is a positive power of* $2\}$

Of course, the fact that the language can be generated by a non-context-free grammar does not necessarily mean that it cannot also be generated by a context-free grammar. However, in this case, it can be shown that no context-free grammar exists which generates the language, though we will not attempt to prove it here. Other fairly simple-looking languages that can also be shown not to be context free are

1. $\{a^n b^n c^n \mid n \geq 0\}$
2. $\{a^n \mid n$ is prime$\}$
3. $\{ww \mid w$ is in $\{0, 1\}^*\}$

even though the similar looking, though slightly simpler, languages

1. $\{a^n b^n \mid n \geq 0\}$
2. $\{ww^R \mid w^R$ is w reversed and w is in $\{0, 1\}^*\}$

are context free.

What concerns us here, however, is the more practical problem of whether the types of features normally found in programming languages can be generated by context-free grammars, and the answer is that to a very large extent they can!

One feature that has to be considered, however, is the role of *types* in programming languages. Pascal and Ada are examples of strongly typed languages that require a high degree of type compatibility in various contexts. For example, the Pascal fragment

```
var x : integer;
begin x := '?'
```

is incorrect since x may only be assigned an integer value. Similarly, if p is declared as

```
procedure p (i,j: integer);
```

then it may not be called thus

```
p(3,4,5)
```

with three parameters instead of two. Similarly, if the array A is declared as

```
var A[1.10] of integer;
```

then it may not be accessed thus

```
A[2,3] := 0
```

The above three examples all illustrate misuse of Pascal. However, it is not possible to write a context-free grammar that generates *all* legal Pascal programs, but *none* with the types of faults illustrated. It is worth noting that a type-0 grammar to generate *exactly* all legal Pascal programs exists and *could* be used as the basis for a parser. However, this is impractical for two reasons:

1. The non-intuitive nature and lack of transparency of type-0 grammars – consider, as an illustration of this, the grammar G_3 referred to at the start of this section.
2. The nature of the automaton corresponding to a type-0 grammar – a Turing machine – with its ability to read its input as many times as necessary.

The second point suggests that a parser based on a type-0 grammar would have all the power, and all the inefficiencies, of a Turing machine including having to read from, and write to, an arbitrarily long tape in an arbitrary way.

Despite their limitations, context-free grammars *are* used as the basis for parsers. A context-free grammar generating a superset of a language may be used as the basis for a parser, *as long as* the parser is enhanced by actions to perform type checking of the sort illustrated in the examples above. In practice, this means setting up symbol and type tables into which information pertaining to declarations and definitions of variables and types is inserted, as it becomes available. The information in these tables may then be accessed at a later stage when the variables and types are applied. For some languages, e.g. ALGOL 68, this means that the compilation cannot, in general, be completed in a single pass over the source code, since some of the information required to analyse an expression, for instance, may not be available until later in the program text. Most languages, however, can be compiled in a single pass.

Most parsers therefore consist of two parts:

1. A part that checks that the input conforms to a context-free grammar generating a superset of the language. This part can be produced 'automatically' from the grammar.
2. A part consisting of actions, called by the first part, to check additional constraints on the input.

The context-free grammar can be enhanced to represent these two aspects by adding rules to the grammar. One way of doing this is to use an *attribute grammar*, an example of which is illustrated in the following.

Suppose we wished to be able to specify the values of expressions defined by the grammar with the following productions:

1. *<expr> ::= <expr> '+' <term>*
2. *<expr> ::= <term>*
3. *<term> ::= <term> '*'<factor>*
4. *<term> ::= <factor>*
5. *<factor> ::= constant*
6. *<factor> ::= '('<expr>')'*

where terminals such as operators are surrounded by quotes to show that this is the actual representation of the terminal as distinct from the *name* of a terminal such as 'constant' that represents a (not necessarily finite) set of actual representations.

Attributes can be associated with some of the terminals and nonterminals in the grammar. Since all the attributes correspond to values of subexpressions or the complete expression, it is natural to call them *VAL*, where no confusion can arise, and *VAL1*, *VAL2*, etc. where it is necessary to distinguish between the values corresponding to different symbols in a production. The attributes are referred to as *synthesised attributes* since they are used to move values up the syntax tree or (to look at it another way) to calculate attribute values corresponding to the left side of a production from attribute values on the right of the production. Attributes that move information in the opposite direction, i.e. down the tree or from the right to the left side of productions, are referred to as *inherited attributes*.

The context-free grammar augmented by attribute rules to specify the value of an expression in terms of the value of its components is given below. The upward arrow at the start of each attribute name is an indication that the attribute is synthesised rather than inherited:

1. *<expr>* ↑ *VAL* ::= *<expr>* ↑ *VAL1* '+' *<term>* ↑ *VAL2*
   [rule: ↑ *VAL* = ↑ *VAL1* + ↑ *VAL2]*
2. *<expr>* ↑ *VAL* ::= *<term>* ↑ *VAL*
3. *<expr>* ↑ *VAL* ::= *<term>* ↑ *VAL1* '*' *<factor>* ↑ *VAL2*
   [rule: ↑ *VAL* = ↑ *VAL1* × ↑ *VAL2]*
4. *<term>* ↑ *VAL* ::= *<factor>* ↑ *VAL*
5. *<factor>* ↑ *VAL* ::= *constant* ↑ *VAL*
6. *<factor>* ↑ *VAL* ::= '(' *<expr>* ↑ *VAL* ')'

with the convention that, where an attribute with the same name appears in more than one position in a production then the two instances have the same value.

An attribute grammar to specify the type rules of a language such as Pascal is complex, as it involves specifying the equivalence of sets of symbol table information appearing as attributes throughout the syntax tree. However, the type constraints in Pascal can, in principle, be described in terms of attributes in a similar way to which the value of the expression defined by the above grammar is specified.

While an attribute grammar *specifies* consistency rules, it is not difficult to convert these to *actions* to check that the consistency rules are obeyed. It is not difficult, in principle, therefore, to implement an attribute grammar in terms of a context-free parser supplemented by additional actions. However, a naive implementation of an attribute grammar for a typical programming language would be very inefficient, if only because of the copying of, possibly large, tables which would have to take place.

As we will see later, attribute grammars may also be used to define source code metrics in a way from which it is easy to produce tools to measure the values of the metrics. Attribute grammars have an equivalent power to type-0 grammars and are much more transparent. They were first identified by Knuth and have been used as the basis for programming environments, the detection of anomalies in programs and as a basis for a software development paradigm.

2.8 **The parsing problem**

So far, we have discussed how a grammar may be used to generate sentences of a language, and how it may be used to define the syntax of a language. In the compilation process, the *parsing problem* consists of finding a derivation (if one exists) of a particular sentence using a given grammar. Thus it is not so much a matter of finding the sentences generated by a grammar, but of finding a derivation of the given sentence using the grammar or, alternatively, reporting that none exists. In most cases a leftmost derivation or a rightmost derivation will be sought, which will usually be unique. Where the derivation is not unique (in the case of an ambiguous grammar, for example), rules must be available (disambiguating rules) to determine which of the derivations is required. Thus the outcome of the parsing problem is always well defined.

Of course, users would not be satisfied with a compiler that merely reported that a string did not belong to the source language, and then terminated without performing further analysis. In practice, the compiler will also indicate the last symbol read before it was clear that the string was not in the source language, and it will then continue with the analysis after making whatever assumptions seemed most appropriate in the circumstances.

The simplest way to picture the parsing problem is to imagine the sentence symbol at the top of a large sheet of paper and the sentence to be analysed at the bottom. The parsing problem then consists of drawing a syntax tree, which uses the subtrees corresponding to the productions of the grammar, to join the sentence symbol to the sentence. There are a number of ways of tackling the problem. One would be to start at the top with the sentence symbol and work towards the sentence at the bottom of the page (*top-down parsing*); another would be to start at the bottom of the page with the sentence and to work towards the sentence symbol at the top (*bottom-up parsing*). A mixture of the two approaches might also be tried (the *mixed approach*). Horizontal and diagonal approaches are also possible, for example, from left to right or right to left or even top right to bottom left or whatever. Solutions to the problem could be deterministic in the sense that once a part of the tree had been drawn it would never have to be rubbed out, or nondeterministic which would allow parts of the tree already constructed to be erased if necessary.

Many different parsing methods have been developed in the history of programming language implementation with a variety of the above characteristics. Early top-down parsing methods were often non-deterministic and quite inefficient, but nowadays parsing is usually highly efficient, taking a time proportionate to the length of the sentence being parsed. Programs are nearly always parsed from left to right though the idea of a backward (or right to left) parse may sometimes seem attractive. Top-down parsing is more intuitive than bottom-up parsing, though bottom-up parsing has greater generality and enjoys better tool support. Both methods have their advocates, and will be discussed in detail in chapters 4 and 5 respectively.

2.9 Semantics definition

Apart from introducing the notion at the start of this chapter, we have said little about language semantics and how they are defined. Static semantics (type checking, etc.) which we discussed in section 2.7 were treated more or less as if they were extensions of syntax. The need to be able to define the meaning of (the effect of executing) a piece of program, is just as important as being able to define what constitutes a legal program, and the study of semantics has applications in program verification as well as in compiler technology. However, there is, as yet, no universally accepted method for defining semantics. Possibilities include:

- *denotational semantics* based on functional calculus, in which the operations in the language are mapped on to well-defined mathematical notions, which are used to describe the effect of the program in terms of inputs and outputs;
- *axiomatic semantics* based on predicate calculus, in which the effects of the computation are described in terms of relationships between the values of variables before and after particular operations have taken place;
- *operational semantics* in which the operations in the language are described in terms of the actions of some abstract machine executing the program.

All of the above methods have been used to define some or all of various programming languages. However, many language definitions still use informal (and possibly ambiguous) methods to define semantics, and, despite the obvious dangers of such an approach, we will do the same here in the absence of any totally satisfactory, and easily implementable, method of defining programming language semantics.

2.10 Summary

This chapter has been principally concerned with programming languages and their definition. In particular we have:

- introduced the notion of a grammar, and shown how it is used to generate a language;

- defined and discussed the significance of the Chomsky hierarchy of grammars;
- illustrated the notions of leftmost and rightmost derivations and syntax trees;
- discussed the significance of ambiguity in grammars;
- discussed the limitations of regular and context-free grammars;
- introduced the idea of actions in a parser to check noncontext-free aspects of languages;
- introduced the idea of an attribute grammar;
- introduced the parsing problem and general approaches to solving it;
- outlined three possible methods of defining language semantics.

Further reading

Grammars are used in virtually all compiler texts to define languages. Context-free grammars were introduced by Chomsky (1956) in relation to natural languages. Regular expressions were developed by Kleene (1956). The unambiguous grammar for the *if-statement* is given in Aho, Sethi and Ullman (1985), page 175. Attribute grammars were developed by Knuth (1968a) and were used to define Pascal by Watt (1977). Terry (1997) compares various methods of defining programming language semantics.

Exercises

2.1 Describe each of the following sets of strings in English:

(a) $\{a^n \mid n \geqslant 0\}$
(b) $\{a^m b^n \mid m, n \geqslant 1\}$
(c) $\{x^n y^n z^n \mid n \geqslant 0\}$
(d) $\{x^m y^n z^m \mid m > 0, n > 1\}$
(e) $\{x^m y^n z^p \mid m, n, p > 0\}$

2.2 Describe each of the following regular expressions in English:

(a) $x^* y^*$
(b) $x x^* y y^*$
(c) $(x \mid y)^*$
(d) $(a \mid b) a^* b^*$
(e) $(a^* \mid b^*)^*$

2.3 State, giving reasons, which of the following grammars are regular (S is the sentence symbol in each case and with the usual convention regarding the naming of terminals and nonterminals):

(a) $S \rightarrow aX$
$\quad S \rightarrow bY$
$\quad X \rightarrow x$
$\quad X \rightarrow xX$
$\quad Y \rightarrow y$
$\quad Y \rightarrow yY$

(b) $S \rightarrow aX$
$\quad S \rightarrow bY$
$\quad X \rightarrow x$
$\quad X \rightarrow xX$
$\quad Y \rightarrow y$
$\quad Y \rightarrow Yy$

(c) $S \rightarrow AB$
$\quad A \rightarrow a$
$\quad A \rightarrow aA$
$\quad B \rightarrow b$
$\quad B \rightarrow bB$

(d) $S \rightarrow xSy$
$\quad S \rightarrow xy$

2.4 State which of the grammars in exercise 2.3 generate regular languages and, in the cases where the language generated is regular but the grammar given is not, give a regular grammar for the language.

2.5 For the grammar

$$S \rightarrow S + x$$
$$| x$$

give a rightmost derivation for

$$x + x + x + x$$

Give reasons why this derivation is unique.

2.6 For the grammar

$$statement \rightarrow \textbf{if } expr \textbf{ then } statement \textbf{ else } statement \,|$$
$$\textbf{if } expr \textbf{ then } statement \,|$$
$$other$$

show that the sentence

$$\textbf{if } expr \textbf{ then if } expr \textbf{ then } other \textbf{ else } other$$

has two rightmost and two leftmost derivations. Show also that the string can be derived from the grammar with productions

> *statement* → *matched* |
> *unmatched*
> *matched* → **if** *expr* **then** *matched* **else** *matched* |
> *other*
> *unmatched* → **if** *expr* **then** *statement* |
> **if** *expr* **then** *matched* **else** *unmatched*

2.7 Write down a grammar that generates all the strings (including the empty string) over the alphabet *{0, 1}*.

2.8 Consider the grammar with the following productions (PROGRAM is the sentence symbol):

> *PROGRAM* → **begin** *DECS*; *STATS* **end**
> *DECS* → *d*; *DECS*
> | *d*
> *STATS* → *s*; *STATS*
> | *s*

Give the leftmost and rightmost derivations of

> **begin** *d*; *d*; *s*; *s* **end**

2.9 An identifier in FORTRAN consists of a sequence of up to six letters and digits, of which the first character must be a letter. Derive

(a) a regular expression for an identifier,
(b) a type-3 grammar generating exactly all the FORTRAN identifiers.

2.10 Most languages have a conditional statement similar to that in exercise 2.6 above. Explain how the potential ambiguity is avoided or resolved in some languages with which you are familiar.

CHAPTER 3

Lexical analysis

3.1 **Introduction**

In this chapter we discuss what is, conceptually, the first phase of compilation, lexical analysis, the principal function of which is to group sequences of characters in the source text into language symbols. In particular, we will:

- outline the main features of a typical lexical analyser;
- show how simple lexical analysers may be readily built based on regular expressions and their related automata;
- show how the lexical analyser generator Lex may be used to produce lexical analysers;
- discuss some of the lexical 'problems' that arise in well-known programming languages.

3.2 **Basic ideas**

Lexical analysis, as has been mentioned, is the phase of compilation in which language symbols are formed from sequences of characters. For example, in C there are six types of symbols:

1. *Keywords* such as const, char, if, else, typedef.
2. *Identifiers* such as sum, main, printf.
3. *Constants* such as 28, 3.141529, 017 (octal).
4. *String literals* such as "Katherine", "bannockburn".
5. *Operators* such as +, −, ++, >>, /=, &&.
6. *Punctuators* such as {,], ..., ;.

Each of these types of symbol is formed during lexical analysis by the lexical analyser (or lexer).

Lexical analysis is a fairly straightforward process and corresponds to what the human reader would do automatically. The relatively simple nature of the symbols means that they can always be represented by regular expressions or equivalent type-3 grammars and, as we will see, it is not difficult to produce the type of recognisers required, from the corresponding regular grammars. Indeed, as we will also see, the process of producing the lexer is easily automated and tools are readily available to produce lexers from regular grammars or regular expressions. The study of lexical analysis does, however, give a good deal of insight into the rather more difficult problem of syntax analysis.

In addition to recognising the symbols of the language the lexical analyser will usually perform one or two other simple tasks such as

- deleting comments,
- inserting line numbers,
- evaluating constants,

though there are arguments that the last of these is better left to the machine-dependent back end of the compiler.

3.3 **Symbol recognition**

It is important to realise that the lexical analyser is *only* concerned with recognising language symbols in order to pass them on to the syntax analyser. It is not concerned at all with the order in which symbols appear. It would not detect an error, for example, in the following sequence of symbols

```
64 const char typedef >> +
```

as each of the symbols is perfectly correct in itself. If would be up to the syntax analyser to realise that they did not form the start (or even part) of any program. Nor would the lexical analyser have any understanding of the scope of variables, etc., so that it could not distinguish between the use of the identifier sum to represent two different variables in different functions. To the lexical analyser sum would denote the same identifier each time it occurred. It would not even be identified as a variable, as opposed, for example, to a function name, at the lexical analysis phase.

For the purposes of lexical analysis, regular expressions are a convenient method of representing symbols such as identifiers and constants. For example an *identifier* might be represented as

letter(letter| digit)*

and a *real number* (in some language) might be represented as

(+ | – |)digit*.digit digit*

In either case, it is relatively simple to write code to recognise the symbol. For an identifier the code would be:

```
#include <stdio.h>
#include <ctype.h>
```

```
main()
{char in;
in = getchar();
if (isalpha(in))
in = getchar();
else error();
while (isalpha(in) || isdigit(in))
in = getchar();
}
```

where `in` is the value of the character just read and the functions `isalpha()` and `isdigit()` check for a letter and a digit, respectively. `error()` takes some appropriate actions in an error situation. The code is easy to write: check for symbols which must appear and use a while loop to implement the * operator.

In a similar way the code to recognise a real number would be:

```
#include <stdio.h>
#include <ctype.h>

main()
{char in;
in = getchar();

if (in=='+'||in=='-')
in = getchar();

while (isdigit(in))
in = getchar();
if (in=='.')
in = getchar();
else error();

if (isdigit(in))
in = getchar();
else error();

while (isdigit(in))
in = getchar();

printf("ok\n");
}
```

Notice there are three situations to deal with, and how each is represented in the code:

1. Characters that may appear optionally ('+', '–') – no error if they do not
   appear, just read the next character.
2. Characters that must appear (the decimal point and the digit after it) – if
   they do not appear call the `error` function.
3. Characters that may appear zero or more times (a digit before the point or
   after the first digit after the point) – set up a while loop to check each
   occurrence and read the next character, no need to call the `error`
   function

The code is easy to write – it can be written almost as fast as one can write!
Moreover, its production can readily be automated.

Instead of writing the code from the regular expression, the finite automaton
corresponding to the regular expression could be used. A finite automaton (FA) is
simply a finite set of states together with transitions between them defined by
characters read from an input string. One state is defined to be the *start state* and
a set of one or more of the states is defined to be the *final state(s)*. The FA is said
to *accept* the input string if, starting in the start state and performing the appropriate transitions as it reads each character of the input string, it is in a final
state when it has read the complete string. More formally an FA is defined as a
quintuple

$$M = (K, \Sigma, \delta, S, F)$$

where

K is the set of states,
Σ is the alphabet from which the input strings are formed,
δ is the set of transitions,
$S(S \in K)$ is the start state,
$F(F \subseteq K)$ is the set of final states.

The transitions, δ, may be defined in terms of a table, defining a *next* state for
each state and each possible input character; or they may be defined graphically.
For example, the FA to recognise an identifier may be defined as shown in Figure
3.1 in which there are two states, *state 1* the start state, indicated by the arrow,

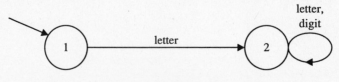

Figure 3.1

and *state 2* the (single) final state. Reading a letter in *state 1* leads to *state 2* and, thereafter, reading any number of digits or letters leads back to *state 2*.

The FA representation can readily be used to produce a recogniser. For example, the following code implements a recogniser for an identifier:

```
#include <stdio.h>
#include <ctype.h>

int main()
{int state;
char in;
state = 1;
in = getchar();

while (isalpha (in) || isdigit (in))
{switch (state)

{case 1:    if (isalpha(in))
              state = 2;
            else error();
            break;

 case 2:    state = 2;
            break;
} in = getchar();
}

return (state == 2);
}
```

The while loop ensures that the code terminates as soon as anything other than a letter or a digit is read. The switch statement has one element for each state in the automaton, and within each element all the transitions from that state are represented. In the second switch element there is no need to check the input since the while condition ensures that it is not reached unless the last character read is either a letter or a digit. The assignment of 2 to the state is also not strictly necessary but serves to make the transition explicit.

The real number, defined as a regular expression earlier in this section, may also be represented by an FA as in Figure 3.2 and coded in a manner similar to that used above giving:

```
#include <stdio.h>
#include <ctype.h>
```

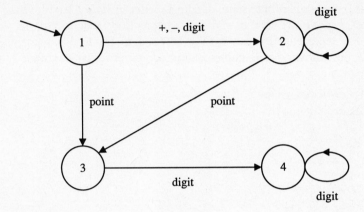

Figure 3.2

```
int issign (char sign)
{return (sign == '+' || sign == '-');
}

int main()

{int state;
char in;

state = 1;
in = getchar();

while (isdigit(in)||issign(in)|| in == '.')
{switch (state)
{
case 1:    if (isdigit (in)|| issign (in))
           state = 2;
           else if (in == '.')
           state = 3;
           break;
case 2:    if (isdigit(in))
           state = 2;
           else if (in == '.')
           state = 3;
           else error();
           break;
case 3:    if (isdigit(in))
           state = 4;
           else error();
           break;
```

```
case 4:    if (isdigit(in))
               state = 4;
               else error();
               break;
    }
    in = getchar();
    }

    return(state == 4);
    }
```

where `error()` has the same meaning as before, and `sign()` has the value `true` when its parameter is + or –, and `false` otherwise.

3.4 Lex

The construction of symbol recognisers, either from their regular expression definitions or from finite automata that accept them, is so simple that, with the aid of appropriate tools, it can be readily automated. The best known, and the most widely used, tool for this purpose is Lex, originally developed for use in conjunction with the parser generator YACC in a Unix environment, but now also available in its public domain equivalent Flex, and in other environments such as PC Windows and Macintosh. Originally Lex required the actions accompanying the analysis to be written in C, or possibly RATFOR (a version of FORTRAN), but now versions of Lex allow other languages to be used such as Turbo Pascal and C++. The various versions of Lex are very similar, though not identical, and the examples in this book have been checked out using the Unix version of Lex.

A notation very similar to that of regular expressions is used for the definition of symbols input to Lex. The notation differs from that of regular expressions for two principal reasons:

1. It allows the more efficient representation, in terms of number of characters used in the representation, of some types of symbols.
2. It extends the power of the regular expression notation in certain, fairly limited, respects.

As an example of the former, regular expression notation cannot represent the notion of 'every character from an alphabet but one', without listing all the other characters in the alphabet! An example of the latter is where the Lex notation allows the notion of a symbol appearing only in a particular context, a feature which is required to analyse certain (possibly unfortunate) features of FORTRAN.

To define an identifier in the Lex notation, a `letter` and a `digit` may first be defined

```
letter  [a-z]
digit   [0-9]
```

These are known as *definitions* in Lex. Notice that it is not necessary to list each of the characters in the range a-z or 0-9. The following *is* then used to define an identifier

```
identifier {letter}({letter}|{digit})*
```

where | and * mean the same as in regular expressions, and curly brackets are used to surround notions that have already been defined. If some action were to be taken each time an identifier was recognised (the usual situation for a lexical analyser) then this would be expressed in a *rule* such as

```
{identifier}    {printf("identifier recognised\n");}
```

Each time {identifier} is recognised, the single statement (which could have been compound, but not a sequence of statements)

```
{printf("identifier recognised\n");}
```

is executed.

The complete input to Lex to produce an analyser that recognised identifiers and executed the above statement each time one was encountered, would be

```
letter     [a-z]
digit      [0-9]
identifier {letter}({letter}|{digit})*
%%
{identifier}    {printf("identifier recognised\n");}
%%
```

Assuming the above was the content of the file firstlex.1, then the analyser would be produced by the command, as follows

```
lex firstlex.1
```

which would result in a C version of the resultant analyser appearing in lex.yy.c, which may then be compiled thus

```
cc -o firstlex lex.yy.c -11
```

to put the object code in firstlex, the name of the parameter following the -o flag. Notice that the Lex library parameter (-11) must appear. firstlex may then be executed with data from a file containing a C program, `cprog`:

```
firstlex <cprog
```

the input being redirected from the keyboard (the standard input channel) to the file `cprog`. Hence the '<'. Output would be to the screen, or could also be redirected

```
firstlex <cprog >idents
```

A slightly more interesting analyser would be produced from the following Lex input:

```
letter          [a-z]
digit           [0-9]
identifier      {letter}({letter}|{digit})*
%%
{identifier}    {printf("identifier %s on line %d\n", yytext,
                yylineno);}
%%
```

which makes use of two Lex variables, `yytext` whose value is the textual representation of the last symbol recognised, and `yylineno` which keeps a running count of the end-of-lines encountered and whose value is the current line number. There are a number of such variables available in Lex and YACC and some of the more useful ones are listed in Table 3.1 in section 3.6.

The output from the analyser produced from the above input would be a sequence of lines of the form:

```
identifier input on line 1
```

The general form of the input expected by Lex is

definitions
%%
rules
%%
user functions

of which the second part must be present, though the other two parts need not, unless required. Consecutive parts must be separated by a line containing

%%

in the leftmost positions.

The Lex input to produce an analyser to identify and print occurrences of real numbers defined as previously by the regular expression

(+ | – |)digit*.digit digit*

could be

```
digit      [0-9]
realno     [+\-]?{digit}*\.{digit}+
%%
{realno}   {printf("real%s on line %d\n",yytext,yylineno);}
```

This example illustrates two points:

1. Input characters that are also used as part of the notation must be preceded by the '\' character (alternatively they could be enclosed in double quotes) where ambiguity could arise – in this case '–' '.' are 'escaped' in this way. However there is no need to escape the first occurrence of '+' as no ambiguity arises.
2. '+' (as part of the notation) is used to denote one or more occurrences of what precedes it. This does not make the notation any more powerful than that used for regular expression, but it can make it more compact and easier to understand.

At this stage it is useful to illustrate, by means of examples, the main features of the regular expression-like notation used in the input to Lex:

`a`	represents a single character
`\a`	represents a when a is a character used in the notation (thus avoiding any ambiguity)
`"a"`	also represents a where a is a character used in the notation
`a|b`	represents a or b
`a?`	represents zero or one occurrence of a
`a*`	represents zero or more occurrences of a
`a+`	represents one or more occurrences of a
`a{m,n}`	represents between m and n occurrences of a
`[a-z]`	represents a character set
`[a-zA-Z]`	also represents a (larger) character set
`[^a-z]`	represents the complement of the first character set
`{name}`	represents the regular expression defined by name
`^a`	represents a at the start of a line
`a$`	represents a at the end of a line
`ab\xy`	represents ab when followed by xy

Some of the above points are illustrated in the following example which will produce an analyser to recognise (slightly simplified) constants, identifiers, strings and certain language words in a Pascal program – other language words will simply be recognised as identifiers. The Lex input would be

```
digit           [0-9]
intconst        [+\-]?{digit}+
realconst       [+\-]?{digit}+\.{digit}+(e[+\-]?{digit}+)?
letter          [A-Za-z]
identifier      {letter}({letter}|{digit})*
whitespace      [ \t\n]
stringch        [^']
string          '{stringch}+'
otherch         [^0-9a-zA-Z+\-' \t\n]
othersymb       {otherch}+
%%
program         printf("program recognised\n");
var             printf("var recognised\n");
begin           printf("begin recognised\n");
for             printf("for recognised\n");
to              printf("to recognised\n");
do              printf("do recognised\n");
end             printf("end recognised\n");
{intconst}      printf("integer %s on line %d\n",yytext,
yylineno);
{realconst}     printf("real %s on line %d\n",yytext,
yylineno);
{string}        printf("string %s on line %d\n",yytext,
yylineno);
{identifier}    printf("identifier %s on line %d\n",yytext,
                yylineno);
{whitespace}    ; /*no action*/
{othersymb}     ;/*no action*/
%%
```

Notice that whitespace may be any sequence of spaces, newlines and tabs and that \n and \t are used to denote the newline and tab 'characters' respectively in a similar way to which they are used in printf statements in C. Notice, however, that the escape symbol \ is being used in the opposite sense to that which we saw earlier – to indicate a notational use of t and n, rather than representing the characters themselves. In practice the (inconsistent) uses of the escape character do not seem to cause any confusion. A string is defined to be any sequence of characters, not including a quote, surrounded by quotes. othersymb is a sequence of any characters not already mentioned. Notice that null actions are associated both with whitespace and othersymb. This is because, if these symbols are not recognised in the second part of the Lex input, Lex will print them out on the standard output channel, i.e. in among its other output, producing a rather untidy result.

Suppose the analyser produced by Lex had the following Pascal program as input:

```
program double (input, output);
var i: 1..10;
begin
  writeln('number':10, 'timestwo':10);
  for i:= 1 to 10 do
    writeln (i:10, i*i:10);
  writeln
end.
```

then the output would be

```
program recognised
identifier double on line 1
identifier input on line 1
identifier output on line 1
var recognised
identifier i on line 2
interger 1 on line 2
interger 10 on line 2
begin recognised
identifier writeln on line 4
string 'number' on line 4
int 10 on line 4
```

and so on.

Notice that the language words were recognised as such, and not as identifiers. This is because Lex accepts the *first* match in the rules section and it is therefore important that the language words were defined first in the rules part above. Notice also that double is recognised correctly as an identifier and the first two letters are *not* recognised as the language word do. This is because Lex always looks for the longest match, and only if there are two of the same length does it take the first one.

Lex can be called from a C program through the function call yylex(). The following example of a Lex input illustrates how C code can be integrated in to the analyser produced by Lex:

```
%{
int chars = 0, lines = 0;
%}
%%
\n ++lines;
```

```
.    ++chars;
%%
main()
{yylex();
printf("number of characters = %d, number of lines =
%d\n", chars, lines);
}
```

As well as functions appearing in the third part of the input, declarations or other code may appear in the first part, as long as it is indented or surrounded by '%{' and '%}'. Any such code is just copied across to the C program produced by Lex. It is probably preferable to use '%{' and '%}' to surround such code rather than relying on indentation, the purpose of which may not be so clear. If these symbols *are* used they *must* appear on their own at the start of a line, in each case. It must also be remembered that *all* indented lines will be ignored by Lex and copied across to the C program unaltered. Forgetting, or not being aware of this, is a common source of error.

Notice the 'catchall' regular expression denoted by the period which will, in this case, match any character other than the newline character. In general, it will match any predefined symbol, not already matched.

The maximum and average lengths of words in a piece of text could be obtained from the analyser formed by the following Lex input:

```
%{
int letters = 0, words = 0, len = 0, length;
%}
word        [a-zA-Z]+
space       [ \n]
ws          {space}+
%%
{word}      {++words; length = yyleng;
            letters = letters+length;
            if (length > len) len = length;}
ws          ;/*do nothing*/
.           ;/*do nothing*/
%%
main()
{yylex();
printf("maximum word length = %d,average word length = %f\n",
   len, letters/words);
}
```

Notice the use of yyleng to give the length of the last symbol read. If the analyser had been required to terminate at the end of the first sentence the input to

Lex could have been:

```
%{
int letters = 0, words = 0, len = 0, length;
%}
word      [a-zA-Z]+
space     [ \n]
ws        {space}+
eos       [!?.]
%%
{word}    {++words; length = yyleng;
           letters = letters+length;
           if (length > len) len = length;}
{eos}     yywrap();
ws        ;/*do nothing*/
.         ;/*do nothing*/
%%
main()
{yylex();
printf("maximum word length = %d,average word length = %f\n",
   len, letters/words);
}
```

the effect of calling `yywrap()` being to terminate the analysis.

Another simple example of the use of Lex is to produce a tool to add line numbers to source code. Consider the following Lex input:

```
%{
int lineno = 1;
%}

line [^\n]*\n
%%
{line}    {printf("%d %s", lineno++, yytext);}
%%
main()
{yylex();
}
```

The output will be the source code read with each line, including blank lines, prefixed with a line number starting at 1.

Perhaps surprisingly, the recognition of commentary in a language (always a lexical matter) is not usually simple. The problem tends to arise from the characters that are used to surround the commentary and are therefore not allowed to appear within it. Of course, it is possible to define a regular expression for commentary (in C for example) but this is difficult, as we shall see, and is therefore error prone. A preferred solution is simply to write a piece of code to recognise the start of a comment and then to consume all the characters within the commentary until the end of the commentary is reached. After all, the contents of the commentary are of no possible interest to the compiler! The following fragment of a Lex input shows one method of dealing with commentary in C:

```
%%
"/*" {char in;
   for (;;)
   {
   while ((in = getchar()) ! = '*');
   /* do nothing more */
   while ((in = getchar()) =='*');
   /* consume *'s */
   if (in == '/')
   break;
   /* end of commentary*/
   }
   }
```

The above code takes care to ignore *s that are not followed by a / and /s that are not preceded by a *. The code could also be enhanced to detect the occurrence of EOF (end of file) within commentary.

Commentary may also be defined as a regular expression for input to Lex, as follows:

```
comment    "/*""/"*([^*/]|[^*]"/"|"*"[^/])*"*"*"*/"
```

and the complexity of this requires some explanation. The "/*" at the start, and the "*/" at the end simply denote the pairs of characters required at the start and end of commentary, leaving

```
"/"*([^*/]|[^*]"/"|"*"[^/])*"*"*
```

representing what may appear within commentary. The "/"* on the left represents the fact that there may be any number (including zero) of occurrences of "/" at the start, and the "*"* on the right that there may be any number (including zero) of occurrences of "*" at the end – the two uses of '*' here can be confusing. The middle part represents a sequence of zero or more segments, each of which either:

- contains no occurrences of "/" or "*";
- only contains "/" when it is not preceded by "*";
- only contains "*" when it is not followed by "/".

So it is not so bad after all! Whether the complexity of the commentary structure is inherent in its definition or reflects the limitations of the Lex notation is not so clear. The language for commentary is in fact regular, as is shown by the above, but regular does not necessarily mean 'simple'. String literals in many languages are also difficult to define – see the Pascal example above. They are even more complex in C!

3.5 Other uses for Lex

Lex may be used to analyse source code in a large number of ways. However, it is worth mentioning now that many types of code analysis are better performed with a tool based on a parser generator rather than a lexical analyser generator. Types of analysis that are concerned with the syntactic structure of a program, rather than its lexical structure, are generally performed more simply by a parser-based tool than a lexical-based tool. This does not mean that the syntactic structure of a program cannot be analysed in all sorts of clever ways with a lexical tool, just that many of these types of analyses are more simply, and more reliably, performed by a parsing tool. For example, analysis of statement usage, nesting structure, variable cross-referencing, etc., are all concerned with the syntactic, rather than the lexical, structure of the language. As a general rule, if the construction of an analysis based on Lex seems complex, consideration should be given to using YACC instead. There is rarely any need for stacks, flags and other devices, often used to try to turn a syntactic problem into a lexical one!

Types of analysis that *are* concerned with the lexical structure of program include:

- identification of language words;
- identification and evaluation of constants;
- identifying all the *distinct* identifiers in a program (note *not* variables);
- counting the number of lines of commentary in a program;
- computing the number and average length of literals in a program.

For example, we might wish to count the number of non-comment lines of code (NCLOC). This would be a count of the number of lines of code, excluding blank lines and lines containing only commentary. The input to Lex might be:

```
%{
int ncloc =0, count =0;
%}
```

```
comment      "/*""/"*([^*/]|[^*]"/"|"*"[^/])*"*"*"*/"
space        [ \t]
newline      \n
%%
{comment}    ;\*do nothing*\
{space}      ;\*do nothing*\
{newline}    {if (count > 0) ncloc = ncloc+1; count = 0;}
.            count = count + 1;
%%
main()
{yylex();
printf("number of non-comment lines of code (NCLOC) = %d", ncloc);
}
```

where count is incremented for every character read apart from spaces, tabs, and comment characters. If it is non-zero at the end of a line, ncloc is incremented.

The average number of characters per line has been suggested as a useful metric. This together with NCLOC may give a better idea of the size of a program than NCLOC on its own. For consistency, perhaps we should compute the average number of characters per non-comment line (excluding comments), and we should ignore blank lines. If so the Lex input would be:

```
%{
int nochars = 0, ncloc = 0, count = 0;
%}
comment      "/*""/"*([^*/]|[^*]"/"|"*"[^/])*"*"*"*/"
space        [ \t]
newline      \n
%%
{comment}    ;\*do nothing*\
{space}      ;\*do nothing*\
{newline}    {if (count > 0) ncloc = ncloc+1; count = 0;}
.            {count = count+1; nochars = nochars+1;}
main()
{yylex();
printf("number of characters per non-comment lines of code
                        (NCLOC) = %f", ncloc/nochars);
}
```

Other size metrics may be evaluated in the same way, for example, total numbers of lines of code (LOC), number of commented lines of code (CLOC) and total number of characters (NCHAR) are all suitable for collection during lexical analysis. Other size metrics such as number of functions, number of statements, number of statements per line, etc., are better suited to collection during syntax analysis and can be based on YACC. Most complexity metrics, as we will see, are also better collected during syntax analysis.

As well as performing certain measurements during lexical analysis, it is also possible to look for features of the code which are undesirable for some reason (sometimes referred to as defects). For example, very long or very short identifiers are often cited as being inappropriate in code that is intended to be readable. Readability is regarded as an important quality characteristic of code that is likely to be read many times, for example for maintenance purposes. It is not difficult to spot short or long identifiers during lexical analysis, as we will see. Of course, it is also desirable that identifiers should be meaningful, but this is much more difficult to check automatically!

The following Lex input could be used to identify long and short identifiers:

```
%%
letter      [a-zA-Z]
digit       [0-9]
identifier  {letter}({letter}|{digit})*
{identifier} {if (yyleng == 1)
            printf (
            "identifier %s is one character long\n",
            yytext);
            if (yyleng > 8)
            printf (
            "identifier %s is greater than eight
            characters long\n", yytext);}
```

Lengths of constants may also be checked in a similar way to see that they do not exceed the limits imposed by the implementation. However, it is often felt that such checks are not appropriate for the front end of a compiler to perform, since the front end should be machine and implementation independent, as far as possible.

A large number of 'quality' checks can usefully be made on source code such as:

- inappropriate use of goto;
- high control flow complexity;
- undue depth of nesting;
- arbitrary constants in expressions;

the last being considered less desirable than associating an identifier with the constant value. Most of these checks, however, are better done during syntax analysis and we will discuss some of them in chapter 5.

We include one more example just to show the range of tools that can be produced by Lex. We do not know of any programming languages that allow the use of Roman numerals to represent integers, but the inclusion of such a feature would not cause any great problem for the lexical analyser, though, presumably, it would lead to much confusion among the human users of the language!

We first note that a superset of the Roman numerals may be defined by a regular expression namely

$$M^*(CM\,|\,CD\,|\,DC^*\,|\,C^*)\,(XC\,|\,XL\,|\,LX^*\,|\,X^*)\,(IX\,|\,IV\,|\,VI^*\,|\,I^*)$$

which is easily obtained by considering how the thousands, hundreds, tens and units may be expressed. The expression generates *all* Roman numerals and some strings that are not Roman numerals such as

VIIIIII

which has too many *I*s. Such strings could be avoided by replacing the last part of the regular expression by

$$IX\,|\,V\,|\,VI\,|\,VII\,|\,VIII\,|\,IV\,|\,I\,|\,II\,|\,III\,|\,\varepsilon$$

to which could be added *IIII*, (which is usually only seen on clock faces), if desired. A similar treatment to the first three parts of the regular expression would also eliminate illegal strings, so it is possible to write down a (rather complex) regular expression representing *exactly* all the Roman numerals. To be precise, the above expression would have to be further amended to eliminate the possibility of the empty string ε being accepted as a Roman numeral. As far as Lex is concerned, the transformations are not really necessary as some of the checks required to eliminate illegal strings can be coded into the actions. The following is the Lex input required to evaluate a Roman numeral:

```
%{
int value = 0;
%}

thousands   M*
hundreds    CM|CD|DC*|C*
tens        XC|XL|LX*|X*
units       IX|IV|VI*|I*
%%
{thousands}{value = value + yyleng * 1000;}
{hundreds}  {if (!strcmp(yytext, "CM"))
             value = value + 900;
             else  if(!strcmp(yytext, "CD"))
                 value = value+400;
                 else  if (yytext [0] == 'D')
                     value = value+500+(yyleng -1)* 100;
```

```
                                 else value = value + yyleng * 100;}
{tens}         {if (!strcmp(yytext, "XC"))
               value = value+90;
               else  if (!strcmp(yytext, "XL"))
                     value = value+ 40;
                     else  if (yytext [0] == 'L')
                           value = value+50+(yyleng-1)*10;
                           else    value = value + yyleng * 10;}
{units}        {if (!strcmp(yytext, "IX"))
               value = value + 9;
               else  if (!strcmp(yytext,"IV"))
                     value = value + 4;
                     else  if (yytext [0] == 'V')
                           value = value+5+(yyleng-1);
                           else value = value + yyleng;}
%%
main()
{yylex();
printf("value of numeral is%d\n", value);
}
```

To include checks for too many Cs, Xs or Ls, something like the following would be required:

```
{hundreds}  {if (!strcmp(yytext, "CM"))
               value = value + 900;
               else  if(!strcmp(yytext, "CD"))
                     value = value+400;
                     else  if (yytext[0] = 'D')
                           if (yyleng > 4)
                           printf("too many C's\n");
                           else value=value+500+(yyleng-1)*100;
                     else if(yyleng>4)printf("too many C's\n");
                     else value = value + yyleng * 100;}
```

The use of strcmp is a little counter intuitive since it is defined to produce 0 if its two parameter strings are identical. This would be equivalent to *false* in C so the value has to be inverted using the ! operator.

3.6 Interface with YACC

yylex() can be used to return a value to whichever function called it. While, in the examples we have considered, this was usually main(), it will often be the parser produced by YACC, so the appropriate actions on recognising language symbols may be as follows

```
">=" return symbol(GE);
```

where `symbol()` maps `GE` on to a unique integer representation. Language words such as `if, else, for` can be matched similarly

```
if    return symbol (if)
else  return symbol (for)
```

as long as these rules appeared before that for an identifier. However, there are advantages, from an extensibility point of view, in recognising *all* strings of this form as follows

```
{letter}{letter|digit}* return lookup (yytext)
```

where `lookup()` is a function to search a table of language words for the value of `yytext`, and to return the integer representation of an identifier or the language word recognised.

Sometimes, it will be necessary to pass the text of the symbol just recognised, as well as its syntactic class to the parser. Suppose, for example the parser analysed arithmetic expressions and also contained actions to evaluate the expressions, then the lexical analyser would need to pass the value of each number as it read it to the parser. The relevant part of the input to Lex might then be

```
{number}   {yylval = atoi (yytext); return NUMBER;}
```

`yylval` being a YACC variable which is used to associate an attribute with the current symbol. The C function `atoi` converts from string to integer and is available in `stdio.h`.

We will discuss the issues of integrating the outputs of Lex and YACC, further in chapter 5. In the meantime, Table 3.1 summarises the names specific to Lex mentioned so far.

Table 3.1

Lex name	Use
yytext	Text of last symbol recognised
yyleng	Number of characters in last symbol recognised
yylval	Value associated with last symbol recognised
lex.yy.c	C file that Lex produces

3.7 **Lexical difficulties**

Despite the overall simplicity of the lexical analysis process, a small number of language features make the production of lexical analysers a little more difficult than has been suggested up to now. Most of these features belong to one of the following classes:

- Language words being available for use as identifiers.
- The interpretation of certain character sequences being context dependent.

Both FORTRAN and PL/1 allow language words to be used as user-defined identifiers. This has the advantage of not requiring the user of the language to know *all* the language words before he/she can write a program. COBOL, on the other hand, has over 100 language words, the exact number depending on the version of COBOL that is being used, and none of these can be redefined by the user. Allowing language words to be used as identifiers, however, leads to difficulties for the lexical analyser, and perhaps at times for the human reader too. Consider, for example, the FORTRAN fragment

```
IF(I) = 1
```

which can only be interpreted as an assignment to an array called `IF`, though this is not certain until the end of the line is reached. Up to that point, it could be the start of the if-statement

```
IF(I) 1,2,3
```

In addition to allowing language words to be used as user-defined identifiers, FORTRAN also regards spaces within identifiers as being non-significant and does not (unlike most languages) use spaces as symbol separators. Consider

```
DO 7 I = 1,5
```

which is the start of a do-statement. However, up to the point where the ',' is read the characters

```
DO 7 I
```

could be an identifier.

In order to resolve these ambiguities, a lexical analyser for FORTRAN needs to be able to perform some lookahead and, presumably, this is why Lex provides facilities for matching strings, provided they are followed by a particular sequence. In FORTRAN the lookahead is usually limited, and never extends beyond the current statement. In early versions of FORTRAN, at least, only limited (and short) forms of expression were allowed as subscripts of arrays, and this helped to limit the amount of lookahead that had to be considered.

In PL/1 language words are also (in the main) not reserved and because of the more structured nature of the language (compared with FORTRAN) an arbitrary amount of lookahead can be required to resolve local ambiguities. For example

```
IF (I) = THEN + THEN;
```

where the expression 'I' may be arbitrarily complex, is an assignment statement, whereas

```
IF (I) = THEN + THEN THEN
```

is an if-statement. Similarly

```
DO WHILE(P=0);
```

is a do while-statement whereas

```
DO WHILE(P) = 0...
```

is a do-statement with a control variable `WHILE (P)`.

In ALGOL 68 – a language we do not hear so much about these days – there are problems brought about by the fact that the way in which certain sequences of characters should be grouped in to symbols depends on the context in which they appear. For example, the sequence

```
⇐
```

may denote the operator symbol '⇐' or it may also appear in the declaration of the operator '<' in

op ⇐...

In the latter case '<' and '=' would be two separate symbols as far as the syntax analyser is concerned. In the example shown, the only context required to distinguish between the two interpretations of the character sequence is the occurrence of the word **op** immediately before the two characters. However, distinguishing between the two interpretations is not nearly so straightforward when the symbol sequence appears later in a list of operator declarations, for example in the following situation

op ⇒...,⇐...

Another interesting feature of ALGOL 68, from the lexical point of view, is the issue of formats. Formats, for controlling input and output, are delimited by $ signs, and within formats the lexical structure of the language is quite different from elsewhere in the language. What is more, formats themselves may contain expressions with a lexical structure equivalent to that of expressions outside formats, and expressions within formats may contain formats, and so on to any depth. An example of a format would be

```
$n(x-1)x,dd$
```

in which the second x means a space (its normal meaning within a format) while the first x is part of an expression, indicated by the n preceding it.

A lexical analyser for ALGOL 68 needs to be able to operate in two modes, one for 'normal' ALGOL 68 text and one for text within formats, and the two modes must be able to call each other recursively. This may sound complex, but is not so hard to implement in practice!

3.8 Summary

This chapter has been concerned with lexical analysis as part of the compilation process, as well as in other applications. In particular, we have:

- shown how lexical analysers may be produced from regular expressions and finite automata;
- demonstrated how Lex may be used to produce lexical analysers;
- shown how Lex may be used to produce simple text measurement tools;
- discussed how Lex interfaces with YACC;
- given examples of language features that complicate the process of lexical analysis.

Further reading

Lexical analysis is well covered in all of the introductory compiler texts mentioned at the end of chapter 1. The standard reference to Lex is Lesk (1975). Lex also tends to be described in some detail in the documentation accompanying Unix systems, though textbooks that describe it in detail are rather sparse, the main one being Levine, Mason and Brown (1992), mentioned previously. Many compiler texts provide an outline of the tool, but few provide enough information to use it for a serious application. The most comprehensive source of information on source code metrics such as NCLOC is Fenton and Pfleeger (1996).

Exercises

3.1 Explain why lexical analysis is usually a relatively slow phase of the compilation process.

3.2 Are values of constants required during syntax analysis? Give a reason for your answer.

3.3 Suggest a finite automaton for recognising FORTRAN identifiers that are no more than six characters (letters and digits) long, and begin with a letter.

3.4 For each of the following regular expressions, define the corresponding finite automata:

(a) *l(l| d)**

(b) *d*.dd**

(c) *(a| b| c)xx*(a| b| c)*

3.5 Give a type-3 grammar corresponding to each of the regular expressions in exercise 3.4.

3.6 From the regular expression definition of real number

$$(+| - |)digit^* .digit\ digit^* (e(+| - |)digit.digit^*|)$$

derive

(a) a finite automaton accepting a real number;

(b) C code to recognise a real number based on the finite automaton.

3.7 From the regular expression definition of real number in exercise 3.6 derive a type-3 grammar generating a real number.

3.8 Consider binary strings consisting of an even number of 1s. Derive a finite automaton accepting such strings and hence derive

(a) regular expression for such strings;

(b) the Lex input to detect such strings.

3.9 Suggest methods of recovering from lexical faults.

3.10 Suggest an alternative to mutually recursive procedures to handle the two lexical modes of ALGOL 68 and discuss the advantages and disadvantages of this approach over the recursive procedure approach.

CHAPTER 4

Top-down parsing

4.1 Introduction

In this chapter, we discuss the concepts involved in top-down parsing and how they are implemented. Top-down parsing methods are more intuitive than bottom-up methods, and this is a good reason to consider them before bottom-up methods. Bottom-up methods, however, have the advantages of having better tool support and being more widely applicable than top-down parsing methods. They will be described in chapter 5.

This chapter will:

- investigate the decision criteria used in top-down parsing;
- identify the class of context-free grammars on which top-down parsing can be based;
- demonstrate simple methods of producing top-down parsers from suitable grammars;
- illustrate the transformation of grammars into an appropriate form for top-down parsing;
- discuss the advantages and disadvantages of top-down parsing;
- outline the use of context-free grammars as a framework for compile-time actions.

4.2 The decision criteria

Recall that the parsing problem consists of finding a derivation (if one exists) of a particular sentence using a given grammar. In the case of top-down parsing, it is nearly always a *leftmost derivation* that is required while, in the case of bottom-up parsing, it is usually a *rightmost derivation* that is sought. Recall also, that in top-down parsing we start with the sentence symbol and *generate* the sentence, while in bottom-up parsing we start with the sentence and *reduce* it to the sentence symbol. We will assume that the sentences to be generated, or reduced, will be read from left to right, though backward passes which read sentences from right to left are a theoretical possibility.

In section 2.5, we considered the language:

$\{x^m y^n \mid m, n > 0\}$

generated by the productions:

$S \rightarrow XY$
$X \rightarrow xX$
$X \rightarrow x$
$Y \rightarrow yY$
$Y \rightarrow y$

to show how the sentence:

xxxyy

may be derived (or generated) by a leftmost derivation, namely:

$S \Rightarrow XY \Rightarrow xXY \Rightarrow xxXY \Rightarrow xxxY \Rightarrow xxxyY \Rightarrow xxxyy$

The first step of the derivation is straightforward, since the sentence symbol S appears on the left side of only one production, so it can be written down quite simply:

$S \Rightarrow XY$

The second step, however, is not so simple since the leftmost nonterminal in the sentential form (X) appears on the left side of more than one production (two in this case). However, it should be remembered that when parsing takes place the outcome, the sentence generated, is always known. In this case it is:

xxxyy

and since it contains more than one x, the next production to be used should be:

$X \rightarrow xX$

Similarly, the third step in the derivation should apply the same production giving:

xxXY

The fourth step is:

$xxXY \Rightarrow xxxY$

and shows the production:

$$X \rightarrow x$$

being used for the first time, since this is the last x to be generated. The fifth step:

$$xxxY \Rightarrow xxxyY$$

shows the production:

$$Y \rightarrow yY$$

being applied since there will be further ys generated. The final step in the derivation:

$$xxxyY \Rightarrow xxxyy$$

applies the production:

$$Y \rightarrow y$$

since there will *no* further ys generated.

In the above example, the derivation is readily found from a knowledge of the sentence to be generated; though at most stages of the derivation a knowledge was required of *two* symbols beyond those generated so far. For some grammars more than two symbols (even an arbitrary number!) are required in order to identify a correct derivation. In what follows we will seek grammars that require at most a single symbol of *lookahead* at each stage of a derivation, in order to identify the correct production to apply.

Another useful way of showing the steps of a top-down derivation is shown in Table 4.1. The characters of the sentence are considered one at a time and are used to drive the parsing process. Once a character of the sentence has been generated it is shown as crossed out, as part of the input string. At each stage of the parse,

Table 4.1

Input string	Production	Sentential form
xxxyy	$S \rightarrow XY$	XY
xxxyy	$X \rightarrow xX$	xXY
̶xxxyy	$X \rightarrow xX$	xxXY
̶x̶xxyy	$X \rightarrow x$	xxxY
̶x̶x̶xyy	$Y \rightarrow yY$	xxxyY
̶x̶x̶x̶yy	$Y \rightarrow y$	xxxyy
̶x̶x̶x̶y̶y		

three items are shown, the input sentence with leading characters crossed out as appropriate, the production currently being applied, and the sentential form as it currently stands. When the parse is complete, all the characters in the input sentence have been crossed out and the sentential form equals the original sentence read in.

At each stage, the first symbol in the input string not crossed out is defined to be the *input symbol* and is used to drive the parse. It is advanced one each time a terminal is generated in the sentential form. During a parse the *lookahead symbol* is defined to be either the current input symbol or the end marker, a special symbol assumed to lie after the end of the sentence, usually represented by the $\perp$ symbol. Parsing decisions in top-down parsing are usually based on the lookahead symbol (or sequence of symbols), though more general methods exist in which the history of the parse so far is also taken into account.

4.3 **LL(1) grammars**

In this section we will investigate the properties of grammars that support top-down parsing with a single symbol of lookahead. Grammars will be assumed to be unambiguous so that a unique leftmost derivation of each sentence in the language exists. The aim will be to identify, for each nonterminal that appears on the left side of more than one production, disjoint sets of lookahead symbols in such a way that each set contains the lookahead symbols consistent with the application of exactly one of the alternative right sides. The choice of which production to use to replace a given nonterminal will be determined by the lookahead symbol, and the disjoint set to which it belongs. The union of the various disjoint sets, for a particular nonterminal, need not be the complete alphabet over which the language is defined. If the lookahead symbol does not belong to any of the disjoint sets then a syntax error must be present.

The set of lookahead symbols associated with the application of a particular production will be referred to as its *director symbol set*. Before defining the notion of a director symbol set, we will first define two other notions:

1. A *starter symbol* for a given nonterminal is defined to be any symbol (for example a terminal) which may appear at the start of a string generated by the nonterminal.
2. A *follower symbol* of a given nonterminal is defined to be any symbol (terminal or nonterminal) that can follow the nonterminal in any sentential form.

Computation of starter symbol sets can be quite time consuming and computationally expensive, and is always performed during parser generation, rather than each time the parser is executed. However, there are some situations in which the computation is relatively straightforward. For example if a grammar had only two productions for *T*:

$$T \rightarrow aG$$
$$T \rightarrow bG$$

with the usual convention regarding terminals and nonterminals, then the starter symbol sets are:

Production	Starter symbol set
$T \rightarrow aG$	{a}
$T \rightarrow bG$	{b}

In general, where a production starts with a terminal, its starter symbol set simply consists of that terminal. However, the fact that a production does not start with a terminal does not prevent a starter symbol set being computed for it. For example, if the productions for *R* (in the same grammar) were

$$R \rightarrow BG$$
$$R \rightarrow CH$$

then the starter symbol sets for these two productions cannot be determined 'at a glance'. However, if the only productions for *B* were

$$B \rightarrow cD$$
$$B \rightarrow TV$$

then it could be deduced that the starter symbol set for

$$R \rightarrow BG$$

was the set

$$\{a, b, c\}$$

since these are all starter symbols for *B*.

While *c* is clearly a starter for *B* from its first production, the set {a, b} also has to be included since *a* and *b* are starters of *T*. In general the situation can be even more complex. We might have, for example, a sequence of productions such as

$$A \rightarrow BC; B \rightarrow DE; D \rightarrow FG; F \rightarrow HI; H \rightarrow xY$$

which would imply, among other things, that *x* was a starter symbol for

$$A \rightarrow BC$$

Another complication arises when nonterminals may generate the empty string. For example we could have

$A \rightarrow BC$
$B \rightarrow \varepsilon$

in which case the starter symbol set for $A \rightarrow BC$ will include starters of C, as well as any starters of B (given by productions not shown). If B and C could both generate the empty string then the application of this production would be indicated by lookahead symbols that were followers of A as well as starters of BC. The *director symbol set* of a production is chosen to be the set of *all* terminals which as lookahead symbols would indicate the application of that production in a top-down parse, so that the director symbol set for

$A \rightarrow BC$

would include all *followers* of A as well as starters of BC.

Consider the following example concerning a grammar with the productions:

$S \rightarrow Ty$
$T \rightarrow AB$
$T \rightarrow sT$
$A \rightarrow aA$
$A \rightarrow \varepsilon$
$B \rightarrow bB$
$B \rightarrow \varepsilon$

The director symbol sets for the productions with alternative right sides are

Production	Director symbol set
$T \rightarrow AB$	$\{a, b, y\}$
$T \rightarrow sT$	$\{s\}$
$A \rightarrow aA$	$\{a\}$
$A \rightarrow \varepsilon$	$\{b, y\}$
$B \rightarrow bB$	$\{b\}$
$B \rightarrow \varepsilon$	$\{y\}$

The director symbol set for the production $B \rightarrow \varepsilon$ is $\{y\}$ since y can follow B, and similarly the director symbol set for $A \rightarrow \varepsilon$ is $\{b, y\}$ since b can follow A, as can y when B generates the empty string.

There is an algorithm (see further reading at the end of the chapter) to find the director symbol sets of all productions of a grammar. The complexity of the algorithm is mainly caused by the need to allow for symbols generating the empty string, and we do not describe the algorithm here. Once all the director symbol sets have been computed, then they may be compared for overlap, and we define an *LL(1) grammar* to be one in which, for each nonterminal that appears on the left side of more than one production, the director symbol sets of all the productions in which it appears on the left side are disjoint. The term LL(1) is made up as follows. The first L means reading from Left to right, the second L means using Leftmost derivations, and the 1 means with one symbol of lookahead.

The grammar referred to above is clearly LL(1) since the lookahead symbol sets for *T*, *A* and *B* are each disjoint. LL(1) grammars form the basis of the top-down parsing methods that are described in this chapter. Languages described by LL(1) grammars can always be parsed deterministically, i.e. without ever having to undo any production once it has been applied, as long as the director symbol sets for all alternative right sides of productions have been computed. They are *not* the most general set of grammars that may be used for deterministic top-down parsing but they are the ones normally used. Non-deterministic top-down parsing, based on backtracking, is no longer considered a viable procedure, though in the early days of compilers it was widely used with languages such as FORTRAN. LL(k) grammars, which require k symbols of lookahead to distinguish between alternative right sides of productions, are also no longer considered practical from a parsing point of view.

An *LL(1) language* is one that may be generated by an LL(1) grammar. It follows therefore that top-down parsing with a single symbol of lookahead is possible for any LL(1) language. We will now consider some 'theoretical' results concerning LL(1) grammars and languages, before considering the more practical issues of implementing them.

First, as we have seen, there is an algorithm to determine whether a given grammar is LL(1), so a grammar may be checked for 'LL(1)-ness' before an attempt is made to produce a top-down parser based on it. However, perhaps surprisingly at first sight, there is no algorithm to determine whether a language is LL(1) or not, i.e. whether it possesses an LL(1) grammar or not. This means that a non-LL(1) grammar may have an equivalent LL(1) generating the same language, or it may not, and there is no algorithm that, given an arbitrary grammar, will determine whether the *language* generated by the grammar is LL(1) or not. Of course, algorithms exist which work for special cases such as if the grammar is LL(1) then the language is certainly LL(1); and to spot certain classes of grammars which never generate LL(1) languages. However, in general, the problem is undecidable, or unsolvable, in the same sense as the problem of whether a language is ambiguous is unsolvable, and the Halting problem for Turing machines is unsolvable.

The above result is important, for we will see that there are grammars which are not LL(1) which nonetheless generate languages that are LL(1), i.e. the grammars have equivalent LL(1) grammars. This means that grammars often have to be transformed before they can be used in connection with top-down parsing. In fact, the grammars usually used in language definitions or in textbooks are rarely LL(1) and are not, therefore, immediately usable for efficient top-down parsing.

It is all the more unfortunate, therefore, that there is no algorithm to tell if a grammar has an equivalent LL(1) grammar, which means that there cannot be an algorithm to find the equivalent LL(1) grammar, if it exists, *in all cases*. However, in this imperfect world we sometimes have to make do with imperfect algorithms, so that, while there exists no algorithm to perform the transformation in general (i.e. for every case), there do exist algorithms that will work in a great many cases, and will *never* produce a wrong answer. However, they may occasionally get into an endless loop.

It is worth noting that there is one feature of grammars which, if present, prevents them from being LL(1), namely left recursion. Consider the productions:

$$D \rightarrow Dx$$
$$D \rightarrow y$$

Then, writing *DS* for the director symbol set:

$$DS(D \rightarrow Dx) = \{y\}$$
$$DS(D \rightarrow y) = \{y\}$$

where the second director symbol set follows immediately from the production, and the first one follows also since *D* is a starter of the right hand side. Clearly no grammar that exhibits left recursion in this way can be LL(1). Suppose, however that the *only* production for *D* was:

$$D \rightarrow Dx$$

then, of course, the director symbols for *D* would not enter into the algorithm to detect 'LL(1)-ness'. The use of this production could never lead to any terminal strings of the language, since there would be no way of getting rid of the nonterminal *D* once it appeared in a sentential form. A grammar with productions that cannot be used, or are unnecessary for some reason, is often referred to as *unclean*, and we will assume from here on that all grammars we consider are 'clean'.

The left recursion may be indirect, involving two or more productions. For example, the set of productions

$$A \rightarrow BC$$
$$B \rightarrow DE$$
$$D \rightarrow FG$$
$$F \rightarrow AH$$

exhibit indirect left recursion involving each of the nonterminals *A*, *B*, *D* and *F*. Of course there must be non-recursive rules for at least some of *A*, *B*, *D*, *F* to ensure the grammar is clean. As for direct left recursion, any grammar involving indirect left recursion will have overlapping director symbol sets for some of its nonterminals and therefore cannot be LL(1). Thus no left recursive grammar is LL(1). This is not as serious a problem as it may at first appear, as it will be shown (in section 4.5) that *all* left recursion in grammars may be replaced by right recursion, without altering the language generated.

Grammar transformations, whether performed automatically or by hand, are a necessary part of LL(1) parsing and, many would say, one of its limitations. However, given a suitable grammar, writing an LL(1) parser is simple. Some even say you can write one as fast as you can write, using the well-known method of *recursive descent* which will be described in the next section.

4.4 **Recursive descent**

The parsing method known as *recursive descent* involves the use of recursive procedure calls and operates in a top-down manner – hence the name! Suppose, for example a grammar for a programming language had PROGRAM as the sentence symbol and a single rule having the sentence symbol on the left side:

> *PROGRAM→ begin DECLIST comma STATELIST end*

words in upper case letters denoting nonterminal symbols and words in lower case letters denoting terminal symbols, as usual. Use of recursive descent parsing would consist of checking for each of the symbols on the right side of the production in turn. The occurrence of *begin* would be checked directly (by calling the lexical analyser), *DECLIST* would be checked by calling a function (conveniently called DECLIST), *comma* would be checked directly with the aid of the lexical analyser, *STATELIST* would be checked by calling a function called STATELIST, and finally *end* would be checked directly, again with the aid of the lexical analyser.

Suppose the other productions of the grammar were

> *DECLIST→   d semi DECLIST*
> *   d*
> *STATELIST→ s semi STATELIST*
> *   s*

where *d* may be thought of as standing for a declaration and *s* may be thought of as standing for a statement, but both being considered as terminals, in this instance.

The recursive descent method may only be applied to LL(1) grammars and clearly the grammar is not LL(1) since:

> *DS (DECLIST→ d semi DECLIST) = {d}*
> *DS (DECLIST→ d) = {d}*

which are not disjoint, and similarly for the productions for *STATELIST*. The grammar therefore has to be transformed. To perform the necessary transformation to the productions for *DECLIST*, it should first be realised that the two productions, between them, generate sequences of the form:

> *d*
> *d semi d*
> *d semi d semi d*

and so on, the last *d* always being generated by the second rule for *DECLIST* and the others by the first rule. The complete set of such sequences may be written:

> *d(semi d)* *

as a regular expression. We may think of each of the sequences as beginning with a *d* followed by either the *empty string*, or *semi* followed by whatever may constitute a *DECLIST*. Therefore, it is possible to rewrite the two productions as:

> *DECLIST→ dX*
> *X→ semi DECLIST*
>   ε

X being a new nonterminal in the grammar.

In a similar way the productions for STATELIST may be rewritten:

> *STATELIST→ sY*
> *Y→ semi STATELIST*
>   ε

Y being another new nonterminal.

The transformations to the grammar are not completely obvious. The simplest way to spot them is to consider the *language* generated by the productions to be transformed, as was done above. However, this type of transformation is so common that it is readily spotted and performed, either manually or automatically. It is often referred to as *factorisation* because of its similarity to the corresponding algebraic process. In fact, it is useful to think of grammars as a type of algebra with associated transformation rules that do not affect the language generated.

The productions of the transformed grammar are:

> *PROGRAM→ begin DECLIST comma STATELIST end*
> *DECLIST→ dX*
> *X→ semi DECLIST*
>   ε
> *STATELIST→ sY*
> *Y→ semi STATELIST*
>   ε

and to show it is LL(1) we only have to consider the director symbol sets for the two productions for X, and the two productions for Y. For the productions with X on the left side these are:

    $DS(X \rightarrow semi\ DECLIST) = \{semi\}$
    $DS(X \rightarrow \varepsilon) = \{comma\}$

by considering followers of X (when it generates the empty string). *comma* is a follower of *DECLIST* from:

    $PROGRAM \rightarrow begin\ DECLIST\ comma\ STATELIST\ end$

and any follower of *DECLIST* is a follower of X, from the production:

    $DECLIST \rightarrow dX$

so comma is a follower of X, and therefore a director symbol of:

    $X \rightarrow \varepsilon$

Similarly:

    $DS(Y \rightarrow semi\ STATELIST) = \{semi\}$
    $DS(Y \rightarrow \varepsilon) = \{end\}$

since *end* is a follower of *STATELIST* from:

    $PROGRAM \rightarrow begin\ DECLIST\ comma\ STATELIST\ end$

and any follower of *STATELIST* is a follower of Y from the production:

    $STATELIST \rightarrow sY$

Since, in each case, both sets of director symbols are disjoint, the grammar is LL(1).

We now write functions for each of the nonterminals of the grammar *PROGRAM, DECLIST, X, STATELIST, Y*. The functions are written in C, but any other language which allows recursive functions could be used.

```
void PROGRAM()   /*corresponds to PROGRAM*/
{ if (token! = begin)
  error();
  token = lexical();
  DECLIST();
  if (token! = comma)
```

```
        error();
        token = lexical();
        STATELIST();
        if (token! = end)
        error();
}

void DECLIST()
{  if (token! = d)
    error();
    token = lexical();
    X();
}

void X()
{  if (token == semi)
    {   token = lexical();
        DECLIST();
    }
    else if (token == comma)
    ;    /*do nothing*/
    else error();
}

void STATELIST()
{  if (token! = s)
    error();
    token = lexical();
    Y();
}

void Y()
{  if (token == semi)
    {   token = lexical();
        STATELIST();
    }
    else if (token == end)
    ;    /*do nothing*/
    else error();
}

main ()
{ token = lexical();
    PROGRAM();
}
```

The call of lexical() causes the lexical analyser to deliver the next symbol to the parser and error() is called when a syntax error has occurred. It is assumed that some sort of error recovery (which we do not specify here) is performed when error() is called. semi, comma, begin and end are pre-set constants whose values are the post-lexical analysis representations of these symbols.

The order in which the functions have been written corresponds to the order of the productions in the grammar. For compilation by Borland C compiler they would need to be preceded by the following function prototypes to allow for functions applied before their declarations:

```
void DECLIST();
void STATELIST();
void X();
void Y();
```

Recursion (though indirect) is present in the productions of the grammar and hence in the parser. Of course if none of the productions contained recursion, the language generated would be very restricted and consist only of a finite number of sentences. However the recursion in the parser can be costly, and may be avoided as follows. Rewrite the productions of the grammar in an extended notation which includes the * notation with its usual meaning of zero or more occurrences of what precedes it. The productions may then be written as:

PROGRAM → begin DECLIST comma STATELIST end
DECLIST → d (semi d)*
STATELIST → s(semi s)*

a more compact, and perhaps a more readable, representation of the grammar. The notation is sometimes referred to extended Backus–Naur notation, the original notation being equivalent to the Backus–Naur notation used originally to define ALGOL 60 in the ALGOL 60 Report.

A parser based on these productions will use iteration rather than recursion. The main() and PROGRAM () functions are the same as previously and the DECLIST() and STATELIST() functions may be rewritten as follows. There is no need now for the functions X and Y.

```
void DECLIST()
{ if (token! = d)
    error();
    token = lexical();
    while (token == semi)
    {token = lexical();
    if (token! = d)
```

```
      error ();
      token = lexical();
      }
}

void STATELIST()
{   if (token! = s)
    error();
    token = lexical();
    while (token == semi)
    {token = lexical();
    if (token! = s)
    error ();
    token = lexical();
    }
}
```

where `lexical()`, `error()`, `semi`, `comma`, `begin` and `end` have the same meanings as previously.

Right recursion can always be transformed to iteration in this way, and the process may be automated. Left recursion may not appear in an LL(1) grammar and, as we have demonstrated, may be transformed into right recursion. Therefore, as far as left or right recursion is concerned, an iterative, rather than a recursive, parser may always be produced.

However, a grammar for a type-2 (but not type-3) language will contain middle recursion (for bracket matching, etc.) and this cannot (so easily) be replaced by iteration. Consider, for example the grammar for an expression, with the following productions in which terminals are enclosed in quotes to avoid confusion between the terminals '*', '(' and ')' and the subsequent use of the same symbols as a metasymbols:

$$E \rightarrow E \;'{+}'\; T$$
$$E \rightarrow T$$
$$T \rightarrow T \;'{*}'\; F$$
$$T \rightarrow F$$
$$F \rightarrow '('E')'$$
$$F \rightarrow 'x'$$

which can be transformed to LL(1) form

$$E \rightarrow TX$$
$$X \rightarrow '{+}' TX$$
$$X \rightarrow \varepsilon$$

$T \rightarrow FY$
$Y \rightarrow$ '*'FY
$Y \rightarrow \varepsilon$

$F \rightarrow$ '('E')'
$F \rightarrow$ 'x'

Replacing recursion by iteration, where possible, we have

$E \rightarrow T($'+'$T)^*$
$T \rightarrow F($'*'$F)^*$
$F \rightarrow$ '('E')'
$F \rightarrow$ 'x'

However, the (indirect) middle recursion involving E, T, F remains and cannot be removed. The recursive descent functions corresponding to these productions also (not surprisingly) contain recursion, as well as iteration (in the case of E and T). The following implementation is based on the productions above enhanced by an extra production to introduce a sentence symbol that does not appear on the right side of any production. These are:

$S \rightarrow E$
$E \rightarrow T($'+'$T)^*$
$T \rightarrow F($'*'$F)^*$
$F \rightarrow$ '('E')'
$F \rightarrow$ 'x'

and the functions are

```
void E()
{  T();
   while (token == plus)
   {token = lexical();
   T();
   }
}

void T()
{  F();
   while (token == times)
   {token = lexical();
   F();
   }
}
```

```
void F()
{  if (token == obracket)
   {token=lexical();
   E();
   if (token == cbracket)
   token=lexical();
   else error();
   }
   else if (token == x)
   token = lexical();
   else error();
}

main ()
{ token = lexical();
E();
}
```

where plus, times, obracket, cbracket and *x* are the post-lexical analysis representation of the symbols +, *, (,) and *x* respectively. Again, in order to compile the functions, prototypes for E, F and T would have to appear at the start of the code.

One way to minimise the effect of the middle recursion is for the parser to have an explicit stack which can be used for storing return addresses for function entry and exit; and this approach is likely to be more efficient than the more general mechanism for handling recursion provided by the high-level implementation language.

4.5 Grammar transformations

Another major limitation of recursive descent parsing, as well as other methods of LL(1) parsing, is that grammar transformations are so often required. Two types of transformations are involved:

1. Removal of left recursion.
2. Factorisation.

4.5.1 *Removal of left recursion*

Left recursion, as we have seen, can always be removed from a context-free grammar. However, care should be taken in removing it lest the meanings of the strings generated by the productions concerned are changed. For example, in transforming the following productions from left recursive form to right recursive form:

$$E \rightarrow E + T$$
$$E \rightarrow T$$

it might seem that they should be transformed into

$$E \rightarrow T + E$$
$$E \rightarrow T$$

which does not affect the strings generated. This indeed may be all that is required. However, if the meaning of the strings is important, as it could be if a compiler was being constructed, or the expression was being evaluated, then the left recursive form would generate the sequence

$$T + T + T + T$$

as follows:

$$E \Rightarrow E + T \Rightarrow E + T + T \Rightarrow E + T + T + T \Rightarrow T + T + T + T$$

implying left to right evaluation of the expression, with the following bracketing:

$$((((T + T) + T) + T) + T)$$

while the right recursive form would generate the expression as follows:

$$E \Rightarrow T + E \Rightarrow T + T + E \Rightarrow T + T + T + E \Rightarrow T + T + T + T$$

implying right to left evaluation of the expression with the following bracketing:

$$(T + (T + (T + (T + T))))$$

It depends on the meaning of the operator + whether the order of evaluation of the expression will affect its value and, for the arithmetic operator + (at least for integers), the order of evaluation does not matter. However, a compiler will usually define a particular order of evaluation for arithmetic expressions that is likely to be the simplest and most efficient to implement. Left to right evaluation is, in most circumstances, considered simpler to implement than right to left evaluation, and seems more natural, so that the left recursive productions above are preferable to the right recursive ones, from this point of view at least.

Perhaps it should be pointed out that, while it would not be impossible to base a left to right evaluation of the expression on the right recursive rules given above, it would be awkward and unnatural to implement, and is something to be avoided, if at all possible.

What is really required is a right recursive grammar that implies left to right evaluation, and this is where the transformation used earlier comes in to its own, since the rules

$E \rightarrow TX$
$X \rightarrow + TX$
$X \rightarrow \varepsilon$

have the advantages of being right recursive and suggesting left to right evaluation. For example, the expression

$T + T + T + T$

is generated thus:

$E \Rightarrow TX \Rightarrow T + TX \Rightarrow T + T + TX \Rightarrow T + T + T + TX \Rightarrow T + T + T + T$

implying the bracketing:

$((((T + T) + T) + T) + T)$

Unfortunately, the transformation involved in transforming

$E \rightarrow E + T$
$E \rightarrow T$

into

$E \rightarrow TX$
$X \rightarrow + TX$
$X \rightarrow \varepsilon$

may not seem very natural. It is certainly not so simple as merely reversing the order of the symbols in the first production. However, as has already been pointed out, it is not so hard if we think in terms of the *language* generated by the rules. In general, the rules:

$P \rightarrow Pa$
$P \rightarrow b$

generate the language:

ba^*

and may also be generated by the productions:

$P \rightarrow bX$
$X \rightarrow aX$
ε

and this result can easily be extended. A more general case is where there are a number of left recursive productions for P and a number of productions for P which are not left recursive, for example:

$P \rightarrow P\alpha_1, P \rightarrow P\alpha_2, P \rightarrow P\alpha_3, ..., P \rightarrow P\alpha_n$
$P \rightarrow \beta_1, P \rightarrow \beta_2, P \rightarrow \beta_3, ..., P \rightarrow \beta_m$

where the β's do not contain P. These productions generate:

$$(\beta_1 | \beta_2 | \beta_3 | ... | \beta_m)(\alpha_1 | \alpha_2 | \alpha_3 | ... | \alpha_n)^*$$

which is also generated by the set of productions:

$P \rightarrow \beta_1, P \rightarrow \beta_2, P \rightarrow \beta_3, ..., P \rightarrow \beta_m$
$P \rightarrow \beta_1 Z, P \rightarrow \beta_2 Z, P \rightarrow \beta_3 Z, ..., P \rightarrow \beta_m Z$
$Z \rightarrow \alpha_1, Z \rightarrow \alpha_2, Z \rightarrow \alpha_3, ..., Z \rightarrow \alpha_n$
$Z \rightarrow \alpha_1 Z, Z \rightarrow \alpha_2 Z, Z \rightarrow \alpha_3 Z, ..., Z \rightarrow \alpha_n Z$

where Z is a new nonterminal, and the productions are now right (rather than left) recursive. The most general case is the above but with indirect, rather than direct, recursion. The algorithm to remove indirect left recursion is first to replace indirect left recursion with direct left recursion (which can always be done, though we do not give the algorithm here) and then proceed as described above.

The main point of the above discussion is that there is an algorithm to remove left recursion from grammars and replace it with right recursion; and that the process can be performed automatically (i.e. by a program). Use of a program, of course, makes the process more reliable, being less subject to human error. The possibility of an error in the transformation program itself should not, of course, be overlooked, but frequent use of the program should lead to confidence in it.

4.5.2 *Factorisation*

We now turn to the second type of transformation that has to be performed to the productions of grammars in order to make them LL(1). As we have seen, this is referred to as factorisation and is illustrated by the following example. Consider the grammar with productions:

$P \rightarrow aPb$
$P \rightarrow aPc$
$P \rightarrow d$

which is clearly not LL(1) since the first two productions both have a as a director symbol. The problem is removed by transforming the productions into:

$P \rightarrow aPX$
$X \rightarrow b$
$X \rightarrow c$
$P \rightarrow d$

in which aP has been factored out and X is a new nonterminal. Another example is shown by the productions:

$P \rightarrow abQ$
$P \rightarrow acR$

which can be transformed into:

$P \rightarrow aX$
$X \rightarrow bQ$
$X \rightarrow cR$

The process seems simple enough and one might imagine that it could always be performed, and that there would exist an algorithm that would transform any grammar requiring factorisation into an LL(1) grammar. However, a further example shows that this may not be the case. Consider the productions:

$P \rightarrow Qx$
$P \rightarrow Ry$
$Q \rightarrow sQm$
$Q \rightarrow q$
$R \rightarrow sRn$
$R \rightarrow r$

which is not an LL(1) grammar since the first two productions both have s as a director symbol. Before it is possible to factorise, Q and R should be substituted for, in the first two productions, using the last four. This replaces the first two productions with:

$P \rightarrow sQmx$
$P \rightarrow qx$
$P \rightarrow sRny$
$P \rightarrow ry$

which may then be factorised, giving:

$$P \rightarrow sP_1$$
$$P \rightarrow qx$$
$$P \rightarrow ry$$

where

$$P_1 \rightarrow Qmx$$
$$P_1 \rightarrow Rny$$

The full set of productions is then:

$$P \rightarrow sP_1$$
$$P \rightarrow qx$$
$$P \rightarrow ry$$
$$P_1 \rightarrow Qmx$$
$$P_1 \rightarrow Rny$$
$$Q \rightarrow sQm$$
$$Q \rightarrow q$$
$$R \rightarrow sRn$$
$$R \rightarrow r$$

The productions are now still not LL(1) since both the productions for P_1 have s as a director symbol. The problem is identical to the one we had with P originally, and we could proceed as we did then. This would involve substituting for Q and R using the last four productions then factorising by introducing a new variable P_2, only to find exactly the same problem with P_2 as we had with P_1 and P. The process would never terminate, but the grammar would get larger and larger. Of course in section 4.3 we have already pointed out that no algorithm exists to transform any grammar for an LL(1) language into LL(1) form. Therefore it is not surprising that factorisation is not always possible, *even* when the language is LL(1). The fact that the algorithm gets in to a loop and does not produce an LL(1) grammar does not tell us whether the language is LL(1) or not.

The language whose grammar is given above is *not* LL(1) and can be expressed as

$$\{s^i q m^i x \mid s^i r n^i y\}$$

which cannot be parsed top-down, from left to right since given an s as the lookahead symbol, there is no way of telling whether it should be balanced with an m or an n without arbitrary amount of lookahead to see the q or r.

The example above was a little contrived and does not represent the type of feature likely to be found in programming languages. For example, on encountering an opening bracket in a programming language, there is usually only one symbol likely to represent the corresponding closing bracket. Most programming languages, or to be more precise the context-free aspects of them, are LL(1) and are therefore capable of being parsed by recursive descent. The problem lies in the fact that the grammars normally used to represent programming languages are often not LL(1), so that grammar transformations are usually necessary before recursive descent parsers may be constructed. In the next section, we will discuss this more fully, as well as other advantages and disadvantages of LL(1) parsing.

4.6 Advantages and disadvantages of LL(1) parsing

The reason why LL(1) parsing by recursive descent is appealing to many people is its naturalness, and the method is extensively taught as an introduction to, and a framework for, compiling programming languages. In addition, it is easy to implement and to have confidence in its correctness. As well as performing the parsing process, the functions written may also contain actions to perform *type* checking and other forms of checking, as well as synthesis actions such as storage allocation and code generation.

However, we have also identified some disadvantages of recursive descent parsing, such as the inefficiency of function calls and the need to perform grammar transformations, without even knowing whether suitable transformations exist or not. The problem is not just finding the transformations but ensuring that they are performed correctly. There are therefore good reasons for using tools to perform the transformations rather than relying on a purely manual approach. Other disadvantages of recursive descent parsing are:

- the very large parsers often produced;
- the tendency for actions which are part of different phases of compilation to appear in the same function bodies.

The latter feature does not, unfortunately, tend to produce the best overall structure for a compiler.

The following are the requirements for effective use of recursive descent:

- A good grammar transformer that will *usually* be able to transform a grammar into LL(1) form – we have already seen that, for theoretical reasons, the transformer will not be able to perform the transformation for every possible input.
- The ability to represent the equivalent of the recursive descent parser in tabular form. This means that the parser, instead of entering and leaving functions as it checks the input text, will instead merely move about the tabular equivalent of the grammar, stacking return addresses as necessary.

Good transformers exist and are at times combined with tools to form the LL(1) 'tables'. In addition, the same tools may allow users to define actions to be performed at particular stages of the parse, in terms of the *original* grammar. There is considerable advantage in allowing the actions to be specified with respect to the original, rather than the transformed, grammar, since it is usually easier for the user to think in terms of the original, more natural grammar, than in terms of the less natural LL(1) grammar produced by the transformer. Earlier examples should bear this out. In particular, while left recursion will not appear in the transformed grammar, it may well appear in the original grammar, and indeed provides the most natural framework for specifying compile-time actions such as generating code to evaluate expressions from left to right. In practice, the rather unnatural nature of the transformed grammar should not really impinge on the compiler writer in any way. In the next section we show how actions to specify compile-time activities may be defined in a grammar.

4.7 **Embedding actions in grammars**

A classical way of breaking down arithmetic, and other, expressions prior to generating machine code is to form postfix notation. As an example of postfix (sometimes referred to as reverse Polish) notation, the (infix) expression

$(a + b)*(c + d)$

is represented as

$ab + cd + *$

in postfix notation. Notice that there are no brackets and no operator precedence in postfix notation. Also, if a postfix expression is evaluated from left to right, the operands of each operator are known before the operator is encountered. This makes postfix a notation from which it is relatively simple to produce object code.

Consider the expression grammar with the following productions:

$S \rightarrow EXP$
$EXP \rightarrow TERM$
$EXP \rightarrow EXP + TERM$
$EXP \rightarrow EXP - TERM$
$TERM \rightarrow FACT$
$TERM \rightarrow TERM * FACT$
$TERM \rightarrow TERM/FACT$
$FACT \rightarrow -FACT$
$FACT \rightarrow VAR$
$FACT \rightarrow (EXP)$
$VAR \rightarrow a \mid b \mid c \mid d \mid e$

so that expressions generated by the grammar include:

(a + b)*c
a*b + c
a*b + c*d*e

In what follows, we will assume the existence of an environment in which actions embedded in a grammar will be executed each time the parser analyses code generated by the corresponding part of the grammar. In order to generate postfix expressions three actions, which will be denoted by *A1*, *A2* and *A3*, need to be placed in the grammar as follows:

S → EXP
EXP → TERM
EXP → EXP + <A1> TERM<A2>
EXP → EXP − <A1> TERM<A2>
TERM → FACT
TERM → TERM *<A1> FACT<A2>
TERM → TERM/<A1> FACT<A2>
FACT → − <A1> FACT<A2>
FACT → VAR<A3>
FACT → (EXP)
VAR → a | b | c | d | e

angle brackets being used to delimit the actions.

All operators require to be stacked (action *<A1>*) in order that they may be printed at an appropriate time (action *<A2>*). Variables (*VARs*) on the other hand are just read and printed (action *<A3>*). There are *no* other actions. The stack may be defined and initialised as:

```
char stack [3];
int ptr = 0;
```

and a variable to assign the latest symbol to

```
char in;
```

The three actions are then

```
<A1>
{  stack[++ptr] = in;
}

   <A2>
{  printf("%c",stack [ptr--]);
}
```

```
<A3>
{ printf("%c", in);
}
```

The actions seem to be remarkably simple and, to be honest, we have simplified the situation a little by specifying variables to consist of a single character only. What also seems surprising, at first sight, is that the actions do not seem to take account of the differing precedences of the operators involved. However, the operator precedence is implied in the original grammar and there is no need for the actions to know anything about operator precedence, or about the use of brackets. Notice that there are no actions associated with the production containing brackets.

As an example, consider how the following expression would be transformed by the actions in the grammar:

$$(-a + b)^* (c + d)$$

To see how the various actions are used it is useful to show the effect of generating the above expression by the grammar including the actions:

$$(-<A1>a<A3><A2> + <A1>b<A3><A2>)^*<A1>(c<A3> + <A1>d<A3><A2>)<A2>$$

showing how the actions are interspersed with reading the characters of the string. The effect of the actions can be represented as in Table 4.2.

The complete output is given by reading the rightmost column from the top down, and the top of the stack is assumed to be on the right. The stack need only

Table 4.2

Character read	Action	Stack contents	Output
(			
– (minus)	A1	– (minus)	
a	A3	–	a
	A2	–	– (minus)
+	A1	+	
b	A3	+	b
	A2	+	+
)			
*	A1	*	
(		*	
c	A3	*	c
+	A1	*+	
d	A3	*+	d
	A2	*	+
)	A2	*	*

be of depth three since there are only three *different* levels of operator precedence (monadic, additive and multiplicative). A larger number of operator precedence levels would require a deeper stack. Also right recursion would have required an arbitrary sized stack!

Of course, the algorithm is dependent on the availability of a parser-generating tool to produce code to read the input, and to perform the actions appropriately. However, such tools are available, and provide a powerful means of writing parsers to read, and perform actions on, any input that can be represented as a context-free grammar. Source code is a typical example of such input, and the operations that may be performed on it are many and varied, such as generation of object code, variable cross-referencing and various types of measurement. What we have tried to illustrate is that many of the operations that are typically performed on source code are simply and naturally expressed as actions in a context-free grammar. Through expressing them in this way and with the use of suitable tools, the production of compilers and related tools may be greatly simplified. Not only are compilers relatively simple to write, but they are also simple to understand and hence to modify, leading, it is to be hoped, to a high degree of confidence in their correctness.

In the chapters that follow, we will deal in more detail with bottom-up parsing methods, and their associated tools. The benefits of using a grammar as the framework for compile-time actions will become apparent.

4.8 Summary

This chapter has been concerned with top-down parsing. In particular we have:

- defined LL(1) grammars and languages;
- shown how recursive descent parsers may be built from LL(1) grammars;
- shown how certain grammars may be transformed into LL(1) form by the removal of left recursion and factorisation;
- identified the principal advantages and disadvantages of recursive descent parsing;
- illustrated how compile-time actions may be embedded in a parser.

Further reading

The LL(1) terminology is attributed to Knuth (1971) and the properties of such grammars have been investigated by Foster (1968). Recursive descent compiling dates back to the 1960s and has been attributed to Lucas (1961). It was extensively used to produce portable Pascal compilers in the 1970s, Wirth (1971), and an example of a recursive descent compiler for Pascal has been published by Welsh and Hay (1986).

A number of compiler texts have been published over the years which are based exclusively on recursive descent parsing, including Ullmann (1994). Terry (1997) describes a tool to support recursive descent parsing and provides a copy of it with his text. The algorithm to determine whether a context-free grammar is LL(1), and to produce a parsing table for it, is described in Aho, Sethi and Ullman (1985).

Exercises

4.1 Give an example of a grammar which is not LL(1) but which generates an LL(1) language.

4.2 Explain why

(a) an ambiguous grammar cannot be LL(1);
(b) a grammar containing left recursion cannot be LL(1).

4.3 Show that each of the following languages are LL(1) by providing an LL(1) grammar in each case:

(a) $\{x^n ay^n \mid n>0\}$
(b) $\{x^n ay^n \cup x^n az^n \mid n>= 0\}$
(c) $\{x^n ay^n \cup z^n ay^n \mid n> = 0\}$

($\cup$ is the usual 'set union' operator)

4.4 Discuss the relative advantages and disadvantages of left recursion in grammars from a parsing point of view.

4.5 Consider the two sets of productions

(a) $DECLIST \rightarrow d\ semi\ DECLIST$
     $DECLIST \rightarrow d$
(b) $DECLIST \rightarrow DECLIST\ semi\ d$
     $DECLIST \rightarrow d$

together with the sentence

$d\ semi\ d\ semi\ d$

For each of the sets of productions (a) and (b), state which d is produced by the second production
$DECLIST \rightarrow d$

4.6 Give LL(1) grammars for each of the following languages

(a) $\{0^n a1^{2n} \mid n \geqslant 0\}$
(b) $\{\alpha \mid \alpha$ is in $\{0, 1\}^*$ and does not contain two consecutive 1's$\}$
(c) $\{\alpha \mid \alpha$ consists of an equal number of 0's and 1's$\}$

4.7 Is the grammar with the following productions LL(1) or not? Give a reason for your answer.

$S \rightarrow AB$
$S \rightarrow PQx$
$A \rightarrow xy$
$A \rightarrow m$
$B \rightarrow bC$
$C \rightarrow bC$
$C \rightarrow \varepsilon$
$P \rightarrow pP$
$P \rightarrow \varepsilon$
$Q \rightarrow qQ$
$Q \rightarrow \varepsilon$

where S is the sentence symbol.

4.8 Describe the language generated by the grammar in exercise 4.7.

4.9 Transform the grammar with the following productions into LL(1) form:

$S \rightarrow EXP$
$EXP \rightarrow TERM$
$EXP \rightarrow EXP + TERM$
$EXP \rightarrow EXP - TERM$
$TERM \rightarrow FACT$
$TERM \rightarrow TERM^* FACT$
$TERM \rightarrow TERM/FACT$
$FACT \rightarrow - FACT$
$FACT \rightarrow (EXP)$
$FACT \rightarrow VAR$
$VAR \rightarrow a \mid b \mid c \mid d \mid e$

4.10 Show where the actions defined in section 4.7 to produce postfix notation would appear in the transformed grammar of exercise 4.9.

CHAPTER 5

Bottom-up parsing

5.1 **Introduction**

In this chapter, we describe bottom-up parsing and how it is implemented. In particular, we will:

- illustrate the steps involved in bottom-up parsing, and identify the decision criteria involved;
- show how a parsing table can be used to drive the bottom-up parsing process;
- show how the parsing table may be constructed for particular classes of grammars;
- summarise the main features of bottom-up parsing;
- introduce the parser generator tool, YACC, and show how it can be used to produce a range of simple syntax-oriented tools;
- discuss some of the practical issues involved in using YACC.

5.2 **Basic ideas**

The parsing problem consists of finding a derivation (if one exists) of a particular sentence using a given grammar. In the case of bottom-up parsing, a rightmost derivation is usually sought, and we will illustrate how this may be done with grammar used in section 4.2 to illustrate leftmost derivations. Recall that the language:

$$\{x^m y^n \mid m, n > 0\}$$

was generated by the productions:

$$S \rightarrow XY$$
$$X \rightarrow xX$$
$$X \rightarrow x$$
$$Y \rightarrow yY$$
$$Y \rightarrow y$$

and we consider again how a derivation (in this case a rightmost derivation) of the sentence

xxxyy

may be found.

The derivation will be:

$$S \Rightarrow XY \Rightarrow XyY \Rightarrow Xyy \Rightarrow xXyy \Rightarrow xxXyy \Rightarrow xxxyy$$

Notice that the same number of steps are involved as for the leftmost derivation, and each production is used the same number of times, though the order in which the productions are used is different. In bottom-up parsing, however, the steps of the derivation are not identified in the order shown, but in the *opposite* order, and the rightmost *parse* corresponding to the above derivation would be written:

$$xxxyy \Rightarrow xxXyy \Rightarrow xXyy \Rightarrow Xyy \Rightarrow XyY \Rightarrow XY \Rightarrow S$$

At each step a production of the grammar is applied, the right side of the production being replaced by its left side, which consists of a single symbol. Assuming that the sentence

xxxyy

is read from left to right, it is not immediately obvious why the first x is not replaced by X at the first step of the parse, using the corresponding production of the grammar, or why the first y is not replaced by Y in a similar way at the fourth step. Clearly some other information is required, apart from the productions of the grammar, in order to perform the parse. We will now look at the bottom-up parsing process in more detail.

In bottom-up parsing right sides of productions are not recognised until they have been completely read, and there is a need, therefore, to store partially recognised right sides of productions until they can be replaced by their corresponding left sides. A stack is a suitable structure for storing these partially recognised strings. Therefore, a detailed description of the bottom-up parsing process involves showing the contents of this stack, as well as the information shown in connection with top-down parsing in section 4.2. The steps of the parsing process may be thought of as consisting of two types of action:

1. Putting the last symbol read on top of the stack – a *shift* action.
2. Replacing the string on top of the stack by applying a production of the grammar – a *reduce* action.

We are now ready to look at the parse described above in more detail. The various steps are shown in Table 5.1. The top of the stack is to the right, and the last column indicates whether a shift or reduce action takes place. A *shift action*

Table 5.1

Input string	Stack	Production	Sentential form	(S/R)
xxxyy			xxxyy	
∗xxyy	x		xxxyy	(S)
∗∗xyy	xx		xxxyy	(S)
∗∗∗yy	xxx		xxxyy	(S)
∗∗∗yy	xxX	X → x	xxXyy	(R)
∗∗∗yy	xX	X → xX	xXyy	(R)
∗∗∗yy	X	X → xX	Xyy	(R)
∗∗∗∗yy	Xy		Xyy	(S)
∗∗∗∗∗y	Xyy		Xyy	(S)
∗∗∗∗∗y	XyY	Y → y	XyY	(R)
∗∗∗∗∗y	XY	Y → yY	XY	(R)
∗∗∗∗∗y	S	S → XY	S	(R)

involves consuming a symbol from the original string and stacking it, while a *reduce action* involves a change to the top of the stack and to the sentential form. At the start of the parse the sentential form is simply the sentence to be read and the stack is empty, while at the end of the parse the sentential form is the sentence symbol, the string has been completely read, and the stack contains the sentence symbol alone.

Although the above representation shows the effects of each of the parser moves clearly, it goes no further in explaining when shift and when reduce actions should take place, and which, of possibly several, reduce actions should take place. A *necessary* condition for a reduce action is that the right hand side of some production is on the top of the stack, otherwise a shift action will take place and the next symbol will be read on to the top of the stack. However, the occurrence of the right hand side of a production on top of the stack is not a *sufficient* condition for a reduction to take place. In the illustration above, when x appeared alone on the stack, near the start of the parse, it was *not* reduced to X, though the reason for this is not clear.

In addition, it may be possible to identify the right side of more than one production from the string of symbols on the top of the stack, so there may be two or more possible reductions, at a particular stage of a parse. If, at a particular stage of a parse, either a shift or a reduce action seems possible, there is said to be a *shift–reduce conflict* in the parse. If two or more reduce actions seem possible at a particular point in a parse there is said to be a *reduce–reduce conflict*. In order to arrive at a deterministic parsing method there has to be a way of resolving shift–reduce and reduce–reduce conflicts that arise. In practice, these conflicts are resolved using information of one or other, or both, of the following types:

- previous history of the parse;
- lookahead information.

As with top-down parsing, a single symbol of lookahead information is often used to resolve conflicts. In addition, information concerning the history of the parse so far may be used to resolve conflicts. In the example above it was the lookahead of *y* which determined that the reduction using

$$X \rightarrow x$$

should be applied, and, similarly, the lookahead $\perp$ (end marker) which determined that the reduction using

$$Y \rightarrow y$$

should be applied.

A grammar that has the property that all left to right bottom-up parsing conflicts are capable of resolution based on a fixed amount of information concerning the parse so far, and a limited amount of lookahead is said to be LR(k), where the L means reading from Left to right, the R means using Rightmost derivations, and the k means with k symbols of lookahead. An LR(k) language is one that may be generated by an LR(k) grammar.

If only one symbol of lookahead is required, the usual situation, the grammar or language is LR(1).

LR parsing will be illustrated further by means of another example. Consider the grammar with productions:

1. $E \rightarrow E + T$
2. $E \rightarrow T$
3. $T \rightarrow T*F$
4. $T \rightarrow F$
5. $F \rightarrow (E)$
6. $F \rightarrow x$

in which E is the sentence symbol. The grammar (as it stands) may be used as a basis for bottom-up parsing as is shown by parsing the following sentence (Table 5.2).

$$x + x + x^*x$$

The first x to be put on the stack is reduced to F then to T then to E whereas the second and third xs are reduced to F then to T and the fourth one to F only! The first and second xs have the same lookahead and their different treatment is based on the history of the parse so far. In the case of the third and fourth xs the lookahead symbols are different ($*$ and $\perp$ respectively) but again the different treatment is based on the parse history. The criteria for deciding whether to shift or reduce or, for a reduce action, which production to reduce by, can be contained in a table, usually referred to as the parse table (or parsing table). We gloss over how the parse table is formed for the moment, and explain first how it is used to determine the course of the parse. The parse table is formed once, when the compiler is constructed, and used to drive each parse, thereafter. Since the parse table is

Table 5.2

Input string	Stack	Production	Sentential form	(S/R)
$x + x + x^*x$			$x + x + x^*x$	
$*+ x + x^*x$	x		$x + x + x^*x$	(S)
$*+ x + x^*x$	F	$F \rightarrow x$	$F + x + x^*x$	(R)
$*+ x + x^*x$	T	$T \rightarrow F$	$T + x + x^*x$	(R)
$*+ x + x^*x$	E	$E \rightarrow T$	$E + x + x^*x$	(R)
$*+x + x^*x$	$E+$		$E + x + x^*x$	(S)
$*+*+ x^*x$	$E+ x$		$E + x + x^*x$	(S)
$*+*+ x^*x$	$E+ F$	$F \rightarrow x$	$E + F + x^*x$	(R)
$*+*+ x^*x$	$E+ T$	$T \rightarrow F$	$E + T + x^*x$	(R)
$*+*+ x^*x$	E	$E \rightarrow E+ T$	$E + x^*x$	(R)
$*+*+x^*x$	$E+$		$E + x^*x$	(S)
$*+*+*x$	$E+ x$		$E + x^*x$	(S)
$*+*+*x$	$E+ F$	F->x	$E + F^*x$	(R)
$*+*+*x$	$E+ T$	T ->F	$E + T^*x$	(R)
$*+*+*x$	$E+ T^*$		$E + T^*x$	(S)
$*+*+*x$	$E+ T^*x$		$E + T^*x$	(S)
$*+*+*x$	$E+ T^*F$	F->x	$E + T^*F$	(R)
$*+*+*x$	$E+ T$	T->T^*F	$E + T$	(R)
$*+*+*x$	E	E->$E+ T$	E	(R)

formed by a tool such as YACC, there is no need for the user, or even the compiler developer, to understand how it is formed. However, we will discuss the issues involved in due course.

5.3 Using the parse table

The parse (or parsing) table used for bottom-up parsing is rectangular, with a row for each of the states (always a finite number) in which the parser may be, and a column for each terminal and nonterminal in the grammar. Table 5.3 shows a simple example of a parse table.

At the start of the parsing process, the parser is in state *1* with the first symbol in the input string as the input symbol. Each parsing step will be driven by the table entry identified by the *current state* and the *input symbol*. A table entry may be of one of two types:

1. A *shift* entry of the form *Sm*, causing the parser to perform a shift action and to change state to the state *m*.
2. A *reduce* entry of the form *Rn*, causing the parser to perform a reduce action, using production *n*.

Blank entries in the table correspond to syntax errors in the input and, if desired, a distinct error message may be associated with each blank entry. In practice, parsing tables may be very large, and are often compressed with the consequent cost of eliminating the distinct blank entries, and increasing the time

Table 5.3

	E	T	F	+	*	(	)	x	⊥
1	S2	S5	S8			S9		S12	
2				S3					
3		S4	S8			S9		S12	
4				R1	S6		R1		R1
5				R2	S6		R2		R2
6			S7			S9		S12	
7				R3	R3		R3		R3
8				R4	R4		R4		R4
9	S10	S5	S8			S9		S12	
10				S3			S11		
11				R5	R5		R5		R5
12				R6	R6		R6		R6

to access elements of the table. In any case, precise error messages provided by parser are often of limited value since the parser has no idea *what the user intended* when an error is discovered.

The parse table represents the language dependent part of the parser and the rest of the parser is largely, or completely, language independent, consisting of a *driver program* that interprets the data in the parse table and performs appropriate actions. While the language dependent part of the parser (the parsing table) may be rather large, the language independent part may be quite small, and is often ported from one compiler to another. We will now describe the actions of the driver.

In describing the actions of the driver, it is convenient to think of the driver making use of two stacks referred to as the *symbol stack* and the *state stack*, the symbol stack being equivalent to the stack that we described in the examples in the last section. In fact, only one stack is required, the state stack, but the use of the symbol stack helps to explain the actions of the driver.

At each stage of the parse the parser will be in one of its finite number of states and this, together with the *input symbol* (either the lookahead symbol or a nonterminal just reduced to), identifies an element in the parse table. Assuming a syntax error has not occurred, this entry will be a shift or a reduce action. At the start of the parse, the parser will be in state *1* and the input symbol will be the first symbol in the sentence to be parsed. When the table entry identified is a *shift action*, the following actions will take place:

- The symbol corresponding to the column in which the entry appears will be stacked on the symbol stack.
- The parser will move to the state indicated by the shift entry and *this* state will be stacked on the state stack.
- If the input symbol is a terminal, it is accepted and the next terminal in the sentence (or the end marker) becomes the input symbol.

When the table element identified is a *reduce action* the following actions will take place:

- *n* symbols are removed from the symbol stack and *n* states from the state stack, where *n* is the number of symbols on the right side of the production involved.
- The parser moves to the state on top of the state stack.
- The input symbol becomes the symbol on the left side of the production identified in the reduce entry.

We will now follow through the parse of

$$x + x + x * x$$

again, a step at a time, showing how all the parser steps are determined by the parsing table given in Table 5.3. At each stage, we show the contents of the symbol and state stacks.

Initially

Input string	State stack	Symbol stack	Sentential form
$x + x + x * x$	1		$x + x + x * x$

State is *1*, input symbol is *x*; from the parse table, shift to state *12*, stack *12* on the state stack and stack *x* on the symbol stack, accept *x*:

Input string	State stack	Symbol stack	Sentential form
$\cancel{x} + x + x * x$	1, 12	x	$x + x + x * x$

State is *12*, input symbol is + ; from the parse table, reduce by production *6*, remove one state from state stack (since there is only one symbol on the right side of production *6*) and one symbol from the symbol stack (for the same reason); the input symbol becomes *F*.

Input string	State stack	Symbol stack	Sentential form
$\cancel{x} + x + x * x$	1		$x + x + x * x$

State is *1* (again), input symbol is *F*; from the parse table, shift to state *8*, stack *8* on the state stack and stack *F* on the symbol stack:

Input string	State stack	Symbol stack	Sentential form
$\cancel{x} + x + x * x$	1, 8	F	$F + x + x * x$

State is *8*, input symbol is + ; from the parse table, reduce by production *4*, remove one state from the state stack and one symbol from the symbol stack; the input symbol becomes *T*:

Input string	State stack	Symbol stack	Sentential form
$\ast + x + x \ast x$	1		$F + x + x \ast x$

State is *1* (again), input symbol is *T*; from the parse table, shift to state *5*, stack *5* on the state stack and stack *T* on the symbol stack:

Input string	State stack	Symbol stack	Sentential form
$\ast + x + x \ast x$	1, 5	T	$T + x + x \ast x$

State is *5*, input symbol is +; from the parse table, reduce by production *2*, remove one state from the state stack and one symbol from the symbol stack; the input symbol becomes *E*.

Input string	State stack	Symbol stack	Sentential form
$\ast + x + x \ast x$	1		$T + x + x \ast x$

State is *1* (again), input symbol is *E*, from the parse table, shift to state *2*, stack *2* on the state stack and stack *E* on the symbol stack.

Input string	State stack	Symbol stack	Sentential form
$\ast + x + x \ast x$	1, 2	E	$E + x + x \ast x$

State is *2*, input symbol is +, from the parse table, shift to state *3*, stack *3* on the state stack and stack + on the symbol stack; accept +.

Input string	State stack	Symbol stack	Sentential form
$\ast{+}x + x \ast x$	1, 2, 3	$E+$	$E + x + x \ast x$

State is *3*, input symbol is *x*; from the parse table, shift to state *12*, stack *12* on the state stack and stack *x* on the symbol stack; accept *x*.

Input string	State stack	Symbol stack	Sentential form
$\ast{+}\ast + x \ast x$	1, 2, 3, 12	$E + x$	$E + x + x \ast x$

State is *12*, input symbol is +; from the parse table, reduce by production *6*, remove one state from the state stack and one symbol from the symbol stack; the input symbol becomes *F*.

Input string	State stack	Symbol stack	Sentential form
$\ast{+}\ast + x \ast x$	1, 2, 3	$E+$	$E + x + x \ast x$

State is 3, input symbol is F; from the parse table, shift to state 8, stack 8 on the state stack and stack F on the symbol stack.

Input string	State stack	Symbol stack	Sentential form
$\cancel{x}\!\cancel{+}\!\cancel{x} + x * x$	$1, 2, 3, 8$	$E{+}F$	$E + F + x * x$

State is 8, input symbol is $+$; from the parse table, reduce by production 4, remove one state from the state stack and one symbol from the symbol stack; the input symbol becomes T.

Input string	State stack	Symbol stack	Sentential form
$\cancel{x}\!\cancel{+}\!\cancel{x} + x * x$	$1, 2, 3,$	$E{+}$	$E + F + x * x$

State is 3, input symbol is T; from the parse table, shift to state 4, stack 4 on the state stack and stack T on the symbol stack.

Input string	State stack	Symbol stack	Sentential form
$\cancel{x}\!\cancel{+}\!\cancel{x} + x * x$	$1, 2, 3, 4$	$E{+}T$	$E + T + x * x$

State is 4, input symbol is $+$; from the parse table, reduce by production 1, remove three states from the state stack (since there are three symbols on the right side of production 1) and three symbols from the symbol stack (for the same reason, the input symbol becomes E).

Input string	State stack	Symbol stack	Sentential form
$\cancel{x}\!\cancel{+}\!\cancel{x} + x * x$	1		$E{+}T + x * x$

State is 1, input symbol is E; from the parse table, shift to state 2, stack 2 on the state stack and stack E on the symbol stack.

Input string	State stack	Symbol stack	Sentential form
$\cancel{x}\!\cancel{+}\!\cancel{x} + x * x$	$1, 2$	E	$E{+}x * x$

State is 2, input symbol is $+$; from the parse table, shift to state 3, stack 3 on the state stack and stack $+$ on the symbol stack; accept $+$.

Input string	State stack	Symbol stack	Sentential form
$\cancel{x}\!\cancel{+}\!\cancel{x}{+}x * x$	$1, 2, 3$	$E{+}$	$E{+}x * x$

State is 3, input symbol is x; from the parse table, shift to state 12, stack 12 on the state stack and stack x on the symbol stack; accept x.

Input string	State stack	Symbol stack	Sentential form
$\cancel{x}\!\cancel{+}\!\cancel{x}{+}\cancel{x} * x$	$1, 2, 3, 12$	$E + x$	$E + x * x$

State is *12*, input symbol is *****; from the parse table, reduce by production *6*, remove one state from the state stack and one symbol from the symbol stack; the input symbol becomes *F*.

Input string	State stack	Symbol stack	Sentential form
~~x+x+x~~ * x	1, 2, 3	E+	E + x * x

State is *3*, input symbol is *F*; from the parse table, shift to state *8*, stack *8* on the state stack and stack *F* on the symbol stack.

Input string	State stack	Symbol stack	Sentential form
~~x+x+x~~ * x	1, 2, 3, 8	E + F	E + F * x

State is *8*, input symbol is *; from the parse table, reduce by production *4*, remove one state from the state stack and one symbol from the symbol stack, the input symbol becomes *T*.

Input string	State stack	Symbol stack	Sentential form
~~x+x+x~~ * x	1, 2, 3	E+	E + F * x

State is *3*, input symbol is *T*; from the parse table, shift to state *4*, stack *4* on the state stack and stack *T* on the symbol stack.

Input string	State stack	Symbol stack	Sentential form
~~x+x+x~~ * x	1, 2, 3, 4	E + T	E + T * x

State is *4*, input symbol is *****; from the parse table, shift to state *6*, stack *6* on the state stack and stack ***** on the symbol stack; accept *****.

Input string	State stack	Symbol stack	Sentential form
~~x+x+x~~*~~x~~	1, 2, 3, 4, 6	E + T *	E + T * x

State is *6*, input symbol is *x*; from the parse table, shift to state *12*, stack *12* on the state stack and stack *x* on the symbol stack; accept *x*.

Input string	State stack	Symbol stack	Sentential form
~~x+x+x~~*~~x~~	1, 2, 3, 4, 6,12	E + T * x	E + T * x

State is *12*, input symbol is ⊥; from the parse table, reduce by production *6*, remove one state from the state stack and one symbol from the symbol stack, the input symbol becomes *F*.

Input string	State stack	Symbol stack	Sentential form
~~x+x+x~~*~~x~~	1, 2, 3, 4, 6	E + T *	E + T * x

State is *6*, input symbol is *F*; from the parse table, shift to state *7*, stack *7* on the state stack and stack *F* on the symbol stack.

Input string	State stack	Symbol stack	Sentential form
~~x+x+x~~*~~x~~	1, 2, 3, 4, 6, 7	E + T * F	E + T * F

State is *7*, input symbol is ⊥; from the parse table, reduce by production *3*, remove three states from the state stack and three symbols from the symbol stack; the input symbol becomes *T*.

Input string	State stack	Symbol stack	Sentential form
~~x+x+x~~*~~x~~	1, 2, 3	E+	E + T * F

State is *3*, input symbol is *T*; from the parse table, shift to state *4*, stack *4* on the state stack and stack *T* on the symbol stack.

Input string	State stack	Symbol stack	Sentential form
~~x+x+x~~*~~x~~	1, 2, 3, 4	E + T	E + T

State is *4*, input symbol is ⊥; from the parse table, reduce by production *1*, remove three states from the state stack and three symbols from the symbol stack; the input symbol becomes *E*.

Input string	State stack	Symbol stack	Sentential form
~~x+x+x~~*~~x~~	1		E + T

State is *1*, input symbol is *E*; from the parse table, shift to state *2*, stack *2* on the state stack and stack *E* on the symbol stack.

Input string	State stack	Symbol stack	Sentential form
~~x+x+x~~*~~x~~	1, 2	E	E

With the sentence symbol, *E*, on the symbol stack, and the complete sentence read, the parse terminates successfully.

While the symbol stack is useful to illustrate the progress of the parse, its contents do not affect the decisions made by the parser. Rather it is the contents of the state stack that affect the progress of the parse. The states on the stack, at any stage of a parse, correspond to partially recognised right sides of productions that will eventually be reduced to their left sides.

5.4 Forming the parse table

Now that we have seen how the parser makes use of the parse table, this section will be concerned with how the parse table is formed from the context-free grammar involved. The role of the states will be illustrated first by forming the parse table for a simple grammar generating a finite language. Later we will return to the example in the last section, to show how a parse table for a more realistic grammar is formed.

Consider the grammar with productions (P is the sentence symbol):

1. $P \rightarrow bD;Se$
2. $D \rightarrow d;d$
3. $S \rightarrow s;s$

the only sentence generated being:

bd;d; s;se

We will assume, as usual, that the parser is in state *1* at the start of the parse and annotate the grammar to show this (the sentence symbol is P in this case rather than S):

1. $P \rightarrow {}_1bD;Se$
2. $D \rightarrow d;d$
3. $S \rightarrow s;s$

After reading a *b* the grammar will be in state *2* (say) which is shown thus:

1. $P \rightarrow {}_1b_2D;Se$
2. $D \rightarrow d;d$
3. $S \rightarrow s;s$

State *2* lies immediately before a *D* is recognised, and therefore also appears at the start of the production for *D*, giving:

1. $P \rightarrow {}_1b_2D;Se$
2. $D \rightarrow {}_2d;d$
3. $S \rightarrow s;s$

States *3* and *4* also lie in production *1*. Since state *4* lies just before *S*, it also corresponds to the start of the production for *S*, giving:

1. $P \rightarrow {}_1b_2D_{3;4}Se$
2. $D \rightarrow {}_2d;d$
3. $S \rightarrow {}_4s;s$

We can insert eight more distinguishable states in which the parser may reside:

1. $P \rightarrow {}_1b_2D_{3;4}S_5e_6$
2. $D \rightarrow {}_2d_{7;8}d_9$
3. $S \rightarrow {}_4s_{10;11}s_{12}$

The parse of

bd;d;s;se

would proceed as shown in Table 5.4, and the parse is successful.

All the information required to drive the parse is in the annotated grammar, but is more readily represented in tabular form (via the parse table) as in Table 5.5.

The shift entries are readily placed in the parse table. For example, from the start of the right hand side of production *1*, state *1*, with an input symbol *b*, implies shift to state *2* and the other shift entries are equally obvious. As far as the reduce entries are concerned, the state at the end of the production is the state in

Table 5.4

Input string	State stack	Symbol stack	Sentential form
bd;d;s;se	*1*		*bd;d;s;se*
~~bd~~*;d;s;se*	*1, 2*	*b*	*bd;d;s;se*
~~bd~~*;d;s;se*	*1, 2, 7*	*bd*	*bd;d;s;se*
~~bd;~~*d;s;se*	*1, 2, 7, 8*	*bd;*	*bd;d;s;se*
~~bd;d~~*;s;se*	*1, 2, 7, 8, 9*	*bd;d*	*bd;d;s;se*
~~bd;d~~*;s;se*	*1, 2*	*b*	*bd;d;s;se*
~~bd;d~~*;s;se*	*1, 2, 3*	*bD*	*bD;s;se*
~~bd;d;~~*s;se*	*1, 2, 3, 4*	*bD;*	*bD;s;se*
~~bd;d;~~*s;se*	*1, 2, 3, 4, 10*	*bD;s*	*bD;s;se*
~~bd;d;s~~*;se*	*1, 2, 3, 4, 10, 11*	*bD;s;*	*bD;s;se*
~~bd;d;s~~*;se*	*1, 2, 3, 4, 10, 11, 12*	*bD;s;s*	*bD;s;se*
~~bd;d;s~~*;se*	*1, 2, 3, 4*	*bD;*	*bD;s;se*
~~bd;d;s;~~*se*	*1, 2, 3, 4, 5*	*bD;S*	*bD;Se*
~~bd;d;s;s~~*e*	*1, 2, 3, 4, 5, 6*	*bD;Se*	*bD;Se*
~~bd;d;s;se~~	*1*		*bD;Se*
~~bd;d;s;se~~	*1*	*P*	*P*

Table 5.5

	P	*D*	*S*	*b*	*e*	*d*	*;*	*s*	⊥
1				*S2*					
2		*S3*				*S7*			
3							*S4*		
4			*S5*					*S10*	
5					*S6*				
6	*R1*	*R1*	*R1*	*R1*	*R1*	*R1*	*R1*	*R1*	*R1*
7							*S8*		
8						*S9*			
9	*R2*	*R2*	*R2*	*R2*	*R2*	*R2*	*R2*	*R2*	*R2*
10							*S11*		
11								*S12*	
12	*R3*	*R3*	*R3*	*R3*	*R3*	*R3*	*R3*	*R3*	*R3*

which the reduction should take place, so that from the annotated version of production *1*, there should be a reduce by production *1* in state *6*. The reduce actions are put in each column for the reduce state, *as long as* there are no shift actions in the row concerned and, for this reason, the shift actions are always inserted in the table before any of the reduce actions. We will discuss later what happens if any conflicts occur between shift and reduce actions (shift–reduce conflicts) or between two reduce actions (reduce–reduce conflicts). In the above case there are no conflicts and the grammar concerned is said to be LR(0) (L, read from the left; R, using a rightmost derivation; 0, zero symbols of lookahead to resolve conflicts).

Another way of representing the grammar in the above example is by means of a directed graph as in Figure 5.1. This is known as the *characteristic finite state machine* for the grammar; the CFSM for short. As long as *shift* actions take place, it is as if the control of the parse is in the hands of this finite state machine, with the addition that each state, as it is encountered, has its state number put on the state stack. However, when a reduce action takes place the parser behaves rather differently. It then removes an appropriate number of states from the stack and undoes an equal number of moves of the finite state machine. As before, the next input symbol is the one on the right side of the production just used, in the reduction. The CFSM is formed in an exactly analogous way to which the

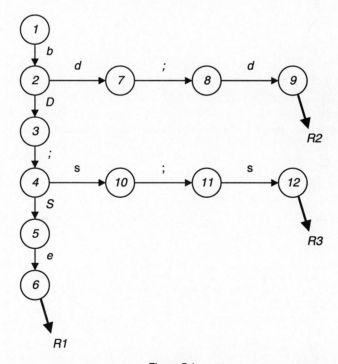

Figure 5.1

annotations were added to the grammar. Some people find the CFSM easier to produce because of its more pictorial nature. The parsing table may also be formed from the CFSM, interpreting each of the moves of the CFSM as shifts in the parsing table, and inserting the reduce moves as before.

In most cases, the reduce actions are not so easy to put in the parse table as the simple example given above suggests. To illustrate the more general approach normally required, we return to the previous example involving the grammar with the productions:

1. $E \rightarrow E + T$
2. $E \rightarrow T$
3. $T \rightarrow T * F$
4. $T \rightarrow F$
5. $F \rightarrow (E)$
6. $F \rightarrow x$

Annotation of the grammar proceeds as follows. First state 1 is placed in its various positions:

1. $E \rightarrow {}_1E + T$
2. $E \rightarrow {}_1T$
3. $T \rightarrow {}_1T * F$
4. $T \rightarrow {}_1F$
5. $F \rightarrow {}_1(E)$
6. $F \rightarrow {}_1x$

Each of the positions in which state *1* has been placed is an example of a *configuration* in the grammar. A *configuration* is defined to be a position on the right side of a production before the first symbol, after the last symbol or between any two symbols.

Configurations corresponding to the same state are indistinguishable from the parser's point of view. State *2* is readily inserted in the grammar and corresponds to a single configuration:

1. $E \rightarrow {}_1E_2 + T$
2. $E \rightarrow {}_1T$
3. $T \rightarrow {}_1T * F$
4. $T \rightarrow {}_1F$
5. $F \rightarrow {}_1(E)$
6. $F \rightarrow {}_1x$

State *3*, since it appears before a nonterminal, corresponds to a set of configurations:

1. $E \rightarrow {}_1E_2 + {}_3T$
2. $E \rightarrow {}_1T$
3. $T {}_{1,3}T * F$

4. $T \rightarrow {}_{1,3}F$
5. $F \rightarrow {}_{1,3}(E)$
6. $F \rightarrow {}_{1,3}x$

At first sight, it may seem strange to have two states corresponding to the same configuration in the grammar (e.g. states *1* and *3* *both* appear at the start of the right side of production *3*). However, as far as the history of the parse is concerned, the two states are *distinguishable* since state *3* always occurs after a +, whereas state *1* does not. We now insert state *4*:

1. $E \rightarrow {}_{1}E_{2} + {}_{3}T_{4}$
2. $E \rightarrow {}_{1}T$
3. $T \rightarrow {}_{1,3}T_{4}{}^{*}F$
4. $T \rightarrow {}_{1,3}F$
5. $F \rightarrow {}_{1,3}(E)$
6. $F \rightarrow {}_{1,3}x$

State *4* appears in two places: at the end of production *1* where it corresponds to a reduce action and, since it is defined to be the state reached from state *3* on reading a *T*, it also appears after *T* in production *3*. Already it looks as if state *4* is going to cause a shift–reduce conflict of some sort!

For a similar reason, state *5* also appears in two places, one corresponding to a reduce action at the end of production *2*, and one corresponding to a shift in production *3* (another potential problem?). Notice that, in production *3*, the states preceding *T* on the right side of the production *appear* in the corresponding order to the states after *T*, i.e. *1* leads to *5*, and *3* leads to *4*.

1. $E \rightarrow {}_{1}E_{2} + {}_{3}T_{4}$
2. $E \rightarrow {}_{1}T_{5}$
3. $T \rightarrow {}_{1,3}T_{5,4}{}^{*}F$
4. $T \rightarrow {}_{1,3}F$
5. $F \rightarrow {}_{1,3}(E)$
6. $F \rightarrow {}_{1,3}x$

State *6* will appear in several places, since it precedes a nonterminal:

1. $E \rightarrow {}_{1}E_{2} + {}_{3}T_{4}$
2. $E \rightarrow {}_{1}T_{5}$
3. $T \rightarrow {}_{1,3}T_{5,4}{}^{*}{}_{6}F$
4. $T \rightarrow {}_{1,3}F$
5. $F \rightarrow {}_{1,3,6}(E)$
6. $F \rightarrow {}_{1,3,6}x$

States *7* and *8* are readily inserted:

1. $E \rightarrow {}_{1}E_{2} + {}_{3}T_{4}$
2. $E \rightarrow {}_{1}T_{5}$
3. $T \rightarrow {}_{1,3}T_{5,4}{}^{*}{}_{6}F_{7}$

4. $T \rightarrow {}_{1,3}F_8$
5. $F \rightarrow {}_{1,3,6}(E)$
6. $F \rightarrow {}_{1,3,6}x$

State *9*, however, is more complex since it appears before a nonterminal and must therefore appear at the start of rules for that nonterminal, and so on recursively. Thus, we have:

1. $E \rightarrow {}_{1,9}E_2 + {}_3T_4$
2. $E \rightarrow {}_{1,9}T_5$
3. $T \rightarrow {}_{1,3,9}T_{5,4}{}^*{}_6F_7$
4. $T \rightarrow {}_{1,3,9}F_8$
5. $F \rightarrow {}_{1,3,6,9}({}_9E)$
6. $F \rightarrow {}_{1,3,6,9}x$

We must take care in inserting state *10*. State *10* will be the *E* successor of *9* and will therefore appear after the *E* in productions *1* and *5*. No further states, however, will be required in productions *2* and *3* to 'remember' whether the production was 'entered' in state *1* or state *9*. This is for what may appear the somewhat arbitrary reason that any new state inserted after the *T* in these productions would correspond to a set of configurations identical to that of some existing state. While it is possible that some type of conflict may occur by not inserting these additional states, this rarely occurs in practice, and the possibility is ignored for the present. After all, it is better not to have a larger parsing table than is necessary!

1. $E \rightarrow {}_{1,9}E_{2,10} + {}_3T_4$
2. $E \rightarrow {}_{1,9}T_5$
3. $T \rightarrow {}_{1,3,9}T_{5,4}{}^*{}_6F_7$
4. $T \rightarrow {}_{1,3,9}F_8$
5. $F \rightarrow {}_{1,3,6,9}({}_9E_{10})$
6. $F \rightarrow {}_{1,3,6,9}x$

No further states are required, as followers of state *9* in productions *4–6*, for arguments similar to those used for not inserting further states in productions *2* and *3*. The remaining states may be inserted straightforwardly in the grammar:

1. $E \rightarrow {}_{1,9}E_{2,10} + {}_3T_4$
2. $E \rightarrow {}_{1,9}T_5$
3. $T \rightarrow {}_{1,3,9}T_{5,4}{}^*{}_6F_7$
4. $T \rightarrow {}_{1,3,9}F_8$
5. $F \rightarrow {}_{1,3,6,9}({}_9E_{10}){}_{11}$
6. $F \rightarrow {}_{1,3,6,9}x_{12}$

The CFSM for the grammar is shown in Figure 5.2. The shifts are readily inserted into the parsing table from the grammar or the CSFM, giving Table 5.6.

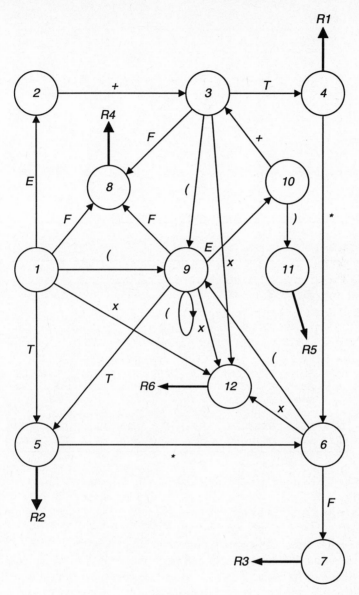

Figure 5.2

Some of the reduces are also readily inserted across the table without producing any conflicts, giving Table 5.7.

The reductions in states *4* and *5*, however, are not so straightforward, as there are already shifts in certain columns in the rows corresponding to these states. For this reason, the grammar is not LR(0), and we must take into account lookahead

Table 5.6

	E	T	F	+	*	(	)	x	⊥
1	S2	S5	S8			S9		S12	
2				S3					
3		S4	S8			S9		S12	
4					S6				
5					S6				
6			S7			S9		S12	
7									
8									
9	S10	S5	S8			S9		S12	
10				S3			S11		
11									
12									

Table 5.7

	E	T	F	+	*	(	)	x	⊥
1	S2	S5	S8			S9		S12	
2				S3					
3		S4	S8			S9		S12	
4					S6				
5					S6				
6			S7			S9		S12	
7	R3	R3	R3	R3	R3	R3	R3	R3	R3
8	R4	R4	R4	R4	R4	R4	R4	R4	R4
9	S10	S5	S8			S9		S12	
10				S3			S11		
11	R5	R5	R5	R5	R5	R5	R5	R5	R5
12	R6	R6	R6	R6	R6	R6	R6	R6	R6

symbols in determining whether to reduce or shift in certain states, i.e. in order to resolve the shift–reduce conflicts. Consider first the situation in state *4*. Either a shift or a reduce action may take place in this state. From Table 5.7 or the CFSM, we see that a *shift* is only appropriate if the lookahead is *. We consider, therefore, what lookahead symbols correspond to a *reduce*.

The reduction, if it takes place, will be to the symbol E, so we consider the symbols that may follow an E (which will be the possible lookaheads in the event of a reduction by production *1*). From production *1*, a + may follow an E, and from production *5* a) may follow an E. In addition a ⊥ may also follow an E, since E is the sentence symbol; and these three symbols [+ , ⊥,)] are the only symbols that may follow an E. We therefore put reduce actions in state *4* in the columns of the parse table corresponding to these symbols only.

As far as state *5* is concerned, * will again be the lookahead symbol when a *shift* should take place, and the lookahead symbols associated with a reduction will again be [+ , ⊥,)], the followers of E. We may now put the reduce actions for productions *1* and *2* in the appropriate columns of states *4* and *5*, giving Table 5.8. Since there are no shift actions in those positions, the shift–reduce conflicts have been resolved.

Although it may not be strictly necessary, the positions of the other reduce actions could also be computed taking into account lookahead symbols. For example, a reduction by production *3* would only be appropriate if the lookahead was a symbol which could follow *T*. Since * may follow *T* from production *3*, and any follower of *E* may be a follower of *T* from production *2*, the complete sets of symbols which may follow *T* are [* , + , ⊥,)]. The *R3* action should, therefore, only appear in those columns for state *7*. Similarly for state *8*, since the reduction is again to *T*, the *R4* actions should only appear in the columns corresponding to [* , + , ⊥,)].

In states *11* and *12* the reduction involved is to the symbol *F* and the symbols which may follow *F* are all the followers of *T*, from production *4*, i.e. the set [* , + , ⊥,)] again. *R5* and *R6* actions should therefore only appear in these columns. The table then becomes the one in Table 5.3 that we used earlier, without showing how it had been derived.

When the parse table is formed taking into account *all possible* follower symbols of the nonterminal on the left side of the production in order to place reduce actions, it is known as the *simple LR(1) table*, or the *SLR(1) table*, and the algorithm used is known as the *SLR(1) algorithm*. If the table formed in this way contains no conflicts then the grammar from which it was produced is known as an *SLR(1) grammar*. Clearly all LR(0) grammars are SLR(1), though as the current example shows, not all SLR(1) grammars are LR(0). Even if a grammar is not SLR(1) it may still be possible to resolve remaining conflicts in some other way, and the grammar may still be LR(1).

Either of Tables 5.8 or 5.3 could be used as the parse table for the grammar we have been discussing. The first one is easier to compute and the second one will support a more efficient parsing process, but only in the following sense.

Table 5.8

	E	T	F	+	*	(	)	x	⊥
1	S2	S5	S8			S9		S12	
2				S3					
3		S4	S8			S9		S12	
4				R1	S6		R1		R1
5				R2	S6		R2		R2
6			S7			S9		S12	
7	R3	R3	R3	R3	R3	R3	R3	R3	R3
8	R4	R4	R4	R4	R4	R4	R4	R4	R4
9	S10	S5	S8			S9		S12	
10				S3			S11		
11	R5	R5	R5	R5	R5	R5	R5	R5	R5
12	R6	R6	R6	R6	R6	R6	R6	R6	R6

It is possible that the use of Table 5.8 would cause a reduction to take place, whereas the use of Table 5.3 would indicate a syntax error. In these circumstances, a syntax error will in fact exist, and the reduction signalled by Table 5.8 would in fact be incorrect. However, even using Table 5.8, a syntax error would still be signalled a short time afterwards. The syntax error would be discovered later, in the sense that a few more parser actions will have taken place than would have been the case if Table 5.3 had been used, but before any further symbols from the input string had been read. From the user's point of view, the syntax error would be discovered at the same stage of the parse in terms of the number of symbols read. In both cases, the syntax error would be discovered on the first inadmissible symbol. Detecting an error on the first inadmissible symbol is one of the desirable features of LR(1) (and LL(1)) parsers. We illustrate the ideas described above by an example based on the grammar we have been discussing.

Consider the following syntactically incorrect input string

xx

Initially

Input string	State stack	Symbol stack	Sentential form
xx	1		*xx*

State is *1*, input symbol is *x*; using either Table 5.3 or Table 5.8, shift to state *12*, stack *12* on the state stack and stack *x* on the symbol stack; accept *x*.

Sentence	State stack	Symbol stack	Sentential form
✶x	1, 12	*x*	*xx*

The state is *12* and the input symbol is *x*. According to Table 5.3, there is a syntax error; however, according to Table 5.8 a reduce by production *6* is indicated. In order to see what happens, we will follow Table 5.8 removing one symbol from the state stack and one symbol from the symbol stack. *F* is then the new input symbol.

Sentence	State stack	Symbol stack	Sentential form
✶x	1		*xx*

The state is *1* and the input symbol is *F*; from the parse table (Table 5.8), shift to state *8*, stack *8* on the state stack and stack *F* on the symbol stack.

Sentence	State stack	Symbol stack	Sentential form
✶x	1, 8	*F*	*Fx*

The state is *8* and the input symbol is *x*; again, according to Table 5.8, a reduce is indicated, this time by production *4*. Remove one state from the state stack and one symbol from the symbol stack; the input symbol becomes *T*.

Sentence	State stack	Symbol stack	Sentential form
＊x	*1*		*Fx*

The state is *1* and input symbol is *T*; according to Table 5.8, shift to state *5*, stack *5* on the state stack and stack *T* on the symbol stack.

Sentence	State stack	Symbol stack	Sentential form
＊x	*1, 5*	*T*	*Tx*

The state is *5* and input symbol is *x*; now Table 5.8 indicates a syntax error.

Although a syntax error may be detected later, in terms of parser moves, using a table with the extra reduces in it such as Table 5.5, the analysis of a program *without* syntax errors will take no longer using this version of the table. The usual approach, therefore, when forming the parse table, is to put the reduces in every column for a reduce state, if this causes no conflicts; and, if it does, to consider *follower symbols* as necessary.

As we have seen, the LR(0) algorithm is successful if there is no need to consider follower symbols at all, and all the reduce actions can be placed in all the columns. The SLR(1) algorithm is successful if the conflicts discovered by the LR(0) algorithm are resolved using the follower symbols in the way we have described. However, on occasion, even this approach does not resolve all the conflicts, and a more general approach is required. In this case, the LALR(1) (lookahead LR(1)) algorithm is performed to try to resolve all remaining conflicts. The LALR(1) algorithm restricts the number of follower symbols that need to be considered for a particular reduction, by using left context (i.e. state) information to identify only those followers that are valid in the state concerned.

Even the LALR(1) algorithm may not succeed in removing all conflicts. This may, of course, be because the grammar is not LR(1) so that it is not possible to form a conflict-free parse table of the type we have been describing. Ambiguous grammars, for example, are not LR(1). However, there exist grammars that are LR(1) and not LALR(1). For these grammars, the parsing table is formed by introducing extra states to the annotated grammar in exactly the circumstances in which we avoided introducing extra states in the example described above, i.e. when more than one state would correspond to the same set of configurations in the grammar. Occasionally such states are required, perhaps even many such states, making the parsing table very large indeed. Fortunately, there are few grammars requiring such a treatment and, as most such grammars appear rather contrived in the context of programming language grammars, we will not give an example of any.

We may now talk about a general algorithm to form an LR(1) parsing table. It proceeds in a number of steps:

1. Try using the LR(0) algorithm to form the parsing table. If it succeeds (i.e. there are no conflicts), the algorithm terminates.
2. If the LR(0) algorithm does not succeed, try the SLR(1) algorithm. If it succeeds, the algorithm terminates.
3. If the SLR(1) algorithm does not succeed, try the LALR(1) algorithm. If it succeeds, the algorithm terminates.
4. If the LALR(1) algorithm does not succeed, try the LR(1) algorithm.

The basic philosophy behind the approach described above is to try the simplest algorithm first and so on. Few programming languages will actually be LR(0), but many will be SLR(1) and the rest almost certainly LALR(1). The number of states will be the same for the LR(0), SLR(1) and LALR(1) grammars, but often considerably more for the LR(1) algorithm. No matter which algorithm is used to form the parse table, the manner in which it is used by the parser is the same.

5.5 Features of LR parsing

Some theoretical results are worth mentioning at this stage:

- There exists an algorithm to determine whether a grammar is LR(k), for a given k.
- There is no algorithm to determine whether there exists a k for which a given grammar is LR(k). The problem is undecidable, in general.
- Any language which is LR(k) for a given k is also LR(1).

However, none of these results is particularly significant from a practical point of view. The third one means that there is no need to consider lookaheads of more than one symbol, from a language point of view, since if a language has an LR(k) grammar, for any k, it also has an LR(1) grammar. What is less obvious, and is not subject to proof, is that, in practice, the available grammar is usually LR(1) anyway, though we will give a few examples shortly of grammars that are LR(2) and not LR(1). However, as we will see, they are readily transformed into LR(1) grammars.

In view of the availability of an LR(1) grammar for all LR(k) languages the first two results are not of great practical significance. At first sight, they may appear to contradict each other. However, the fact that, for a fixed k, there exists an algorithm (similar to the one we have described for $k = 1$) to determine whether the grammar is LR(k), does not imply that there is a terminating algorithm that will find the lowest value of k (should one exist) for which a grammar is LR(k). To put it another way, algorithms exist to determine whether the grammar is LR(1), LR(2), etc., but no matter how large the value of n for which the grammar is found not to be LR(k) for all $k \leqslant n$, it may not be assumed that there cannot exist a value of k larger than n, for which the grammar is LR(k). Therefore, the algorithm may not terminate.

A few typical programming language grammars exhibit non-LR(1) features. Consider, for example, the grammar fragment with productions:

```
1. S→ aL, S
2.      |aL
3. L→ x,L
4.      |x
```

so that the sentences generated are lists of lists of the form:

ax, x, x, x, ax, x

the *same* separator being used for *both* levels of list. The grammar is not LR(1) since on reading the fragment

ax

with the lookahead symbol ',' it is not known whether to shift (as in production *3*), or to reduce (by production *4*). Two lookahead symbols, however, resolve the conflict since the lookahead sequence ',*x*' implies a shift, corresponding to production *3*, while the lookahead pair ',*a*' implies a reduce, corresponding to the end of production *4*. This follows since ', *S*' is a follower of *L* (from production *1* and '*a*' is a starter of *S* (again from production *1*). Also '*x*' is a starter of *L*.

According to the theory presented above, the LR(2) grammar may be transformed to an LR(1) grammar. In this case, the 'simple' transformation of amending the grammar to generate a single list of *x*s and *ax*s (after the first one, which is always an *ax*) makes the grammar LR(1). The grammar is then:

```
1. S→ axF
2. F→ , JF
3.      |ε
4. J→ ax
5.      |x
```

Verification that the transformed grammar is LR(1) is one of the exercises at the end of the chapter and, as for the other exercises, a solution is supplied at the end of the book. The features of the original grammar that prevented it being LR(1) appear to have been the combination of the use of right recursion and the double use of the comma. However, while grammars containing left recursion cannot be LL(1), the corresponding result for LR(1) grammars, namely that they cannot contain right recursion, does not hold in general. It is only in comparatively rare circumstances that right recursion produces problems in LR(1) grammars, and, when it does, it is usually due to a combination of grammar features rather than to the right recursion alone. However, left recursion does have advantages over right recursion in most parsers, as it allows lists to be reduced as they are read in, rather than having to stack complete lists before they can be reduced. For this reason, left recursion is to be preferred to right recursion in most cases.

Ambiguous grammars, of course, cannot be LR(1), and the way in which ambiguity often creeps into grammars is when there are alternative derivations for the empty string, ε. A fairly trivial example of this is shown in the grammar fragment:

$$S \rightarrow A|$$
$$\quad B|$$
$$\quad \varepsilon$$
$$A \rightarrow aA$$
$$\quad \varepsilon$$

so that there are two derivations of ε:

$$S \Rightarrow \varepsilon$$
$$S \Rightarrow A \Rightarrow \varepsilon$$

one of which may easily be removed from the grammar simply by replacing the production

$$A \rightarrow \varepsilon$$

with the production

$$A \rightarrow a$$

without changing its generative power in any way. Such problems are quite common in grammars, but are usually easily dealt with.

Overall, LR parsing has the following desirable features:

- It may be applied to a wide class of grammars and languages.
- Grammar transformations are usually minimal.
- The time required for analysis is linear in the length of the input.
- Syntax errors are discovered on the first inadmissible symbol.
- It is well supported by tools.

Moreover, the tool support usually means that the compiler writer does not have to know in detail how the parse table is formed. In the next section, we discuss in detail how a well-known parser generator tool is used.

5.6 **Introduction to YACC**

In this section, we show, by means of examples, how the parser generator YACC is used to produce parsers from context-free grammars. We also show how such parsers may be used as the basis for a range of analysis tools, including compilers and metric evaluation tools, by embedding source code actions in the grammar rules. YACC (Yet Another Compiler-Compiler) was developed at Bell Laboratories, and will produce an LR parser from any LALR(1) grammar. It is fully compatible with Lex, and actually preceded it by some years, so that in the early days of YACC the user had to produce his or her own hand-coded lexical analyser to go along with the automatically produced parser. This, however, is no longer required and we will demonstrate in the examples how Lex and YACC work together.

The input to YACC is always of the form

```
declarations
%%
rules
%%
user-defined functions
```

However, the *declarations* section and the *user-defined functions* section may be empty. If the *user-defined functions* section is empty, the second %% may be omitted, so that the minimal YACC input is

```
%%
rules
```

The output from YACC is a C program that may be compiled in the usual way. YACC was originally designed to support RATFOR (a version of FORTRAN) as well as C, and nowadays versions of YACC are available to support a number of languages including Borland's Turbo Pascal. YACC is very similar to Lex in many ways though, of course, the types of language construct supported are more general. The language to be parsed is expressed as a context-free grammar using a notation similar to the usual notation for context-free grammars, though with some extensions which will become apparent through the examples. These extensions do not increase the power of the notation, in the sense that it may be used to describe languages that could not be described by means of a context-free grammar, but do make it simpler to describe some languages, and may also make the language description shorter.

As an example, we show how the language of arithmetic expressions may be expressed as YACC input:

```
%left '+' '-'
%left '*' '/'
```

```
%%
expr    :   expr '+' expr
        |   expr '-' expr
        |   expr '*' expr
        |   expr '/' expr
        |   '(' expr ')'
        |   num;
```

Notice that the terminals are surrounded by single quotes and the : is used in place of the more usual -> to separate the left and right sides of the productions. The | is used, as usual, to separate alternative right sides of productions. An extension to the notation in which context-free grammars are expressed is used to define the precedence levels of operators. The first line of the input above defines + and - to have the same level of precedence, since they appear on the same line, and the second line does the same for * and /. In addition, since * and / are on a lower line than + and -, they are defined to have a higher level of precedence than + and -. The occurrence of *left* before each pair of operators indicates that they associate from the left. Therefore

3+4+5

should be evaluated as

((3+4)+5)

which is the method of evaluation normally preferred, and corresponds to the use of left recursion in the grammar. The higher level of precedence of the multiplication operators over the addition operators could alternatively have been expressed (as we have seen) by defining an expression to be a sum of terms, each of which is a product of factors. However, as YACC input, this is not required, and the YACC grammar is shorter, and probably more readable. The grammar rules, on their own, are ambiguous. For example, there is more than one derivation of

3+4+5

but the associativity and precedence rules resolve the ambiguities completely. This illustrates the fact that YACC grammars may be ambiguous (despite the fact that no LR(1) grammars are ambiguous) as long as rules are provided to resolve any ambiguities. Such rules are often known as *disambiguating rules*.

The example above may be extended to include unary operators, whose precedence may not be the same as the binary operators represented by the same symbol. If the unary - was to be included, with higher precedence than the multiplying operators the YACC input would be

```
%left '+' '-'
%left '*' '/'
%left UMINUS
%%
expr  :   expr '+' expr
      |   expr '-' expr
      |   expr '*' expr
      |   expr '/' expr
      |   '-' expr        %prec UMINUS
      |   '(' expr ')'
      |   num;
```

We are now almost in a position to write a YACC input to generate a program to evaluate arithmetic expressions. First, however, we should say something about embedding actions in YACC input. As for Lex, the actions are written in C and normally (though not always) occur at the ends of syntax rules, thus corresponding to *reductions*. For example the syntax rule

```
expr  :   expr '+' expr;
```

could have an action added to become

```
expr  :   expr '+' expr  {$$=$1+$3;};
```

in which the C code is enclosed in curly brackets. The dollar variables are peculiar to YACC and are extremely useful. n is a numerical value (an attribute) associated with the nth symbol on the right side of the production and $$ is a numerical value to be associated with the symbol on the left side. Thus, in the example shown, the value of the dollar variable associated with the expression on the left side of the rule will be the sum of the values of the dollar variables associated with the first and third symbols on the right side of the rule. In this way, values may be passed from the right sides of productions to the left sides, or, looked at a different way, from the bottom of the syntax tree to the top. Finding the values at the terminal nodes of the syntax tree is a matter for the lexical analyser and, in this case, the value at the top of the syntax tree is the value of the complete expression. The value of the complete expression may be printed out.

The YACC input including commentary delimited by /* and */ could be:

```
%token NUMBER
%left '+' '-'
%left '*' '/'
%left UMINUS
```

```
/*precedence for unary minus, greater than that for the
other operators*/


%%      /* rules section*/
s      :    expr
            {printf("%d\n", $1);};
expr   :    expr '+' expr
            {$$=$1+$3;}
       |    expr '-' expr
            {$$=$1-$3;}
       |    expr '*' expr
            {$$=$1*$3;}
       |    expr '/' expr
            {if ($3 == 0) yyerror ("divide by 0");
            else $$=$1/$3;}
       |    '-' expr        %prec UMINUS
            {$$=-$2;}
       |    '(' expr ')'
            {$$=$2;}
       |    NUMBER;
%%
#include "lex.yy.c"

yyerror(s)
char *s;
{printf("%s\n",s);
}


main()
{return yyparse();
}
```

To link in with the lexical analyser produced by Lex, `lex.yy.c` is 'included' before the user-defined functions. Notice that, in the case of division, we test first to see whether the divisor is zero, in which case `yyerror` is called and the program will terminate. The user should supply his or her own version of `yyerror` and of `main` (which must return the value obtained by calling `yyparse()`). They may be as simple as those shown or more complex, if desired. Notice that terminals in the grammar that do not correspond to single characters are 'declared' as `%token`. This provides the link with the lexical analyser. Single character terminals may be passed through automatically by Lex without the need to be explicitly 'recognised'.

The input to Lex for the expression evaluator would be

```
%%
[0-9]+ {yylval = atoi (yytext); return NUMBER;}
[ \t]  ;   /*ignore whitespace*/
.       return yytext[0];
```

where `yytext` is an array containing the characters of the symbol just matched. The C function `atoi` is used to convert this string to an integer, and the symbol NUMBER is returned to provide the link with the parser. The value of the number is assigned to the integer `yylval` through which it is passed on to the parser. Notice that variables that have a special meaning in YACC usually start with the letters `yy`. This helps to avoid any confusion with user-defined variables.

Assuming the Lex and YACC inputs are in `nums.l` and `nums.y`, respectively, the following is required to generate the parser:

```
lex nums.l
yacc nums.y
cc -o nums y.tab.c -ll -ly
```

The `-o` option specifies that the parser should be produced in the file *nums*, and `-//` and `-/y` ensure that the Lex and YACC libraries are included. To execute the parser we require

```
nums <dat
```

where `dat` contains the data (an expression) to be evaluated.

While it is normal practice to put actions at the ends of rules in YACC, it is possible to embed actions in the middle of rules, as long as this causes no ambiguity in the grammar. For example, we can imagine that when an action is embedded in the middle of a rule the simple transformation is made to the grammar of introducing a new nonterminal which generates only the empty string, immediately before the position of the action. If this transformed grammar is still LALR(1) then the parsing table may be formed in the usual way. Consider, as an example, the production (from an LALR(1) grammar):

$$X \rightarrow aLMb$$

with an action embedded between the *L* and the *M*:

$$X \rightarrow aL\{action();\}Mb$$

then as long as replacing this production by the productions:

$X \rightarrow aLNMb$
$N \rightarrow \varepsilon\{action();\}$

does not prevent the grammar being LALR(1), no problem is caused by putting the action in the position shown above.

We may now return to the example in section 4.7 in which actions were placed in an LL(1) grammar to produce postfix (reverse Polish) notation from the usual, infix, notation for expressions. As an input to YACC the grammar could now be written thus:

```
S       : EXP;
EXP     : TERM
        | EXP+{A1();} TERM {A2();}
        | EXP-{A1();} TERM {A2()};};
TERM    : FACT
        | TERM * {A1();}FACT {A2();}
        | TERM/{A1();}FACT {A2();};
FACT    : -{A1();}FACT {A2();}
        |VAR {A3();}
        | ( EXP );
        VAR : a|b|c|d|e;
```

where *A1()*, etc., are function calls corresponding to the actions defined previously in section 4.7. There is no need for the user to worry about the transformations involved in introducing a new nonterminal generating the empty string for each action that is not placed at the end of a rule. YACC will deal with this automatically.

5.7 Evaluation of metrics

In section 3.5 we discussed the evaluation of source code metrics based on compiler tools, and noted that some metrics were lexical in nature, and their evaluation was readily performed by a Lex-based tool. We also pointed out that others were more syntactic in nature, and were naturally evaluated by a YACC-based tool. As an example of how a simple metric evaluation tool may be produced using YACC, suppose that the complexity of an arithmetic expression was defined, somewhat arbitrarily, by the formula:

$A + 2B + 5C$

where A is the number of binary addition and subtraction operators in the expression; B is the number of unary addition and subtraction operators in the expression; and C is the number of multiplication and division operators in the expression.

The Lex and YACC inputs for the tool could be given by the following:

```
var         [a-z]
space       [ \n\t]
morespace   {space}+
%%
{more space}      ;
{var}       {return VAR;}
.           {return yytext[0];}
```

and

```
%token VAR
%left '+' '-'
%left '*' '/'
%%
s    :   expr
{printf("%d\n", $1);};
expr :   expr '+' expr
          {$$ = $1+$3+1;}
        | expr '-' expr
          {$$ = $1 + $3+1;}
        | expr '*'     expr {$$ = $1+$3+5;}
        | expr '/'     expr {$$ = $1+$3+5;}
        | '-' expr
          {$$ = $2+2;}
        | '+' expr
          {$$ = $2+2;}
        |'(' EXP ')'
          {$$ = $2;}
        | VAR
          {$$ = 0;};

%%
#include "lex.yy.c"
yyerror(s)
char *s;
{printf("%s\n",s);
}

main()
{return yyparse();
}
```

It has been assumed in the above, for simplicity, that the expressions are composed of identifiers, brackets and operators, each consisting of a single character. Notice that it is not actually necessary to count the numbers of operators of each type.

A well-known metric, also syntactic in nature, is McCabe's metric. McCabe's metric is based on graph theory, and is equivalent to the cyclomatic complexity of a directed graph. If the control structure of a program (or part thereof) is represented as a directed graph, the value of McCabe's metric is the number of linearly independent paths through the control graph. This turns out to be equivalent to be *the number of decisions in the piece of program plus one*. Since this is an easier notion to understand, we will show how to produce a tool to count the number of decisions in a piece of software. We will use the following subset of Pascal, defined by a grammar in YACC notation, to illustrate how this may be done:

```
proc :          procheading block;

block :         constdec vardec prodecs stmpart;

stmpart :       compoundstat;

compoundstat :  BEGIN stmtseq END;

stmtseq :       statement
                | stmtseq ';' statement;

statement :     compoundstat
                |structstat
                | /*empty statement*/
                |assignstat
                |procstat;

structstat :    condstat
                |whilestat;

condstat :      IF condition
                THEN statement
                ELSE statement
                |IF condition
                THEN statement;

whilestat :     WHILE condition DO statement;
```

Certain nonterminals in the above grammar, such as `condition`, are not expanded, for simplicity. If we equate a condition to a decision (not the way that everyone would interpret a decision!) then we may include actions in the grammar to count the number of decisions, and to print the value of McCabe's metric:

```
proc :          procheading block
                {printf(%d\n, $2+1);};

block:          constdec vardec prodecs stmpart
                {$$ = $4;};

stmpart:        compoundstat
                {$$ = $1;};

compoundstat:   BEGIN stmtseq END
                {$$ = $2;};

stmtseq:        statement
                {$$ = $1;}
                | stmtseq ';' statement
                {$$ = $1+$3;};

statement:      compoundstat
                {$$ = $1;}
                |structstat
                {$$ = $1;}
                | /*empty statement*/
                {$$ = 0;}
                |assignstat
                {$$ = 0;}
                |procstat
                {$$ = 0;};

structstat :    condstat
                {$$ = $1;}
                |whilestat
                {$$ = $1;};

condstat :      IF condition
                THEN statement
                ELSE statement
                {$$ = $4+$6+1;}
                |IF condition
                THEN statement
                {$$ = $4+1;};

whilestat :     WHILE condition DO statement
                {$$ = $4+1;};
```

Notice that all the dollar variables correspond to the 'number of decisions' associated with a nonterminal.

5.8 Using YACC

In this section, we discuss some of the situations that may arise in using YACC. It is possible to find out more about how YACC forms the parse tables by running YACC in 'verbose mode' in order to provide details in

```
y.output
```

To obtain this file in a Unix environment, call YACC with the *-v* option, e.g.

```
yacc -v nums.y
```

The file y.output will contain details of the parser states. For example, the input:

```
%token NUM
%left '+'
%left '*'

%%
expr :  expr '+' expr
     |  expr '*' expr
     |  '(' expr ')'
     |  NUM;
```

will produce:

```
state 0
  $accept: _expr $end

  NUM shift 3
  ( shift 2
  .error

  expr goto 1

state 1
  $accept: expr_$end
  expr: expr_+ expr
  expr: expr_* expr

$end accept
  + shift 4
  * shift 5
  .error
```

```
state 2
  expr: (_expr )

  NUM shift 3
  ( SHIFT 2
  . error

  expr goto 6

state 3
  expr : NUM_ (4)

  . reduce 4

state 4
  expr : expr +_expr

  NUM shift 3
  ( shift 2
  . error

  expr goto 7

state 5
  expr : expr *_expr

NUM shift 3
  (shift 2
  .error

  expr goto 8

state 6
  expr : expr_+ expr
  expr : expr_* expr
  expr : (expr_)

  + shift 4
  * shift 5
  ) shift 9
  .error

state 7
  expr : expr_+expr
  expr: expr+expr_
  expr : expr_* expr
```

```
  * shift 5
  . reduce 1

state 8
  expr : expr_+ expr
  expr : expr_* expr
  expr : expr * expr_    (2)

  .reduce 2

state 9
  expr : ( expr )_       (3)

  .reduce 3

7/3000 terminals, 1/1000 nonterminals
5/2000 grammar rules, 10/5000 states
0 shift/reduce, 0 reduce/reduce conflicts reported
5/1400 working sets used
memory: states,etc. 106/40000, parser 3/70000
5/600 distinct lookahead sets
3 extra closures
14 shift entries, 1 exceptions
4 goto entries
0 entries saved by goto default
Optimizer space used: input 37/40000, output 218/70000
218 table entries, 206 zero
maximum spread: 257, maximum offset: 42
```

This is consistent with the grammar being enhanced by a single rule (rule0) and annotated with the states 0–9, thus

$$
\begin{aligned}
\textit{accept} \quad & :_0\textit{expr}_1 \\
\textit{expr} \quad : \quad & _{0,2,4,5}\textit{expr}_{1,6,7,8} \,{}'+{}'\, _4\textit{expr}_7 \\
& | \quad _{0,2,4,5}\textit{expr}_{1,6,7,8} \,{}'*{}'\, _5\textit{expr}_8 \\
& | \quad _{0,2,4,5}{}'({}'\, _2\textit{expr}_6\, {}')'\, _9 \\
& | \quad _{0,2,4,5}\textit{NUM}_3
\end{aligned}
$$

which together with the precedence and associativity information given in the YACC input, corresponds to the parsing table shown in Table 5.9.

Notice that in state *1*, a reduction only occurs if $\bot$ is the lookahead. Operator precedence and associativity is taken into account by *always* reducing in state *8*. Notice, however, that we do *not* necessarily reduce in state *7* (not when * is the

Table 5.9

	expr	+	*	(	)	NUM	⊥
0	S1			S2		S3	
1		S4	S5				R0
2	S6			S2		S3	
3	R4	R4	R4	R4	R4	R4	R4
4	S7			S2		S3	
5	S8			S2		S3	
6		S4	S5		S9		
7	R1	R1	S5	R1	R1	R1	R1
8	R2	R2	R2	R2	R2	R2	R2
9	R3	R3	R3	R3	R3	R3	R3

lookahead). Notice also that the `y.output` file distinguishes between `goto` when a nonterminal follows, and `shift` when a terminal follows, whereas both were treated similarly in the earlier part of the chapter, and in the table above. It should be clear that in the `y.output` file the underline symbol indicates the configurations in the grammar to which a state belongs, and the period symbol indicates an action on all other input – in many cases a syntax error. Numbers in brackets, to the right of grammar fragments indicate the relevant production numbers.

The last part of the output from `y.output` contains statistics about the grammar and the parsing table formed. For example

```
5/600 grammar rules, 10/1000 states
```

This means that out of a possible 600 grammar rules, the grammar had 5, while out of a possible 1000 states the parser requires 10. The table sizes used by YACC can be increased by using the –N flag, where N is followed by an integer (>40,000 in some installations).

When the input produces shift–reduce or reduce–reduce conflicts, the contents of `y.output` are invaluable for resolving them. For example if the precedence of the operators in the above example had not been included, `y.output` would have been identical to that obtained above up to and including state 6, but the output for states 7 and 8 would have been

```
7: shift/reduce conflict (shift 4 red'n 3) on +
7: shift/reduce conflict (shift 4 red'n 1) on *

state 7
  expr : expr_+expr
  expr : expr +expr_
  expr : expr_* expr
```

```
  + shift 4
  * shift 5
  . reduce 1

8: shift/reduce conflict(shift 4, red'n 2) on +
8: shift/reduce conflict(shift 5, red'n 2) on *
state 8
  expr : expr_+ expr
  expr : expr_* expr
  expr : expr * expr_    (2)

  +shift 4
  * shift 5
  .reduce 2
```

Notice that states are exactly the same in both cases and the only difference is the appearance of shift–reduce conflicts in states *7* and *8* owing to the ambiguities in the grammar that, in this case, are not resolved by precedence rules.

As mentioned previously, an interesting and well-known ambiguity arises with the *if*-statement in C defined as

```
if-statement :if '('expression')' statement
             | if '('expression')'statement else
                statement;
```

which generates the ambiguous statement

```
if (x==3) if (y==5) z = 6; else w = 7;
```

The ambiguity arises since it is not clear whether the **else** corresponds to the first or the second **if**. It is readily shown that the above sentence has two left most or right most derivations and two syntax trees (see exercise 2.6). C is not alone in having this ambiguity; it exists in a number of other languages, including COBOL and C++. To illustrate how YACC would deal with this ambiguity, consider the following input:

```
%token IF, ELSE, EXP
%start statement
%%
statement:  if_statement
          |;
if-statement :IF '(' EXP')' statement
             | IF '(' EXP')' statement EXP statement;
```

where, for simplicity, EXP is assumed to be a terminal, and the empty statement (a special case of the expression-statement in C) is included as the only alternative for the if statement. When YACC is applied to the above, the contents of y.output are:

```
state 0
  $accept: _statement $end
  statement:_

  IF shift 3
  .reduce 2

  statement goto 1
  if_statement goto2

state 1
  $accept: statement_$end

  $end accept
  .error

state 2
  statement: if_statement_ (1)

  .reduce 1

state 3
  if_statement: IF_(EXP) statement
  if_statement: IF_(EXP) statement ELSE statement

  ( shift 4
  .error

state 4
  if_statement: IF(_EXP) statement
  if_statement: IF(_EXP) statement ELSE statement

  EXP shift 5
  .error

state 5
  if_statement: IF(EXP_) statement
  if_statement: IF(EXP_) statement ELSE statement
```

```
      ) shift 6
      .error

   state 6
      if_statement: IF(EXP)_statement
      if_statement: IF(EXP)_statement ELSE statement
      statement : _    (2)

      IF shift 3
      .reduce 2

      statement goto 7
      if-statement goto 2

   7: shift/reduce conflict (shift 8, red'n 3) on ELSE

   state 7
      if_statement: IF(EXP) statement_
      if_statement: IF(EXP) statement_ELSE statement

      ELSE shift 8
      .reduce 3

   state 8
      if_statement: IF(EXP) statement ELSE_ statement
      statement: _(2)

      IF shift 3
      .reduce 2

      statement goto 9
      if-statement goto 2

   state 9
      if_statement: IF(EXP) statement ELSE statement_ (4)
      .reduce 4

   7/3000 terminals, 2/1000 non terminals
   5/2000 grammar rules, 10/5000 states
   1/shift/reduce, 0 reduce/reduce conflicts reported
   etc.
```

corresponding to the grammar being augmented by a single rule (production 0) and annotated thus:

```
accept:         ₀statement₁
statement :     ₀, ₆, ₈if_statement₂
                ₀, ₆, ₈| ;
if_statement: ₀, ₆, ₈IF₃'('₄EXP₅')'₆ statement₇
              |₀, ₆, ₈IF₃'('₄EXP₅')'₆ statement₇ ELSE₈ statement₉
```

The table with shift actions and all of the reduce actions except reduce by 3 (in state 7) is therefore as in Table 5.10.

The SLR(1) algorithm is sufficient to resolve any conflicts in Table 5.10. However, insertion of the R3 action in state 7 is more difficult. If we consider the followers of if_statement these include ELSE and $\perp$, and while there is no problem in putting a reduce in the $\perp$ column, there is already a shift action in the ELSE column. Furthermore, use of the more general LALR(1) and LR(1) algorithms does not resolve the conflict in this case. It should not be surprising to have found an unresolvable conflict in the parse table since, as we have seen, the original grammar was ambiguous. On the contrary, if an unresolvable conflict had not been found, then it would not have been possible to find alternative derivations for any sentences in the language, contradicting the fact that the grammar was ambiguous.

While the grammar for the if-statement presented above is ambiguous, the language it generates is not. That is, there exists an unambiguous grammar that generates the same language, and we could use this grammar as the basis of an LR(1) parser. Such a grammar was presented in section 2.6 but, to many people, would not appear to be the most natural way of representing the language. So, rather than resorting to the use of a rather contrived and unnatural grammar on which to base the parser, it is preferable to make use of the YACC feature that allows parsers to be built for ambiguous grammars. A parser produced by YACC

Table 5.10

State	st	if-st	IF	EXP	ELSE	(	)	$\perp$
0	S1	S2	S3		R2			R2
1	R0							
2	R1	R1	R1	R1	R1	R1	R1	R1
3						S4		
4				S5				
5							S6	
6	S7	S2	S3		R2			R2
7					S8			
8	S9	S2	S3		R2			R2
9	R4	R4	R4	R4	R4	R4	R4	R4

for an ambiguous grammar, will apply the convention that, where a table entry contains a *shift* and a *reduce* action, the *shift* will be performed in preference to the *reduce* in all cases. Thus in the above example the effective parsing table produced by YACC is shown in Table 5.11.

The shift to 8 in state 7 in the ELSE column means that an ELSE will always be assumed to belong to the nearest preceding IF. As this is the convention in C, and in virtually all languages containing this ambiguity, the YACC parser will, thankfully, do the correct thing. Despite the occurrence of the conflict in the y.output file, it is quite safe to ignore it as far as the if-statement is concerned in most languages. However, this should not be taken as a general rule and all other conflicts should be investigated carefully and, in most cases, removed. The fact that YACC has a default action which it will take if the conflict is not resolved is a somewhat mixed blessing, since it is, therefore, easy to ignore conflicts with the risk that the parser will not interpret its input as intended. Most conflicts should be removed unless it is clear that the default action of YACC will be the correct one. In practice, the only conflict that is usually ignored is the one concerning the if-statement.

It is worth noting that, as the examples have shown, ambiguous grammars sometimes provide the simplest and most natural way of representing language features. There is no harm therefore, and sometimes a positive advantage, in using ambiguous grammars, together with disambiguating rules where appropriate, as input to YACC.

As well as reporting shift–reduce conflicts in input grammars, YACC will occasionally report reduce–reduce conflicts. These are much less common than shift–reduce conflicts, and usually arise from something unusual in the language, so it is not so easy to give simple examples of them. They may arise from ambiguities in the grammar; or from unambiguous grammars that generate sentences, *the left part of which* has more than one derivation. Thus it is not possible to distinguish between the alternative derivations of the left

Table 5.11

State	st	if-st	IF	EXP	ELSE	(	)	⊥
0	S1	S2	S3		R2			R2
1	R0							
2	R1	R1	R1	R1	R1	R1	R1	R1
3						S4		
4				S5				
5							S6	
6	S7	S2	S3		R2			R2
7					S8			R3
8	S9	S2	S3		R2			R2
9	R4	R4	R4	R4	R4	R4	R4	R4

part, from a knowledge of the left part plus a single symbol (or even a fixed number of symbols) of lookahead. For example, suppose YACC had the following input:

```
%%
part    :ints
        |reals;

ints  : list1 ':' int;
reals : list2 ':' real;

list1 : list1 ',' ell
      | ell;
list2 : list2 ',' el2
      | ell;

ell   : 'a'|'b'|'p';
ell   : 'x'|'y'|'p';
%%
```

which with the states identified by YACC inserted becomes:

$$\text{\$accept: } {}_0\text{part}_1\perp$$

```
(part :₀ints₂
      |₀reals₃;
```

$$\text{ints} : {}_0\text{list1}_4 \text{ ':' } {}_{13}\text{int}_{17};$$
$$\text{reals} : {}_0\text{list2}_5 \text{ ':' } {}_{15}\text{real}_{19};$$

$$\text{list1} : {}_0\text{list1}_4 \text{ ',' } {}_{14}\text{ell}_{18}$$
$$\qquad | {}_0\text{ell}_6;$$
$$\text{list2} : {}_0\text{list2}_5 \text{ ',' } {}_{16}\text{el2}_{20}$$
$$\qquad | {}_0\text{el2}_7;$$

$$\text{ell}   : {}_0\text{'a'}_8|{}_0\text{'b'}_9|{}_0\text{'p'}_{10};$$
$$\text{ell}   : {}_0\text{'x'}_{11}|{}_0\text{'y'}_{12}|{}_0\text{'p'}_{10};$$

The reduce–reduce conflict is of course in state 10 where p may be reduced either to an ell or an el2 and an arbitrary amount of lookahead is needed to resolve the conflict (as far as the int or the real). The grammar, however, is not ambiguous and there is only one derivation for each sentence. In fact, it could be parsed perfectly easily by a backward pass! When YACC is executed on the grammar with the -v option, part of the contents of y.output is:

```
10: reduce/reduce conflict (red'ns 11 and 14) on :
10: reduce/reduce conflict (red'ns 11 and 14) on ,
state 10
   el1 : p_  (11)
   el2 : p_  (14)


   . reduce 11
```

As for shift–reduce conflicts, YACC has a default action that the parser will execute if the conflict is not resolved; namely, that it always reduces by the first of the two (or more) productions involved. In the example, the two productions are 11 and 14 above so that the parser will *always* reduce by 11. This, however, will only make sense if there are no situations in which the alternative reduction should take place. Consider the following sentence generated by the grammar in the example:

```
p,x,y : real
```

According to the default rule p will be reduced to el1, which will in turn be reduced to list1. The comma will then be read and the next symbol expected will be another el1. However, x is not an example of an el1 and a syntax error will be indicated, although there is none in the sentence input! However, it is difficult to see how YACC could have done anything better. Certainly always reducing by production 14 will give rise to spurious syntax errors in the way we have seen. There is no way out of the problem, other than by performing arbitrary lookahead, and perhaps the fault really lies in the language for making unreasonable demands on the parser! Reduce–reduce conflicts should *always* be investigated, and allowing YACC to take its default action in their presence is unlikely to be satisfactory.

When a parser produced by YACC behaves in an unexpected way, detailed information concerning the steps performed by the parser can be obtained by using YACC in debug mode by setting the -t flag, when it is executed. The debugging information is voluminous and should not be obtained routinely. On occasion, however, its use is the only practical way of sorting out problems that arise in using YACC.

Actions embedded in a YACC grammar may be used to detect non-context-free errors. Although, as we have pointed out, these are usually easier to recover from than context-free errors, it is possible to make YACC behave exactly as if a context-free error had occurred by calling the macro YYERROR.

Error recovery is a complex issue and we will not consider it further here.

YACC, however, provides facilities for implementing relatively sophisticated error recovery strategies as well as the simple, and rarely satisfactory, strategy of aborting the parse as soon as the first context-free error is discovered.

We have introduced the main features of YACC. Features of YACC vary slightly from one implementation to another, and users should consult local information for precise details of how to use YACC, which may differ slightly from what has been described here. In addition, there may be further features that have not been described. On the whole, YACC input is fairly portable as long as some of the archaic features used in early versions of YACC, but not now required, are avoided.

5.9 Summary

In this chapter we have:

- introduced the concept of bottom-up parsing;
- shown how a bottom-up parsing table may be used to drive the parser;
- introduced the notions of shift–reduce and reduce–reduce conflicts in a bottom-up parser;
- shown how the parser states may be identified in terms of configurations in a grammar;
- demonstrated the LR(0) and SLR(1) algorithms for forming the parsing table;
- introduced the parser generator tool YACC;
- shown how compile-time actions may be placed in a YACC grammar;
- shown how problems arising in the use of YACC may be resolved.

Further reading

LR parsing was first introduced by Knuth (1965) and further developed from a practical point of view by De Reemer (1971). The use of LR parsing with ambiguous grammars was developed by Aho, Johnson and Ullman (1975).

YACC is only one (though certainly the best known) of many parser generator tools now available, in many cases via the Internet. It was developed by Johnson (1975) and is described (though not always in sufficient detail) in many of the standard compiler texts such as Aho, Sethi and Ullman (1985) and Bennett (1990). Levine, Mason and Brown (1992), though not strictly a compiler text, describes YACC (as well as Lex) in some detail. Compiler construction using YACC is described in Schreiner and Friedman (1985).

Bison (a relative of YACC) was developed by Stallman (1994) and Gnu Bison is available from many Internet sites via the Free Software Foundation (see further reading section at the end of chapter 1).

Exercises

5.1 Explain why bottom-up parsing is more generally applicable than top-down parsing.

5.2 Explain what is meant by shift–reduce and reduce–reduce conflicts in bottom-up parsing.

5.3 Explain why an ambiguous grammar cannot be LR(1).

5.4 Explain why only *one* of the two stacks (the state stack and the symbol stack) used in the examples is strictly necessary to control the parsing process.

5.5 By forming the parsing table verify that the grammar with the following productions is LR(1) (see section 5.5):

1. $S \rightarrow axF$
2. $F \rightarrow ,JF$
3. $|\varepsilon$
4. $J \rightarrow ax$
5. $|x$

5.6 Show that the grammar with the following productions is not LR(1):

$$S \rightarrow 1S0$$
$$S \rightarrow 0S1$$
$$S \rightarrow 10$$
$$S \rightarrow 01$$

5.7 Show that the grammar with the following productions is not LR(1) but is LR(2):

$$S \rightarrow V := E$$
$$S \rightarrow LS$$
$$L \rightarrow I:$$
$$V \rightarrow I$$

Assume each character is a separate symbol. Suggest how the non-LR(1)-ness of the grammar may be dealt with during lexical analysis.

5.8 Find out how your local version of YACC deals with each of the grammars in exercises 5.6 and 5.7. Investigate the contents of `y.output` in each case.

5.9 Give arguments for and against the use of the macro `YYERROR`.

5.10 Give an example of an unambiguous grammar with which YACC is not able to deal.

CHAPTER 6
Semantic analysis

6.1 **Introduction**

As has already been mentioned in chapter 1, some features of programming languages are not context-free, and therefore cannot be defined by context-free grammars. In this chapter, we will be concerned with aspects of semantic analysis, in particular, the analysis of non-context-free aspects of programming languages. We will therefore:

- identify language features that are not context free;
- show how a context-free parser may be enhanced with table-based actions to check non-context-free features of programming languages;
- discuss practical methods of implementing symbol and type tables;
- take a brief look at issues concerning object-oriented languages.

6.2 **Non-context-free language features**

Each program in a given language will have at least one parse tree (and at least one leftmost and rightmost derivation), which may be used to show its derivation. However, not every parse tree that can be generated by the language grammar corresponds to a valid program. To illustrate the point, there exist parse trees, based on the ANSI context-free grammar for C, corresponding to both of the following programs:

```
#include <stdio.h>

main ()
{
    int first, second;
    first = 4;
    second = 5;
    printf ("%d", first + second);
    }
```

and

```
#include <stdio.h>

main ()
{
   first = 4;
   second = 5;
   printf ("%d", first + second);
}
```

While the first program compiles and executes, the second produces the error messages (in Borland's Turbo C):

```
Error 622.C 5: Undefined symbol 'first' in function main()
Error 622.C 6: Undefined symbol 'second' in function main()
```

The first example is a valid program in C and the second is not, since the variables first and second have not been declared. In other words, the appearance of variables in a program implies that declarations must appear for them somewhere. There are, therefore, constraints on the way in which a derivation may take place. A context-free grammar has no mechanism for specifying such constraints (we do not actually prove this!), and therefore cannot be used to define precisely what constitutes a C program. A context-free grammar can, however, be used to define a superset of all C programs, the superset containing all valid C programs, as well as C programs that are invalid because of non-context-free faults, such as the non-declaration of variables, etc.

Another category of non-context-free fault is illustrated in the following:

```
#include <stdio.h>

main ()
{
   int first;
   int second [5] = {6,8,4,5,2};
   first = second;
   printf ("%d", first);
}
```

The problem, of course, is the non-compatibility of the types on the two sides of the assignment:

```
first = second;
```

On the whole, C is quite tolerant as far as so-called type errors are concerned, and none of the following assignments will cause compiler errors:

```
int p = 4.3;
real x = 2;
int x = 'a';
int x = NULL;
```

In the above examples, integer to real and real to integer conversions are performed as necessary, as well as character to integer conversions, which consist of replacing the character by its ASCII (American Standard Code for Information Interchange) equivalent (which is used to represent it internally, in any case). The philosophy of C is to perform any reasonable type changes inferred by the context, so that usually when a value appears with a type inappropriate to the context, it will be converted into a more appropriate type. The value NULL in the above example is converted to the integer 0. Even C will produce compiler errors when no 'reasonable' conversion can be applied as in the integer array to integer assignment in the above program!

Other languages, such as Ada and ALGOL 68, take a stricter view with regard to types, and few, if any, implicit conversions are allowed, the reason being that, in this way, more programming errors will be detected at compile time. Such languages are said to have *strong typing*. Yet other languages have *dynamic*, as opposed to *static*, types in which case the types of values are not known at all at compile time, but have to be identified at run time. This means that any type conversions also have to be performed at run time, and code has to be generated at compile time to perform them at run time. When we come to deal with code generation, we will find many examples of actions that may be performed at compile time, and other actions for which code has to be generated at compile time in order that they may be performed at run time.

Another type of non-context-free fault that may appear in a program is illustrated by the following:

```
#include <stdio.h>

int bigger(int no1, int no2)
{
    if (no1 > no2) return no1;
    else return no2;
}

main()
{
    int first, second;
    first = 4;
```

```
      second = 5;
      second = bigger (first);
      printf ("%d", second);
  }
```

The function `bigger` is defined to have two parameters but is called within `main` with only a single parameter, resulting in the following error at compile time:

```
Error 624.C 14: Too few parameters in call to 'bigger' in
function main
```

The types of the parameters in a function call should also match the types in the declaration. In C, of course, type changes between `int`, `float` and `char` will be performed automatically. However, a mismatch between an `int` parameter in a function definition and an array of `int` appearing as the corresponding parameter in the function call would give an error.

A similar type of fault can occur with array subscripts as is shown by the following:

```
#include <stdio.h>

main()
{
    int number;
    int matrix [3][2] = { {4,5},
                          {8,9},
                          {11,12}};
    number=matrix [1,1,1];
    printf ("%d", number);
}
```

where the two-dimensional array `matrix` is defined to have two dimensions but is accessed with three.

A slightly different type of context-free fault occurs in connection with the *scope* rules of a language. The scope rules of C are illustrated by the following:

```
#include <stdio.h>

int p = 7;

void fun1()
```

```
{int p = 4;
printf ("local p = %d\n",p);
{int p = 11;
printf ("more local p = %d\n",p);
}
}

void fun2()

{printf ("global p = %d\n", p);
}

main()
{fun1();
fun2();
}
```

which would produce as output

```
local p = 4
more local p = 11
global p = 7
```

However, the following C program is incorrect, since the declaration of the global p has been removed and neither of the other declarations of p are in scope within fun2():

```
#include <stdio.h>

void fun1()

{int p = 4;
printf ("local p = %d\n",p);
{int p = 11;
printf ("more local p = %d\n",p);
}
}

void fun2()

{printf ("global p = %d\n", p);
}
```

```
main()
{fun1();
fun2();
}
```

The above program will fail to compile, giving the error message

```
Error 628.C 14: Undefined symbol 'p' in function fun2
```

The compile-time errors associated with each of the above 'programs' could *not* have been detected by a parser based purely on a context-free grammar. Put another way, a parser built with the aid of YACC would not have detected any of these errors through reaching a 'blank' entry (corresponding to a syntax error) in the LALR(1) parsing table, produced by YACC. Rather it would need to have extra checks, defined by actions in the grammar, to detect these errors. The fact that these types of errors do not lead to an error entry in the parsing table makes them easier to recover from, since, in order to continue the parse, there is no need to make any assumptions concerning the fault made by the programmer. The action that detects the error can merely report the problem and continue parsing. It is also usually simpler to provide meaningful diagnostics for the programmer when non-context-free errors occur, than it is for context-free errors.

In the next section, we will discuss the nature of the actions that have to be added to the parser in order to detect type and scope errors. In principle, these types of faults are easy to detect, since all the information required to detect these faults has already been read by the analyser prior to the point at which the error occurred – if any of the information required to detect the fault occurs after the location of the fault an extra pass or passes has to be performed by the compiler. However, in order for this information to be available when required, tables containing type and scope information have to be used. The design and construction of such tables will be discussed in detail in the next two sections.

6.3 Compiler tables

The two principal tables required by the analyser during compilation are

- the symbol table
- the type table

which will be discussed in detail. Other tables required include

- the function table
- the label table

which will both be mentioned in section 6.3.3.

6.3.1 *Symbol tables*

The principal function of a *symbol table* is to provide a mapping between a *variable* and its *type*. The two basic operations associated with the symbol table are:

1. corresponding to the defining occurrence of variable, e.g.

    ```
    int x
    ```

    the name of the variable, along with its type is inserted in the symbol table.
2. corresponding to an applied occurrence of a variable, e.g.

    ```
    x = 5;
    ```

    The symbol table is searched to find the type of the variable.

The complexity of the symbol table and the routines which operate on it depend on:

- the language being implemented;
- the importance attached to the efficiency of the compiler.

It should be noted, at this stage, that the assumption cannot be made that there may only be a single variable in a program represented by the identifier x, since, in general, there may be any number of variables named x in a program. It is essential, therefore, that, for each applied occurrence of x the symbol table entry corresponding to the *relevant* defining occurrence of x, is identified.

The form of symbol table required to analyse a single C function is straight-forward. Consider the following outline of a C function:

```
void scopes()

{int a,b,c;        /*level 0*/
  ..
  {int a,b;        /*level 1a*/
  ..
  }
  {float c,d;      /*level 1b*/
      {int m;      /*level 2*/
  ..
      }
  }
}
```

The symbol table could be represented by an upwards growing stack, as long as it is searched from the top down each time the entry corresponding to the defining occurrence of an identifier is sought, and entries are removed from the stack as variables go out of scope. Using the above function outline as an illustration, snapshots of the stack at various steps of the analysis are shown in the following.

Initially the symbol table is empty:

```
| |   |          |
|_|___|_____|
```

After the first three declarations have been processed:

c	int
b	int
a	int

After the declarations of level 1a have been processed:

b	int
a	int
c	int
b	int
a	int

Since the symbol table is searched from the top down, the entry corresponding to the most recent (or inner) defining occurrence of a or b will be identified. When the scope corresponding to the declarations 1a is left, the entries corresponding to these declarations must be removed from the symbol table leaving it thus, again:

c	int
b	int
a	int

At the same time the value of the stack pointer is decremented to the value it had before the declarations of level 1a were processed. In order to be able to do this, in general, an array of stack pointers has to be maintained. After processing the declarations of level 1b the stack becomes:

d	float
c	float
c	int
b	int
a	int

and after processing the declarations of level 2

m	int
d	float
c	float
c	int
b	int
a	int

On leaving the scope corresponding to the declarations of level 2, the stack again becomes:

d	float
c	float
c	int
b	int
a	int

and on leaving the scope corresponding to level 1b, it becomes again:

c	int
b	int
a	int

On leaving the function entirely, the symbol table is again empty:

There are several points, which should be noted. First, for variables declared globally (between function definitions) a lower (or outer) level of the stack is required which is present throughout compilation. An *extern* variable (one for which storage has been allocated in another source file) is treated in the same way as a global variable as far as symbol table actions are concerned.

A *static* variable in C is treated the same as an *auto* variable (the ones considered in the example) as far as the symbol table is concerned; though it is treated quite differently when it comes to storage allocation!

In practice, the symbol table would have more than two fields. For example, an extra field could be used to indicate whether the identifier corresponds to a *variable* or a *constant*. In addition, further fields might be used to hold the compile-time address of the variable or constant – though the value of this field will not be known until after storage allocation has taken place.

If a linear search was considered an inefficient way of searching for the defining occurrence of an identifier, then the use of more complex data structures such as binary trees for the various levels of the stack could lead to more efficient search algorithms. While, as far as lexical analysis and syntax analysis are concerned, the methods we have described will take time proportional to the length of the program, this may no longer be the case when it comes to non-context-free analysis (often referred to as *static semantic analysis*). The longer the program is, the larger some of the tables such as the symbol table are likely to be, and the longer *each* symbol table search is likely to take. This means that total compilation time may not be linear in the length of the program, but may be disproportionately long for longer programs.

The stack representation of the symbol table, while adequate for C, will not suffice for languages with more complex scoping rules such as Ada. Consider the following piece of an Ada program:

```
procedure main is
x:integer;
   procedure inner is
   x:character;
   begin x := 'A';
     put (x);
     put (main.x);
   end inner;
begin x:= 4;
   inner;
   put (x);
end main;
```

A call of the procedure `main` would output

```
A 4 4
```

showing that the integer variable `x` declared in `main` is not completely hidden within `inner` but may be accessed by writing `main.x`. Clearly, the symbol table for an implementation of Ada will need to reflect this fact, perhaps by naming sections of the symbol table.

Another interesting feature of Ada, as far as symbol table design is concerned, is the *use* clause, an example of which might be

```
use stack
```

where `stack` is the name of a package containing procedures for adding items to and deleting items from a stack, the names of which the *use clause* would make visible without also making visible the details of how the stack was implemented.

The rules of Ada assert

- an identifier may be made directly visible by a *use clause* only if it would not be directly visible if the clause were not present;
- an identifier made directly visible by a *use clause* must be declared in one and only one package named in the *use clause*.

Bearing these rules in mind, a valid implementation of a *use clause* would be to insert the visible part of the symbol table segment of the package named in the *use clause* 'on top of' (again thinking of the symbol table as a stack) the symbol table, as it currently stands. It would then be removed when the end of the scope of the *use clause* is reached.

Types are not only associated with variables and constants; each element of an expression has a type associated with it including:

- literals such as 3, 23.4, true;
- expressions such as 3 + 4.

The types of literals are usually apparent at lexical analysis (though not always in Ada where determining the type of literals may require some quite complex analysis). For example 3 is clearly (assuming the language is C) of type int and 23.4 is clearly of type float. The types of expressions are determined from the types of their components. Since 23.4 and 34.2 are each of type float, then the expression

```
23.4 + 34.2
```

is also of type float. Similarly the expression

```
23.4 + 5
```

is of type float. This may be explained in one of two ways, depending on the language involved:

- A float plus an int gives a float.
- Addition is only defined for two values of the same type so that the integer 5 has to be converted to type float before the addition can take place.

Implicit type changes can take place in most languages and are sometimes known as *coercions*. They are probably least common in Ada where most type changes have to be explicit. In C an explicit type change is known as a *cast*, an example of which would be

```
x = float (m)
```

which has the effect of converting the (supposed integer) value of m to float before assigning it to x.

In statically typed languages, such as C, all types are known at compile time, and this applies to the types of expressions as well as identifiers and literals. No matter how complex an expression may be its type can be 'built up' at compile time in a number of steps, from the types of its components. This allows (virtually) all type checking to be performed at compile time, leading to the early detection (at compile time rather than at run time!) of many programming errors.

6.3.2 *Type tables*

Within the compiler there has to be a unique way of representing each of the types in a particular program. If the source language allowed only a finite number of types, then a distinct integer could be used to represent each of the allowable types. Some early languages such as FORTRAN could be dealt with in this way, though more recent languages, on the whole, cannot. In considering a suitable representation for types in a program, the following factors usually need to be taken into account:

- The highly structured and recursive nature of many types.
- The common operations which the compiler will have to perform on types.

Common operations on types in C include:

- finding the type of a field of a `struct` or a `union`;
- finding the type of a element of an array;
- finding the type of the result of a function.

The basic types such as `int`, `float` and `char` in C may be represented by integers, while the composite types such as arrays and unions may be represented as structures. For example, the `typedef`

```
typedef struct {
                int day;
                int mth;
                int year;
                }dob;
```

might be represented by the structure shown in Figure 6.1 while the `typedef`

```
typedef long int [9][19] matrix;
```

might be represented as shown in Figure 6.2, and so on.

This type of representation will allow the typical operations performed on types identified above to be performed with comparative ease. It just remains to define an array (the type table) that maps *type names* on to pointers to type structures. Since type names, as used in the program, have a scope, just like other

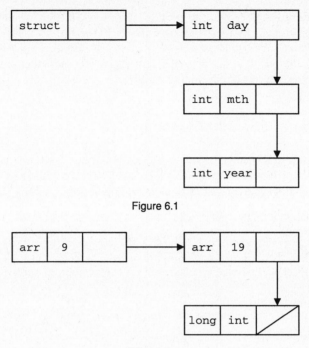

Figure 6.1

Figure 6.2

names, the table would need to be 'scoped' in a similar way to the symbol table. In simple cases, a stack-based structure would be appropriate.

6.3.3 *Other tables*

A number of other tables are required during compile time depending, to some extent, on the language being compiled. Typically these might be:

- a function table;
- a label table.

A function is, in some ways, like a type in that it has subtypes – the types of its parameters and the type of its result – associated with it. At code generation time it is also allocated an address, and all this information is kept in a compile-time table that will be 'scoped' according to the scope rules of the language.

Control structures in a high-level language, as we shall see in chapter 8, have to be represented in object code by means of jumps (conditional or otherwise) and labels, so that the object version of the source program will have both user-defined and compiler-defined labels contained in it. The structure of many languages allows a stack-type table to be used in order to relate *applied* and *defining* occurrences of labels. From what has been said, there are likely to be a number of stacks being used at compile time (as well as those required at run time). Stack management, in the sense of allocating sufficient space for each stack, becomes complex, as the number of stacks rises above two, and there are considerable benefits in being able to merge a number of stacks into a single stack structure. Fortunately, the scope rules of many languages are such that there is ample opportunity for merging stacks in this way.

6.4 Implementing inheritance in C++

It is appropriate at this stage to say something about the issues involved in implementing object oriented programming languages, and we will take as an example C++. The principal characteristics of object oriented programming languages are:

- data abstraction and encapsulation;
- polymorphism;
- inheritance.

Data abstraction is illustrated by classes in C++. Consider the following example:

```
class complex
{
float real, imag;
public:  complex (float = 0.0, float = 0.0);
         complex (const complex&);
         float get_real() const;
         float get_imag() const;
};
```

The class `complex` is defined along with some operations to construct a `complex` and to find its real and imaginary parts. *Polymorphism* is illustrated by the constructor function, which behaves differently depending on whether it has two `float` parameters, or one `complex` parameter. Polymorphism allows different functions or procedures to have the same name, as long as the types and numbers of their parameters are not identical. This means that, in a given instance, the precise function can be identified from the types of its parameters. The notion of polymorphism is already present in many languages for operators that may have different meanings, depending on the types of their operands. A simple example would be the operator + in C which has different meanings, depending on whether its operands are `float` or `int`. Polymorphic functions are simply an extension of this idea to functions, and are no more difficult to implement.

Inheritance is illustrated by the following example:

```
class addcom: public complex
{public: adds (const complex&, const complex&)
}
```

in which the new class `addcom` is defined which *inherits* all the properties of `complex` but, additionally, possesses an addition operator.

If the new class may only inherit from one parent class, as in Java, this corresponds to *single inheritance*, and the new class has all the fields and methods (akin to functions) of its parent class plus the fields and methods which belong to it alone. In Java, a class may contain the definition of a method with the same name as a method of its parent class, in which case the method of the parent class will *not* be inherited but will be overridden by the method of the class with the same name – assuming the method of the parent class is not an abstract one.

The implementation of inheritance is based on object *content* rather than on object *type* and is therefore a dynamic (performed at run time), rather than a static (performed at compile time) matter. However, in the case of single inheritance, it is fairly straightforward. *Multiple inheritance*, on the other hand, in which a class may have more than one parent class, is more difficult to implement. An example of multiple inheritance might be an implementation of a stack that inherited methods from an abstract *stack* class and a concrete *array* class. For a discussion of the issues involved, the reader is referred to the further reading section at the end of the chapter.

6.5 Summary

This chapter has been concerned with how language features that cannot be defined by a context-free grammar may be analysed and implemented. In particular we have:

- shown that non-context-free language features are normally related to the type and scope rules of the language;
- shown how a symbol table may be used to store information required to identify non-context-free faults in a program;
- demonstrated how the symbol table structure depends on the language being compiled, and shown the form it might take for a C compiler;
- suggested how the symbol table might be optimised;
- discussed the role that a type table takes in a compiler, and suggested a possible form for it;
- discussed the need for various other compile-time tables;
- indicated how typical features of object-oriented languages, such as C++ and Java, may be implemented.

Further reading

The use of symbol tables is described in all of the introductory books on compiler construction that have been mentioned previously. Data structures for symbol tables and algorithms for searching them are discussed in Aho, Hopcroft and Ullman (1974). Type equivalence is an important and non-trivial issue as far as type tables are concerned, and its resolution for Pascal is discussed in Welsh, Sneeringer and Hoare (1977). The implementation of single and multiple inheritance in object-oriented languages is discussed in Wilhelm and Maurer (1995).

Exercises

6.1 Give a list of features of C, or whatever language you know best, that are not context free.

6.2 Would you expect the symbol table for a C program to have many distinct stack levels at any stage of a parse? Give a reason for your answer.

6.3 In FORTRAN, the type of an identifier can usually be deduced from the first letter of its name. Does this make a symbol table unnecessary? Give a reason for your answer.

6.4 In some languages, e.g. ALGOL 68, variables, etc. can be declared after they have been used. What effect has this on the symbol tables routines?

6.5 In terms of a language with which you are familiar, explain how recursive types are defined.

6.6 What are the main characteristics of object oriented programming languages?

6.7 Give an argument for and an argument against the notion of *multiple inheritance*.

CHAPTER 7
Storage allocation

7.1 **Introduction**

Up until now, we have been mainly concerned with the analysis stage of compilation, and this is where we switch to considering the synthesis stage. While the synthesis stage is largely concerned with code generation, an important, and closely related topic, is that of storage allocation. The relation between code generation and storage allocation is such that storage allocation is normally thought of as a distinct phase of compilation, called by the code generator, as and when necessary. For this reason, and the number of interesting issues specific to storage allocation, we devote a complete chapter to the topic. In this chapter we will:

- discuss the types of objects for which storage has to be allocated;
- consider how the expected lifespan of an object affects the storage allocation mechanism used for it;
- show how storage is allocated for particular language features;
- describe the principal storage allocation models used.

7.2 **Storage issues**

We must first distinguish between objects and their values. The variable x is an object that, at a given time, may have a value associated with it, and it is the storage space for this value with which we will be concerned. The storage allocated for the value of x will have an associated address referred to, as the *address* of x. This address should have the following properties;

- It should be sufficiently large (but not too much larger) to hold any of the range of values that may be taken by x.
- It should be available throughout the lifetime of x.
- It should be expressible in a form that the code generator can use to generate code to access the value of x at run time.

To satisfy the first point, integer values are usually assigned less storage space than real values, and character values may be assigned less space than integer values. However, in the interests of efficient access, it does not always make sense to pack values, individually requiring small amounts of space, into as little space as possible and, in any case, the savings in doing so may be small. Some languages offer the user the choice of 'packing' values or not 'packing' values.

Space is required for the values of records, arrays and pointers. Record values usually require the sum of the space required by their individual fields. Arrays usually require rather more space than the space required for their elements; the overhead depending on the method used to store the array. In addition, some languages allow arrays to have *dynamic bounds* so their size is not known at compile time, but has to be determined at run time. The space required for pointers depends on the implementation.

As far as allocating storage space for the lifetime of a variable, there are three possibilities:

1. The lifetime of the variable is the lifetime of the program and the space for its value, once allocated, cannot later be released. Such storage is referred to as *static storage*.
2. The lifetime of the variable is a particular block, function or procedure in which it is declared, so that the storage allocated may be released when the block, function or procedure in which it is declared is left. Such storage is referred to as *dynamic storage*.
3. Storage may be allocated for values, not necessarily associated with variables, at a particular point in the execution of a program not necessarily corresponding to the start of a block or the entry to a procedure. The storage is then required from that point on until it is released either by a language mechanism or through simply being no longer reachable from the program. However, the moment of this release may, in general, not be detectable at compile time and is only known at run time. Such storage is referred to as *global storage*.

The static storage requirements of a program are completely known at compile time and a suitable amount of space may be allocated. Since there is no possibility of static space being released after it has been allocated, the total amount of space required is the sum of the individual requirements, and no storage 'sharing' is possible. The management of this storage space is straightforward. The storage requirements of a FORTRAN program, for example, are entirely static.

The dynamic storage requirements of a program are more complex since space is allocated on entry to a function (or block or procedure depending on the language concerned) and de-allocated on leaving the function (or block or procedure). There is therefore the possibility of storage space being shared by values corresponding to different functions, etc. It turns out that management of this type of storage space is not as complex as might at first be imagined, and is easily handled by a *stack* mechanism that grows and contracts as space is allocated and de-allocated. We will discuss this in more detail shortly.

The *allocation* of global space is straightforward enough: an area of space (usually referred to as the *heap*) is simply allowed to grow as required. It is the *de-allocation* of this space that is more complex since it does not relate in any simple way to its allocation. There are two main issues concerning the allocation and de-allocation of global storage space:

1. The availability of space for de-allocation has to be detected at run time, inevitably causing a run-time overhead of some sort.
2. As space is de-allocated, holes will appear in the heap, which normally requires *compaction*, if storage is to be used effectively.

The detection of re-allocable space on the heap and its compaction will be discussed later in this chapter (section 7.5). In the meantime, we will merely note that the stack and the heap can be conveniently accommodated together, if they are allowed to grow towards one another as shown in Figure 7.1. The static storage area may then be situated at one or other end of the space as shown. It is only when expansion of the stack and the heap causes them to collide that action need be taken. This will normally involve identification of inaccessible heap storage and compaction of the heap.

As far as the addresses of variables, etc., is concerned, it is sometimes possible, as in the case of static storage, to know run-time addresses at compile time. More often, this is not possible and run-time addresses of values have to be calculated from a number of factors, some of which are known at compile time and some of which are not known until run time. In these cases, those aspects of the address that are known at compile time are often referred to as the *compile-time address* of the value.

In the language C, there are four possible storage classes for variables *static*, *auto*, *extern* and *register*. *Static* variables are allocated static storage for the duration of the program. *Auto* variables (which are the default storage class) require storage as long as the compound statement (C term, corresponding to a *block* in some other languages) in which they are declared is being executed. They are therefore well suited to having their storage allocated on a stack. *Extern* variables will have storage allocated for them in another file. *Register* variables have their value stored in a register, if the compiler is able to do this conveniently, otherwise they are equivalent to auto variables.

In addition to storage being required for variables in a C program, storage for the values that are reachable via pointers may be allocated using `malloc` e.g.:

```
P = malloc(sizeof(int));
```

Figure 7.1

will allocate enough space for an integer value, and will make P point to it. This space *may* be released when it is no longer pointed to by P or any other variable in the program, but, since this situation may not be detectable at compile time, the space allocated by malloc is necessarily on the heap.

7.3 **Static and dynamic storage**

Early programming languages, such as FORTRAN, had static storage, the amount of which was known at compile time. Storage space once allocated was never released, so a very simple storage allocation model that allocated storage, as required, from one end of the available space towards the other was adequate. More modern languages, from ALGOL 60 onwards, usually have a block structure that allows variables declared in different blocks to share storage. A stack-based storage allocation model is therefore appropriate, allowing storage space, once allocated, to be reclaimed later for a different use. The run-time stack used by this model resembles in some ways the stack-based symbol table illustrated in section 6.3, with the important difference that the run-time stack is a run-time, rather than a compile-time, data structure. However, as will be shown, many of the compile-time actions on the symbol table are mirrored by run-time actions on the run-time stack.

To illustrate how space may be allocated on the run-time stack, we will consider again the C function outline that we used in our discussion of symbol tables. The section of the run-time stack required for a single function is known as a *stack frame*, and we will show how the storage space for the frame corresponding to the function scopes might be allocated.

```
    void scopes()

    {int a,b,c;        /*level 0*/
       . .
       {int a,b;        /*level 1a*/
          . .
       }
       {float c,d;      /*level 1b*/
          {int m;       /*level 2*/
             . .
          }
       }
    }
```

In the symbol table context, we were concerned with type information and storing the types of variables – a compile-time issue. At run time, we are more concerned with *values* rather than *types*, and this is reflected in the structure of the run-time stack that stores *values* in a similar way to which the symbol table stores *types*. We will follow through the *execution* of this program fragment, noting how storage may be allocated on the run-time stack, in much the same way as we followed its *compilation*, noting the contents of the symbol table.

Initially the run-time stack is empty:

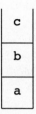

After the declarations of a, b, c (level 0) the run-time stack could look as follows:

c
b
a

where a represents storage space suitable to hold the value of the variable a, etc. After the declarations of level 1a it could appear as:

b
a
c
b
a

On leaving level 1a, at execution time the run-time stack may revert to:

c
b
a

and on entering level 1b it could become:

```
d



c


c

b

a
```

the values of the floats c and d being allocated twice as much space as for the values of the ints a, b and c. On entering level 2 the run-time stack becomes

```
m

d


c


c

b

a
```

and on leaving level 2 (at run time)

```
d


c


c

b

a
```

On leaving level 1b, it reverts to

c
b
a

and is again empty on leaving the function `scopes`.

According to the above description, on leaving a compound statement the storage allocated for the compound statement is simply removed from the stack. To do this, an array of pointers may be maintained pointing to the foot of the stack segments corresponding to the compound statements that are currently being executed.

The calculation of the address of a variable with respect to the foot of the stack frame merely requires a knowledge of the amount of storage occupied by the values of each of the variables below it on the stack – information that (for simple variables at least) is known at compile time.

In practice, the stack frame may not expand and contract as each compound statement or block is entered and left, as implied by the above description. Instead, the maximum storage required for the frame may be allocated as each function is called.

The model we have described is adequate for the storage requirements of a single function but not for a program containing a number of functions that may call each other. For this, a more general model is required. As far as dynamic storage is concerned, at any point during the execution of the program, storage space will only be required for those functions that are currently active. In addition, functions will be left in the opposite order to which they were entered, so the model will not be so different from the one we have just described, the main difference being that the calling hierarchy will not, in general, be known at compile time.

Consider the following C fragment:

```
main()
{ first();
  second ();
}

first ()
{ second();
}
```

It may be seen that `second()` may be called in either of two ways:

1. Directly from `main()`.
2. From `first()`, which has been called from `main()`.

The appearances of the run-time stack corresponding to the two situations are shown in Figures 7.2 and 7.3, respectively. `second()` refers to the section of stack corresponding to the function `second()`, and so on.

From the discussion above, the address of a variable with respect to the foot of the *stack frame* in which it is stored is known at compile time. However, as we have seen, the position of a stack frame with respect to the foot of the stack is not known, in general, at compile time, and has to be evaluated at run time. C programs have the property that (apart from *extern* and global variables) only variables from a single function (the one currently active) can be accessed at run time. Therefore, if a pointer to the start of the current stack frame is maintained at run time, a knowledge of the value of this pointer, together with the address of a variable within the section of stack (known at compile time), is sufficient to calculate the address of the variable, with respect to the foot of the stack.

The pointers to the start of each of the stack frames corresponding to functions currently active, are known as the set of *dynamic stack pointers*. When the function corresponding to the top stack frame is left, control returns to the function corresponding to the stack frame below it, any of whose variables may be accessed. It is necessary, therefore, to retain the values of the dynamic pointers to

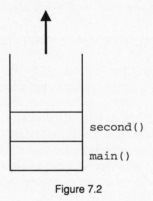

Figure 7.2

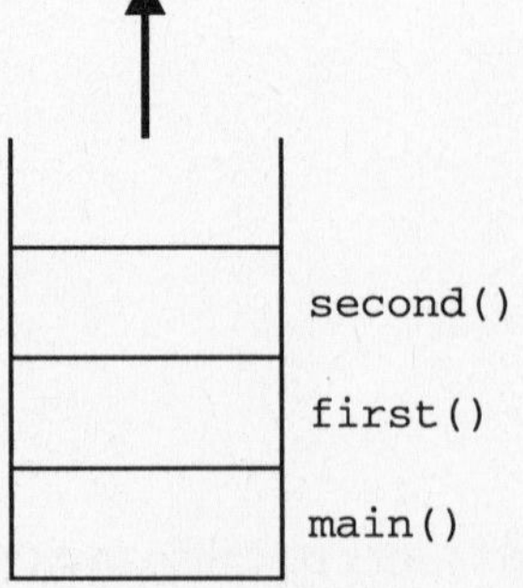

Figure 7.3

each of the stack frames currently on the stack. This may be done by means of an array of pointers as is shown in Figure 7.4.

Maintenance of the array of dynamic pointers requires the following actions at run time:

- Adding the start address of a new stack frame to the pointer array, each time a function is entered.
- Removing the top value of the pointer array each time the function corresponding to the current stack frame is left.

An alternative to using an array of pointers is to store the dynamic pointers in the stack itself.

In C, pointers to the foots of the frames on the run-time stack are only required so that the environment of a call can be recreated after a function call has been left. In Pascal, as in Ada and many other languages, it is also possible – though perhaps not very good practice – to access variables declared in procedures or functions that *statically* enclose the current procedure. Consider, for example, the Pascal outline program:

```pascal
program demo (output);
var x, y: real;
  procedure first;
  var c, d: integer;
    procedure second;
    var p, q: integer;
    begin
      .
      .
    end;
    procedure third;
    var m,n: integer;
    begin
      .
      .
    end;
  begin
  second;
  third
  end;
begin
first
end.
```

By the time second has been called the run time stack might look like Figure 7.5.

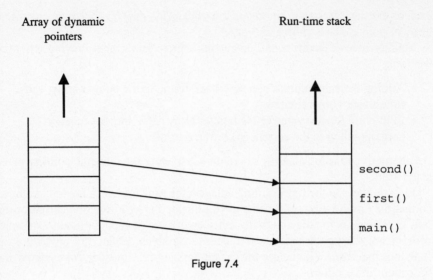

Figure 7.4

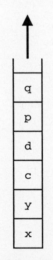

Figure 7.5

In order to facilitate access to variables declared in outer scopes, the Pascal storage model would be likely to have pointers (referred to as static pointers) to each of the currently accessible outer blocks. An array of such pointers is usually called a *display* and would look something like Figure 7.6. However, this will *not* necessarily correspond to an array of pointers to all the procedures that have been entered but not left. For example, suppose third also contained a call

Display   Run-time stack

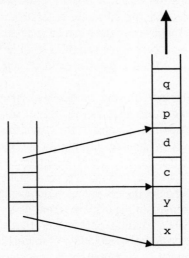

Figure 7.6

of second:

```
program demo (output);
var x, y: real;
  procedure first;
    var c, d: integer;
    procedure second;
    var p, q: char;
    begin
      .
      .
    end;
    procedure third;
    var m,n: integer;
    begin
    second;
      .
    end;
  begin
  second;
  third
  end;
begin
first
end.
```

The situation immediately prior to the call of `second` within `third` would be as in Figure 7.7, whereas immediately after the call it would appear as in Figure 7.8. This illustrates the fact that *display* only provides pointers to the blocks containing variables that are currently accessible, and therefore has *one* pointer to each *static* level whose variables can be accessed. This is illustrated in Figure 7.8 by not providing access to the variables local to `third`, after `second` has been called within `third`, since `second` and `third` are at the same static level!

In the storage allocation model using the display, when a function (or procedure) declared at *the same static level* as the current function is called, it is a matter of updating the value of the pointer on the top of the display, while when a function declared, statically, within the current function is called, it is a matter of pushing a new value on to the display. The same applies in reverse. When a function is left, return may be to a function at the same static level or to one at an enclosing level. In the first case, the top value on the display is updated, while in the second case the top element of the display is removed.

An extreme case is where a function (or procedure) calls itself, a recursive call, which is allowed in many languages, including C-related languages, and Pascal. Here the calling environment and the called environment are at the same level statically, and the top element of the display must be updated on entering and leaving each call. In order to restore the display elements the values of the dynamic pointers may be stored at the foot of each stack frame.

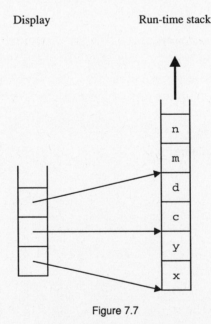

Figure 7.7

Display   Run-time stack

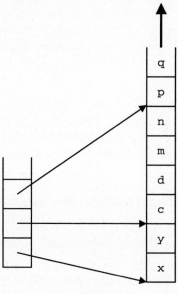

Figure 7.8

7.4 **Compile-time addresses**

The addresses of variables are not, in general, known at compile time. There are a number of reasons for this, some of which will have already become apparent:

- The position of the stack frame, corresponding to a particular function or procedure, on the run-time stack is dependent on the calling order of the functions/procedures.
- The values of array indices are not normally known at compile time, and have to be computed at run time.
- Some values are accessed via pointers, the values of which are not known at compile time.

Although addresses are not known at compile time, some information concerning them is usually known. For example, the following are usually available at compile time:

- The offset of a simple value from the foot of the stack frame.
- The offset of the start of an array from the foot of the stack frame.
- The static depth of the function in which a variable is declared.

The static depth (point 3) is relevant in Pascal and Ada, though not in C.

In the case of C, the compile-time address of a simple variable is simply an offset from the foot of the stack frame. The same applies to the field of a record, since the fields of a record are always stored consecutively, and we assume that the storage required for each of the fields of the record is known. For Pascal or Ada the compile-time address of a simple variable, or a field of a record, would consist of a pair:

(level number, offset)

where *level number* was the static level number of the function or procedure in which the variable or record was declared and *offset* is the offset as for C.

For arrays with static bounds (bounds whose values are known at compile time), the address of an array element may also be expressed as a *level number* and *offset*, or simply an *offset*, depending on the language involved. The offset of an array element from the foot of the stack frame consists of two parts:

1. The offset of the start of the array from the foot of the stack frame.
2. The offset of the array element from the start of the array.

For arrays with static bounds, the first of these will be known at compile time, while the second, in general, will not, since the values of array indices are not normally known at compile time.

Some computation is involved in evaluating addresses of array elements at run time, based on the information known at compile time. The amount of computation, as we will see, depends on the number of dimensions in the array. The situation is illustrated in the following example in Pascal.

Consider the array declaration:

```
var table: array [1..10,1..20] of integer
```

The elements of the array are usually stored *by rows* or, more correctly, *by lexicographic order of the indices*. For example, the values of the elements of table would be stored in consecutive locations in the following order

```
table  [1,1], table [1,2],...,table [1,20],
table  [2,1], table [2,2],...,table [2,20],
              .
              .
              .
table  [10,1], table [10,2],...,table [10,20]
```

The address of a particular array element is calculated as the displacement from the address of the first element of the array, using the formula

$$address(\text{table } [i,j]) = address (\text{table } [l_1,l_2]) + (u_2 - l_2+1)*(i - l_1) + (j - l_2)$$

where l_1 and u_1 are the lower and upper bounds of the first dimension, etc., and each element of the array is assumed to occupy one unit of space. In the example above, the lower bounds are of course 1 in each case, and the upper bounds are 10 and 20 respectively. For a three-dimensional array, arr3, declared as

var arr3 : **array** $[l_1..u_1, \; l_2..u_2, \; l_3..u_3]$ **of** integer

the general formula for the address of an array element arr3[i,j,k] is given by

$$address(arr3[i,j,k]) = address(arr3[l_1,l_2,l_3])+(u_2 - l_2+1)*(u_3 - l_3+1)* \; (i - l_1)+(u_3 - l_3+1)*(j - l_2)+(k - l_3)$$

The expression $(u_r - l_r + 1)$ gives the number of distinct values the rth subscript can take. Thus $(u_3 - l_3 + 1)$, being the number of distinct values that the third subscript can take, is also the distance between array elements that differ by only one unit in the second subscript. Similarly

$$(u_2 - l_2 + 1) \; * \; (u_3 - l_3 + 1)$$

represents the number of distinct pairs of values that the second and third subscripts can take, and hence the distance between elements which differ by only one in the first subscript. The distance between array elements which differ only in the ith subscript is known as the ith *stride*. Thus in the above example the first stride is

$$(u_2 - l_2 + 1) \; * \; (u_3 - l_3 + 1)$$

and the second and third strides are $(u_3 - l_3 + 1)$ and 1 respectively.

From the formula for calculating the offset of an array element from the address of the first element of the array, given above, it is clear that the calculation is relatively simple if the strides are known. For example, for the array arr3, the address of arr3 [i,j,k] is given by

$$address(arr3 \; [i,j,k]) = address \; (arr3 \; [l_1,l_2,l_3]) +s_1 * (i - l_1) + s_2 * (j - l_2) + s_3 * (k - l_3)$$

where s_1, s_2 and s_3 represent the strides

$$(u_2 - l_2 + 1) \; * \; (u_3 - l_3 + 1)$$
$$(u_3 - l_3 + 1)$$
$$1$$

respectively.

Figure 7.9 shows how strides are used to calculate the address of an array element for an array declared (in Pascal) as

```
var N: array [1..10,1..10,1..10] of integer;
```

For languages in which the array bounds are known at compile time, the values of the strides may be computed once (at compile time), thus minimising the computation that has to be performed (at run time) on each occasion an array access occurs. However, it is not possible to simplify the above formula further since differences such as $(i - l_1)$ are not, in general, known at compile time. For languages supporting arrays with dynamic bounds (which are not known until run time) the strides may be evaluated when the array is declared, and stored on the stack, again minimising the amount of computation required for each array access. Although the values of the strides may not be known at compile time, almost certainly the amount of space that the strides will occupy will be known, and space for this can be allocated at compile time. However, the space for the array elements themselves may have to be allocated at run time, since the values of the bounds may be unknown at compile time.

The notion of dynamic arrays (arrays with dynamic bounds) requires a more general model of the run-time stack than the one we have considered up to now. The position of the start of an array, within a stack frame, will not be known, in general. It is therefore convenient to split each stack frame into two parts, a *static part* containing those values whose size is known at compile time and a *dynamic part* containing those values whose size is not known at compile time. All values in the dynamic part will be reachable (through pointers) from values in the static part. The static part of the frame will therefore contain the following values:

- All simple values (*integers, floats*, etc.).
- the static parts of arrays (bounds, strides, pointers to the array elements themselves).
- the static parts (those fields whose size is known at compile time) of records.
- pointers to global values – though the global values will not be held on the stack but on the heap.

```
N[1,1,1]N[1,1,2].N[1,1,10],N[1,2,1]...N[2,1,1]..N[10,10,10]
```

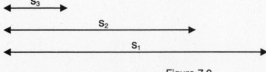

Figure 7.9

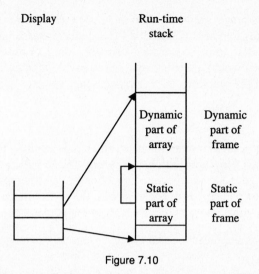

Figure 7.10

The dynamic part of the frame, on the other hand, will contain the elements of arrays. Using this model, even the elements of arrays with static bounds will normally, in practice, be stored in the dynamic part of the frame. Figure 7.10 shows this, more general, model of a stack frame.

As far as accessing an array element is concerned, in this model an extra pointer has to be followed and an offset added, compared with accessing a non-array element. The value of the level number of the frame provides the first pointer from the display. To this is added the offset of the pointer, in the static part of the array, to the start of the array elements themselves, and finally this pointer has to be incremented, *at run time*, to give the address of the particular element of the array.

The compile-time address of the whole array is simply a *level* and *offset* that corresponds to the start of the static part of the array, while the calculation of the run-time address of an array element involves the calculations outlined above. Clearly, array elements are costly in terms of access time, especially for arrays with a large number of dimensions. This cost can be minimised by calculating strides once only, and the cost, in terms of access time, of having arrays with dynamic, rather than purely static, bounds, is that of following one additional pointer at run time, for each access.

7.5 **The heap**

As already mentioned, the heap is used for the storage of values which *may* require to be accessible from the time the storage space is allocated until the program terminates. There is no language mechanism, like block or function exit, that will make the storage space no longer accessible. At first sight, the allocation scheme for such storage would seem to be to allocate space from one end of a linear store towards the other end until all the available space had been used up; and there would seem to be no question of reallocating, or reusing space in any way. This approach would have the severe drawback that, once all the space has been allocated for the first time, the next statement such as

```
string = malloc(4);
```

that attempts to allocate four bytes of space, and return a pointer to it, would cause the program to fail. However, before accepting this as inevitable, it should be realised that storage space may become inaccessible due to program actions such as reassignment to pointers, etc. For example, the space allocated above could become inaccessible *via the variable string* due to the assignment

```
string = newstring;
```

However, there remains the possibility that the space concerned is accessible via some other variable. Consider the effect of executing an assignment such as

```
string1 = string;
```

between the executions of the two assignments above. Assuming there are no other relevant statements, this assignment would make the space allocated by *malloc* accessible via the variable *string1*.

Since there is no way of knowing, in general, at compile time, which path a program will follow at run time, it is not possible to know (at compile time) when the storage space allocated by *malloc* becomes no longer accessible. This means that code to reclaim heap space cannot be generated at compile time, despite the fact that large areas of space allocated on the heap can actually become inaccessible. One way out of this difficulty is to expect programmers to know, from their knowledge of how the code will be executed, when heap storage will become free, and expect them to insert explicit instructions in the source code to de-allocate storage. For example, in C it is possible to write

```
free (string);
```

to deallocate the space to which the variable *string* points. This approach puts a considerable responsibility (and a good deal of extra work) on the programmer. It is therefore worth considering whether some more automatic method of freeing storage may be possible. The language Java takes the view that it is the implementation's, rather than the programmer's, responsibility to free inaccessible storage, and any implementation of Java should provide appropriate mechanisms to do this. Incidentally, Java stores *arrays* on the heap, unlike the storage models we have described so far. Also all *objects* are stored on the heap.

There are two methods potentially available for managing the heap, so as to reclaim unreachable storage. These are known, respectively, as

- *garbage collection;*
- *use of reference counters.*

The first of these is probably the more popular and takes advantage of the fact that there is no need to reclaim any storage space until all available space has been allocated, *and more is required.* For this reason, in many cases zero time will be spent on garbage collection. If, and when, garbage collection is required, it proceeds in two phases:

1. *A marking phase* in which heap storage that is accessible via program variables is marked by inserting values in a bit map.
2. *A compaction phase* in which all the accessible space is moved to one end of the heap, leaving the reusable space in one contiguous block at the other end. Care, of course, must be taken to ensure all pointer values are changed appropriately.

The marking phase is the more interesting of the two and it is worth considering some of the alternative methods for performing it. Some means of 'marking' memory cells that may be accessed via program variables is required. A bit map may be used containing sufficient *bits* to correspond to each cell in the heap. The bit map will not be part of the heap itself, but will be distinct from it. Each *bit* in the bit map may take one of two values:

1. 0 meaning the corresponding memory cell is not able to be accessed via a program variable.
2. 1 meaning the corresponding memory cell may be accessed via a program variable.

At the start of garbage collection, all the elements of the bit map will be set to 0, and, as the execution of the garbage collection algorithm progresses, various elements of the bit map will be set to 1. Eventually all the bit map elements corresponding to memory cells that are reachable via program variables will have been set to 1.

A *simple* garbage collection algorithm makes use of a stack (referred to as the *garbage collection stack*), and proceeds as follows.

Garbage collection 1:

1. The run-time stack is searched in a linear manner until a variable pointing to unmarked cells on the heap is discovered. This may be either a variable itself that is a pointer (into the heap) or a component of a record that is a pointer. The cells on the heap to which this variable points are then *marked* by inserting appropriate bits in the bit map.
2. Some of these cells in turn may be pointers to unmarked cells to the heap, in which case *their* addresses are put on the garbage collection stack.

3. The address on top of the garbage collection stack or, if the garbage collection stack is empty, the address held by the next pointer variable on the run-time stack is followed. Any unmarked cells on the heap to which it points are *marked* and their addresses put on the garbage collection stack.
4. Step 3 is repeated until both the garbage collection stack is empty and *all* the pointer variables on the run-time stack have been processed as described.

Since step 3 always marks an unmarked cell, the algorithm will eventually terminate.

The algorithm described above is intuitive, easy to understand and efficient. It has one big disadvantage. It may not be *feasible* since it requires the use of an arbitrary sized stack at a time when space is at a premium. Otherwise, the garbage collector would not have been called! One would not, of course, expect to be able to perform garbage collection with no working space whatsoever. However, the garbage collection requirements, for a small (and known) amount of working space, could be allowed for in the decision to call the garbage collector in the first place. In fact, garbage collection algorithms with extremely modest space requirements exist, and one such is the following.

Garbage collection 2:

1. Mark all the cells on the heap pointed to directly by values on the run-time stack.
2. Scan the heap from the lower address end to find the first marked pointer pointing to an unmarked cell. *Mark* the cell it points to.
3. Continue scanning the heap marking unmarked cells pointed to by marked cells. Note the address of the cell with the lowest address marked in this way. Call this address *lowest*.
4. Repeat steps 2 and 3 but starting at the address *lowest* so long as at least one cell is marked during a scan. As there are only a finite number of cells to be marked, the algorithm eventually terminates.

In addition to the space required for the bit map, the algorithm requires only three variables representing the:

- current position in a scan;
- the cell being pointed to;
- the lowest address to have been pointed to during the current scan (*lowest*).

However, from a time point of view, the algorithm may be very inefficient. This would be particularly true if the heap contained many backward pointers, and is the penalty to be paid for not making use of a stack.

A compromise between the two algorithms described would be an algorithm that behaves like garbage collection 1 when there is sufficient space to do so and garbage collection 2 otherwise. For example, it could have a *fixed size* stack and behave like garbage collection 1 as long as the stack was sufficiently large. Each time a value had to be added to the stack that would cause the stack to overflow, a value would be allowed to fall out of the bottom of the stack to compensate. The lowest value falling out of the stack in this way would be remembered, and used to initiate a second phase of the algorithm in which it would behave much as garbage collection 2.

Another well-known garbage collection algorithm (see the further reading section at the end of the chapter) considers the heap as a tree structure with pointers from the top to the bottom. Garbage collection starts from the top of the tree and works its way downward. Instead of using a stack to remember pointers yet to be followed, the algorithm uses the pointers in the tree itself, temporarily reversing them as necessary, to provide a route back up the tree. The algorithm turns out to be efficient in time taken *and* in additional storage required.

Other schemes for garbage collection include *generational garbage collection* in which a distinction is made between

- *global objects* that have existed for a relatively long time when the garbage collector is called, whose storage is not necessarily reclaimed;
- *local objects* that have existed for a shorter time, whose storage is always reclaimed.

This scheme clearly reduces the time spent in garbage collection and can be quite effective. Other schemes involve two global areas to reduce the time taken during the compaction phase. References to some of these methods are in the further reading section at the end of the chapter.

Whatever method of garbage collection is used there may be occasions where a program simply runs out of space, and has to terminate unless the system allows recovery in some other way. Programs may also become *garbage collection bound* in that they spend a very significant part of the time performing garbage collection. Soon after garbage collection has been performed and the program is able to resume, the heap fills up, requiring further garbage collection. The overhead of garbage collection in these circumstances can be very significant, and this is where the alternative approach of using *reference counters* may be appropriate. Use of reference counters replaces the unknown, and occasionally very high, overhead imposed by garbage collection, with a constant predictable overhead.

Using reference counters, an attempt is made to reclaim each element of heap storage *immediately* after it can no longer be accessed. Each memory cell on the heap has a reference counter associated with it that contains a count of the number of values that point to it. The count is incremented each time a new value points to the cell and decremented each time a value ceases to point to it. When the counter becomes zero, the cell may be returned to a free list for further allocation. The method can work well but has some limitations:

- Storage associated with data structures such as circular lists cannot be reclaimed.
- The constant overhead associated with the use of reference counters can impose significant penalties on programs with modest storage requirements.

The second point contradicts the *Bauer principle* that 'simple programs' should not have to pay for expensive language facilities that they do not use.

7.6 Summary

This chapter has been concerned with storage allocation for typical programming languages. In particular, we have:

- distinguished between *static*, *dynamic* and *global storage*;
- described the run-time stack model for dynamic storage, including the use of *stack frames* and *display*;
- introduced the notion of the compile-time address;
- described mechanisms for storing and accessing arrays;
- discussed the use of the heap for the storage of global values;
- described alternative methods of garbage collection for reclaiming heap storage when required;
- described how reference counters may be used to control heap storage, and discussed the advantages and disadvantages of using reference counters as an alternative to garbage collection.

In the next chapter, we discuss the principles and methods of code generation.

Further reading

Most compiler books have good treatments of storage allocation issues, for example Loudon (1997) and Terry (1997).

The notion of the run-time stack goes back a very long way to its use in the early ALGOL 60 compilers by Naur (1964) in Denmark, and Randell and Russell (1964) in the United Kingdom. The notion of the heap is slightly more recent and was first required for languages such as SNOBOL 4, LISP 1.5 and ALGOL 68. A good early account of garbage collection algorithms is given by Knuth (1968b), including the Schorr and Waite garbage collection method based on reversing the pointers in a tree data structure. A recent textbook by Appel (1997) describes the main methods of garbage collection, while more comprehensive descriptions appear in Cohen (1981) (survey paper), and Jones and Lins (1996) (a textbook on the subject). Discussion of the implementation of Java is in Lindholm and Yellin (1996).

Exercises

7.1 In many language implementations, characters occupy as much storage space as integers. Give arguments for and against this situation.

7.2 Suggest storage mechanisms appropriate for storing constants.

7.3 A few programming languages offer the facility of 'flexible' arrays with local scope, but whose size may vary at execution time. Suggest what type of storage allocation mechanism would be appropriate for such arrays, and discuss the issues involved.

7.4 Could the display mechanism be replaced by pointers embedded in the stack?

7.5 One of the design aims of Pascal was that 'it should lead to efficient object code on present day computers'. Suggest how the lack of dynamic arrays in the language supports this.

7.6 Explain why compaction of the heap (part of garbage collection) is non-trivial.

7.7 Justify the Java approach of providing a garbage collector rather than making the reclamation of unreachable storage the responsibility of the programmer.

7.8 Discuss whether reference counter or garbage collection management of the heap would be preferable in a real-time environment.

CHAPTER 8

Code generation

8.1 **Introduction**

In this chapter we will consider the code generation phase of compilation. In particular, we will:

- consider various types of intermediate code produced by compilers, and how they are generated;
- discuss the principal types of machine architectures currently in use, and outline the issues involved in producing code for them;
- discuss the issues involved in code optimisation, and how it may be performed at various stages of the compilation process;
- briefly indicate some of the issues concerned with code generator generators.

The emphasis, however, will be on the issues involved in generating code, rather than on providing a comprehensive treatment of code generation, in all its aspects. A detailed treatment of how code is produced for particular machines might do more to obscure the issues than to illuminate them. As usual, references to more complete treatments will be given at the end of the chapter.

8.2 **Production of intermediate code**

As mentioned in section 1.4, there are good reasons for compilers to produce intermediate code, as a first step towards the production of code for an actual machine. Reasons include:

- providing a clear distinction between the machine independent parts of the compiler and the machine dependent parts;
- minimising the effort required to port the compiler to a new environment;
- minimising the effort involved in implementing m languages on n machines;
- ease of optimisation.

Intermediate code can take a number of forms. It may be specific to the language being implemented, e.g. P-code for Pascal, Diana for Ada, bytecode for

Java. Alternatively, it may be specific to the machine on which the implementation is being performed. An example of the latter would be CTL (Compiler Target Language), which was used as an intermediate language on the MU5 machine in the University of Manchester in the 1970s. The intermediate language may be close to the language being implemented, or it may be closer to the machine on which the implementation is being performed. In any case, it will be a linearisation of the syntax tree produced during syntax and semantic analysis, and is formed by breaking down the tree structure into sequential instructions, each equivalent to a single, or a small number of, machine instructions. Machine code may be generated from intermediate code alone, or its production may also require access to symbol table and other compile-time information.

As examples of intermediate codes, we will consider three well-known examples:

1. Three-address code.
2. P-code, a language-specific intermediate code upon which the majority of implementations of Pascal are based.
3. Bytecode used by the Java Virtual Machine.

8.2.1 *Three-address code*

An example of *three-address code* would be

```
a = b op c
```

in which *op* was an arithmetic, or other, operator, b and c its operands (or their addresses) and a an address for the result of applying the operand. The arithmetic expression

$$(a + b)^*(c + d)$$

could be represented by the sequence of three-address code instructions as

```
t₁ = a + b
t₂ = c + d
t₃ = t₁ * t₂
```

where the ts are compiler-generated *temporaries*. Monadic operators could also be handled. For example

$$-m$$

would produce

```
t₁ = -m
```

though, of course in this case there would only be two addresses in the three-address code!

The conversion of expressions to sequences of three-address instructions is readily performed by a YACC-based analyser similar to the one that produced postfix notation described in section 5.6 (based on the example in section 4.7). The YACC grammar with actions is, as before:

```
S     : EXP;
EXP   : TERM;
      | EXP + {A1();} TERM {A2();}
      | EXP - {A1();} TERM {A2();};
TERM  : FACT
      | TERM*{A1();} FACT {A2();}
      | TERM/{A1();} FACT {A2();};
FACT  : - {A1();} FACT {A4();}
      | VAR {A3();}
      | ( EXP );
VAR   : a|b|c|d|e;
```

The actions, however, are not the same as previously. A multi-purpose stack is required capable of storing operators and operands (including temporaries). The actions are:

A1 – stack the operator

A2 – print a three-address code instruction as follows

       print the name of the next temporary to be allocated

       print ' = '

       print the top three elements of stack from the bottom up

       stack the name of the temporary just allocated

A3 – stack the operand

A4 – print a three-address code instruction as follows

       print the name of the next temporary to be allocated

       print ' = '

       print the top two elements of the stack from the bottom up

       stack the name of the temporary just allocated

Three-address code may also be used to represent other aspects of typical programming languages, such as assignments, array accesses, conditional and unconditional jumps. For example, the following could all be examples of three-address code;

```
a := t₁
t₁ = c[i]
goto L
if t₁ goto L
```

Each statement in three-address code has *at most* three addresses, and further forms of instructions exist for assignments involving addresses and pointers, procedure calls, parameter evaluation and so on. High-level control structures such as loops, conditional statements and switch (case) statements are broken down to tests and jumps in order to produce three-address code.

Examples of how control structures compile into three-address code are given by the following:

1. ***if** (expression) statement₁ **else** statement₂*

   The **if**-statement above may be implemented by adding actions to the grammar as follows

   > ***if** (expression) <l1> statement₁ <l2> **else** statement₂ <l3>*

   where the actions are

   > *l1   increment label number*
   > *generate code to jump to label if expression is false*
   > *stack label number*

   > *l2   increment label number*
   > *generate code to jump to label*
   > *unstack label, L_k, say*
   > *set L_k in code*
   > *stack label used in unconditional jump, above*

   > *l3   unstack label, L_j, say*
   > *set L_j in code*

   which would produce the following code:

   ```
        code to evaluate expression
        t₁ = not expression
        if t₁ goto L₁
        code for statement₁
        goto L₂
   L₁   code for statement₂
   L₂
   ```

2. ***while** (expression) statement*

   The while statement above may be implemented by adding actions to the grammar as follows:

   > ***while** <W1>(expression) <W2> statement <W3>*

where the actions are

W1   *increment label number*
       set label in code
       stack label

W2   *increment label number*
       generate code to jump to label if expression is false
       stack label

W3   *unstack label, L_j, say*
       unstack label, L_k, say
       generate code to jump unconditionally to L_k
       set L_j in code

which would produce the following code

```
L₁:  code to evaluate expression
     t₁ = not expression
     if t₁ goto L₂
     code for statement
     goto L₁
L₂:
```

Allocation of labels is non-trivial and requires the use of a compile-time stack. Both backward and forward jumps are involved and the applied and defining occurrences of labels are usually nested in 'the usual way'. However care must be taken at times (for example within *W3*) to deal with cases in which the order that the labels appear on the stack does not quite correspond to the order in which they are required. The label stack may be a compile-time stack of its own, or it may often be merged with other compile-time stacks.

8.2.2 *P-code*

We now turn to the production of another type of intermediate code, namely P-code, a stack-based intermediate code designed specifically for the implementation of Pascal, and widely used for this purpose. P-code instructions each have the following format:

F P Q

F is a function code and *P* or *Q* (or both) may be absent depending on the particular function code. If present, *P* can be used to specify a static block level and Q an offset within a frame or an immediate operand (e.g. constant). Instructions with zero parameters operate on the top elements of the stack and include:

- AND   *applies the Boolean* AND *operator to the top two elements of the stack, removing them in the process, and leaving the result of applying the operator (true or false) on top of the stack;*
- DIF   *applies the set difference operator to the top two elements of the stack, removing them in the process, and leaving the result of applying the operator (a set) on top of the stack;*
- NGI   *changes the sign of the integer value on top of the stack;*
- FLT   *converts the value on top of the stack from integer to real;*
- FLO   *converts the value on the second top position of the stack from integer to real;*
- INN   *tests for set membership, using the top two elements of the stack as parameters and leaving true or false in their place.*

One or two-address instructions are used to load a value on to the top of the stack, or to store the address on top of the stack. For example:

```
LDCI    4    loads integer constant 4
LODI  0 5    loads integer value in address (0,5)
LDA   0 6    loads address (0,6)
STRI  1 4    stores integer in address (1,4)
```

where compile-time addresses are represented as a pair of integers:

(static level, offset)

P-code also includes jump instructions, for example:

```
UJP    L₇    unconditional jump to L₇
FJP    L₈    jump to L₈ if top of stack is false
```

and labels may be set in code, for example:

```
L₄
```

Single instructions are defined in order to be able to apply standard functions to the value on top of the stack, for example:

```
CSP    ATAN
```

which applies the *arctan* function to the value on top of the stack, leaving the result of applying the function in its place, and:

```
CSP     WLN
```

which performs a *writeln* on the file specified by the top element of the stack.

We can now show the P-code that would be produced for the **if** and **while**-statements defined earlier in this section. It is assumed that expression evaluation leaves the computed value of the expression on top of the stack:

1. ***if** (expression) statement$_1$ **else** statement$_2$*

   would generate:

   code to put the value of expression on top of the stack

   ```
   FJP     L₁
   ```

   code to implement statement$_1$

   ```
   UJP     L₂
   L₁
   ```

   code to implement statement$_2$

   ```
   L₂
   ```

2. ***while** (expression) statement*

   would generate

   ```
   L₁
   ```

   code to put the value of expression on top of the stack

   ```
   FJP     L₂
   ```

   code to implement statement

   ```
   UJP     L₁
   L₂
   ```

For each applied occurrence of a variable, code is generated to put the address or the value of the variable, as appropriate, on the stack. For example:

```
LDA     1     7
```

will load the address (1, 7) on top of the stack, whereas:

```
LODI    1    7
```

will load the value of the integer variable with the address (1, 7) on the top of the stack.

The implementation of an assignment involves, in the simplest case, copying the value in the top element of the stack into the address in the second top element of the stack, and removing the top two elements of the stack. This may be performed using the single address instruction:

```
STOI
```

In the more general case involving an array or a record, where a number of consecutively located values have to be copied, the effect of the assignment may be achieved by:

```
MOV     m
```

which will move *m* values, starting from the *source* address, to an appropriate number of addresses starting from the *destination* address, where the source and destination addresses are on the top of the stack. At the same time the two addresses are removed from the stack.

While P-code could be further compiled into machine code for a particular machine, it is more often executed directly, with the aid of an interpreter. The widespread transportation of Pascal from one environment to another in the late 1970s was largely due to the fact that, given a Pascal compiler written in Pascal, all that was required to implement it in a new environment was to write a P-code interpreter for the environment, a task which was supposed to take about a month's work. Many compilers, in fact, stop short of producing actual machine code. In some cases, for example, assembly code is generated, which is subsequently converted into machine code by the system assembler.

8.2.3 *Bytecode*

Bytecode is the intermediate language for the Java Virtual Machine (JVM) and, like P-code for Pascal, is stack based. The Java Virtual Machine is designed to make Java implementations:

- efficient,
- secure, and
- portable,

and this is reflected in the Java run-time system, the main components of which are:

- *the execution engine* which executes the bytecode instructions;
- *the memory manager* which manages the heap in which all *objects* and *arrays* are stored;
- *the error and exception manager* which is used to *catch* run-time failures in a planned and systematic manner;
- *the threads interface* which handles concurrency;
- *the class loader* which loads, links and initialises *classes*;
- *the security manager* which deals with attempts to run 'hostile' programs.

Bytecode instructions for each *class* are contained in *the Java class file*. Each class file contains virtual machine code for the methods (functions/procedures) used by the class, symbol table information (*constant pool* in Java), links to super-classes, etc. For efficiency, the class file is in binary format, though this may be translated into symbolic form for viewing purposes. A strong feature of Java implementations is the *class file verifier* which verifies, among other things, that files from an untrusted source will not cause the interpreter to fail, leave it in an undefined state, or crash the host computer. In particular the *bytecode verifier* is used to check the bytecode within methods for:

- branch instructions that refer to invalid addresses;
- type errors in instruction codes;
- improper stack control with respect to overflow and underflow conditions;
- methods that are called with the wrong number or types of arguments.

It is an important feature of Java implementations that this verification takes place *prior* to execution, thus avoiding potentially expensive run-time checking. However, verification is not cheap and being based on a type of theorem prover, is subject to some theoretical constraints.

There are over 160 different bytecode instructions, many of which only differ in the types of their operands. The retention of type information in bytecode is important from the verification point of view, and the number of instructions available does not allow the same level of support for all the data types! The principal types of bytecode instructions are concerned with:

- stack manipulation;
- performing arithmetic;
- handling objects and arrays;
- control flow;
- method invocation;
- handling exceptions and concurrency.

For example, as in P-code, there are instructions for pushing constants and local variables on to the stack, manipulating the stack itself, and storing values from the stack in local variables:

Instruction	Meaning
iconst_4	load the integer constant 4 on to the stack
iload_4	load the value of local variable number 4 on to the stack
pop	discard the top value on the stack
dup	duplicate top item on the stack
swap	interchange top two values on the stack
istore_4	store the value on top of stack in the local variable number 4

Examples of instructions to perform arithmetic include:

Instruction	Meaning
iadd	add the two integers on the top of the stack
fadd	add the two floats on the top of the stack
fmul	multiply the two floats on the top of the stack

Arrays are accessed using instructions such as:

Instruction	Meaning
iaload	puts the value of an array element on top of stack, assuming the array reference and the index of the index are already on the stack

Conditional and unconditional branch instructions, as well as subroutine entry and table jump instructions, are available. Each takes one or more label parameters. For example;

Instruction	Meaning
ifeq L_1	jump to L_1 if the integer value on top of stack is zero
if_icmpne L_1	jump to L_1 if two integer values on top of the stack are not equal
goto L_1	jump to L_1

These are just a small selection of the rich instruction set offered by the JVM. The JVM could be used, and to some extent is being used, as an intermediate stage for compiling languages other than Java (Ada for example).

We now show how bytecode would be generated for the C control structures that we considered earlier in this section;

1. ***if** (expression) statement₁ **else** statement₂*

   would be represented in bytecode as

   bytecode to put the value of expression on top of the stack

   ```
   ifeq   L₁
   ```

   bytecode to implement statement₁

   ```
   goto   L₂
   L₁
   ```

   bytecode to implement statement₂

   ```
   L₂
   ```

2. ***while** (expression) statement*

   would be represented in bytecode as

   ```
   L₁
   ```

   bytecode to put the value of expression on top of the stack

   ```
   ifeq   L₂
   ```

   bytecode to implement statement

   ```
   goto   L₁
   L₂
   ```

Notice that, in bytecode, *false* is represented by *0* and *true* by *1*. Hence the use of `ifeq` rather than its inverse `ifne`. There is no Boolean type in Java.

The approach adopted by Sun towards the implementation of Java has introduced some interesting and significant new ideas as far as language implementation is concerned. Like the language itself, the implementation method builds on, and extends, established approaches.

In the next section, we consider some of the issues involved in generating actual machine code, by considering the characteristics of some typical machine architectures.

8.3 **Production of machine code**

Before considering other issues, we should look at the two main types of machine architecture currently in use:

- CISC (complex instruction set computer).
- RISC (reduced instruction set computer).

CISCs are designed with the implementation of high-level languages in mind and would therefore seem, at first sight, the ideal candidates as targets for compilers. CISCs have many powerful instructions and are associated with compact object code. Typical characteristics are:

- a wide range of addressing modes to support access to arrays, records, lists, stack frames, etc;
- a small number of registers (usually 16 or less);
- many special purpose registers, for example registers may be reserved for indexation;
- two-address instructions such as $A+B{\rightarrow}A$, where A, B may be complex addresses;
- variable length instructions;
- instructions with side effects, for example auto-increment instructions;
- widely different execution times for instructions;
- control implemented by microgram.

RISCs, on the other hand, tend to have the following characteristics:

- simple addressing modes usually only involving registers;
- many registers, at least 32;
- all registers are 'general purpose';
- three-address instructions but only involving registers, e.g. $r_3 = r_1 + r_2$;
- fixed length instructions (32 bits);
- no side effects, one result per instruction;
- each instruction takes a similar length of time to execute;
- control is hard wired, rather than microprogrammed.

The advantages of RISCs over CISCs are their simplicity and, from the compiler's point of view, the relatively few ways of achieving a given effect (fewer choices to evaluate and choose from at compile time). There are also advantages to be gained from the use of fixed length instructions and the large number of general-purpose registers available. We will not debate the relative merits of CISC and RISC architectures at length, merely observe that the architecture of the target machine is a major issue in deciding code generation strategy.

There are two major issues as far as machine code generation is concerned:

1. Instruction selection.
2. Register allocation.

8.3.1 *Instruction selection*

The primary aim of *instruction selection* is to produce an object program that is semantically equivalent to the source code from which it was derived. In general, there will be more than one way of doing this, and more than one object program equivalent to the source program. The aim of a good code generator should be to implement a low-cost solution to the problem where the cost may be a measure of the size of resultant object code or its efficiency. Instruction selection is not independent of register allocation, since a good instruction selection method may produce poor results, on occasion, owing to a lack of available registers. However, it is normal to perform instruction selection first, and to assume, initially at least, that sufficient registers are available.

Assuming translation is from three-address code, a straightforward approach to instruction selection is to associate a code skeleton with each type of three-address instruction. Translation of each three-address instruction to machine code would then consist of generating code based on the appropriate skeleton. The result, however, is liable to be inefficient for a number of reasons:

- There are likely to be unnecessary load and store instructions.
- No benefit will have been taken of efficient increment instructions.
- No benefit will have been taken of potentially useful context information.

Unnecessary load and store instructions may be suppressed, to an extent, by allowing the code generator access to the contents of registers, etc. The code generator too may be able to spot special cases where 'efficient' instructions, such as autoincrement instructions, should replace a sequence of instructions in one or more code skeletons. In addition, the code generator may be able to use tables of context information to help produce high-quality code. When it comes to choosing between alternative code sequences to be emitted, techniques of *dynamic programming* are often used. These issues would all be considered facets of good code generation, rather than being classified as optimisations, which we will come to later.

8.3.2 *Register allocation*

Register allocation is a critical process as far as the production of quality object code is concerned. It can be assumed that, in general, operations involving the contents of registers will take much less time than the corresponding operations involving values stored in main storage space. This means that registers should be used, as far as possible, for the operands of object code instructions. There are three main types of values that should be held in registers, wherever possible:

1. Frequently used pointers into run-time data structures such as the run-time stack.
2. Values of parameters of functions and procedures.
3. Values of temporary variables used in evaluating expressions.

As far as using registers for pointers into the run-time stack are concerned, this is unlikely to be a problem in the case of RISC architectures, where registers are plentiful and a bank of registers can usually be allocated for this purpose. In the case of CISC architectures, where registers are usually in short supply, this will not always be possible. The usual solution to this problem, in the CISC case, is to use registers only for the most frequently used pointers into the run-time stack, such as the pointer to the foot of the stack, the pointer to the current stack frame and the pointer to the top of the stack. This makes access to local variables, whose values are held in the current stack frame more efficient than access to variables whose values are held in other frames, something that may be exploited by the programmer with a knowledge of implementation details.

Of course, even in the context of RISC architectures, there may be occasions when the bank of registers allocated for frame pointers is insufficient, owing to the dynamic depth of nesting of functions and procedures. There is no way round this, as only a finite number of registers are available, and, if there are insufficient registers, the values of one or more registers will need to *spill* into a non-register memory location.

Parameters of functions and procedures are passed via registers, where possible. However, owing to the unpredictable nature of the dynamic call structure, at compile time, a naive approach to register allocation for parameters would not allow parameter values (or the values of local variables) of one call to be preserved in registers over a call of another procedure (within the current procedure). In RISC architectures with many registers, some or all of these registers may only be accessible through a *register window* which will undertake the task of performing the allocation to particular registers *at run time*. In this way, the parameters and local variables of calling and called procedures need not overlap, at least as long as the call depth and the number of parameters per call is below a certain limit. Knowledge of typical maximum calling depths may be used to ensure that register spillage, owing to long call depths, is extremely rare.

Efficient allocation of *temporaries* (used for example in expression evaluation) to registers is not trivial. In three-address code, new temporaries are allocated each time one is required, but adopting this strategy for registers would not work since there are only a finite number of registers available. Fortunately, many temporaries can usually be allocated to the same register (though not at the same time) and register spillage should rarely occur, at least for RISC architectures. However, detecting which temporaries may share registers requires some analysis of the intermediate code. Roughly speaking, what is required is to detect values in registers that will not be required again, thus making the register free to be used for some other purpose. It must be borne in mind that it is not known, in general, at compile time which particular values will be required later, so a *conservative approach* must be taken. Thus any register value which *may* be required later must not be overwritten.

To consider the matter further, we need to define a few terms. Consider the sequence of three-address code:

```
t₁ = a + b
t₂ = c + d
t₃ = t₁ * t₂
```

As far as this sequence of code is concerned the values of t_1 and t_2 must be preserved until t_3 is evaluated at least. Consider, however, the evaluation of:

$a*b + c*d + e*f$

which would produce the three-address code sequence:

```
t₁ = a * b
t₂ = c * d
t₃ = t₁ + t₂
t₄ = e * f
t₅ = t₃ + t₄
```

Five temporaries are used but clearly the corresponding registers need not all be distinct. For example, the values of t_1 and t_2 are not used again after the third instruction so that the following allocation of temporaries would be valid:

Temporary	Register
t_1	1
t_2	2
t_3	3
t_4	1
t_5	2

We will define variable/temporary to be *live* if it holds a value that (from a conservative analysis) has to be retained for later use. Thus t_1 is live from the time instruction 1 has been executed until instruction 3 is executed, but not thereafter, while t_2 is similarly live from instruction 2 to instruction 3. t_3 is live from instruction 3 until instruction 5. For a piece of sequential code, *liveness analysis* is performed from the end of the code to the beginning.

Intermediate code, of course, will normally contain loops and conditional statements and we should consider how these affect liveness analysis. In addition to its application to temporaries, liveness analysis may be applied to variables that are in regular use, and are to be held in registers. Consider therefore the following piece of code involving a loop, represented in three-address form:

```
1)      n = 0
2)        sum2 = 0
3)        sum3 = 0
4) L₁: t₁ = n<10
```

```
5)      t₂ = not t₁
6)      if t₂ goto L₂
7)      n = n + 1
8)      m = n*n
9)      sum2 = sum2 +m
10)     t₃ = m*n
11)     sum3 = sum3 + t₃
12)     goto L₁
13) L₂:
```

corresponding to the C code

```
n =0;
sum2 = 0;
sum3 = 0;
while (n < 10)
{n = n + 1;
m = n*n;
sum2 = sum2 + m;
sum3 = sum3 + m*n;
}
```

In order to analyse the liveness of the variables in the loop, we must consider which variables are *live* on entering the loop. On entering the loop n, $sum2$ and $sum3$ need to be live, since their values are used within the body of the loop. This is true not only the first time the body of loop is entered, but also on its subsequent executions. Therefore n, $sum2$ and $sum3$ need to be live when the statement

```
goto L₁
```

is executed. In addition, certain other variables may need to be live when the loop is left, though, in what follows, we will ignore this possibility. Further analysis yields the following information concerning the liveness of variables and their possible allocation to registers:

Variable	Live	Register
n	1–12	1
sum2	2–12	2
sum3	3–12	3
t_1	4–5	4
m	8–10	4
t_2	5–6	4
t_3	10–11	4

The above table shows that only four registers are required.

To generalise, the liveness of variables is governed by equations of the form

in[n] = *use[n]* ∪ *(out[n] – def[n])*
out[n] = ∪ *in [s]*

where

use[n]   is the set of all variables whose values are used in statement *n*,
out[n]   is the set of all variables that are live on leaving statement *n*,
def[n]   is the set of all variables that are defined in statement *n*,
in[n]   is the set of all variables that are live on reaching statement *n*,
          and s is a successor statement to n.

The second equation ensures that all possible successor statements to *n* are taken into account, which, for *loops*, would include the initial statement of the loop being considered as a successor of the final statement of the loop.

Equations of the above form exist for each statement in the intermediate code, and the simultaneous solution of these equations provides the sets of variables that are live on entering and leaving each statement. The solution of the equations is an example of data flow analysis, which has a number of applications. It can, however, be an expensive process, at worst taking time proportional to n^4, though, more typically n^2, where *n* is the number of statements involved.

Other issues which should be mentioned include:

- function and procedure calls require their input parameters to be live on entry;
- values of output parameters must be live on leaving function and procedure calls;
- accesses to (anonymous) variables by pointers cannot be handled by data flow analysis;
- access to array elements, whose subscripts are unknown at compile time, can only lead to very conservative data-flow conclusions.

The allocation of variables to registers in a safe way may be seen as a version of the classical *graph colouring problem*, in which colours have to be assigned to nodes of a graph in such a way that no two adjacent nodes have the same colour. A special case of the graph colouring problem is the map colouring problem, in which the states on a two-dimensional map are to be coloured in such a way that no two adjacent states have the same colour.

8.3.3 *Register allocation by graph colouring*

We now describe an algorithm for register allocation based on graph colouring. Each variable that is to be allocated to a register, if possible, may be thought of as a node of an undirected graph, *the interference graph*. An arc is then drawn between two nodes if they cannot share a register. This may occur, for example, because they are live at the same time.

The algorithm proceeds as follows: Suppose there are m registers available. If a particular node N has fewer than m neighbours then, once the rest of the interference graph has been coloured, this node can be coloured using a colour other than one of the ($< m$) colours associated with its neighbours. We may therefore delete this node, along with its associated edges, from the graph and stack them, to be dealt with further in due course. It may be possible to continue in this way until only a single node with no neighbours is left. If so, then we can colour this node in any of the available colours, and proceed to remove the other nodes, and the edges stacked with them from the stack, colouring them as we do so. The colouring will then have been successful.

However, if any node has more than m neighbours, when it is unstacked, spillage may need to occur. However, this is not *necessarily* the case since not all the neighbours of a given node need have distinct colours from each other. A way forward is to mark this node as a possible candidate for spillage, remove it from the graph and stack it like the rest. When it comes to remove this node from the stack, it may be possible to colour it in a colour distinct from all its neighbours, or it may not. If it is not, no register is allocated to it but it is given an address in memory, and spillage has occurred.

An example of the interference graph for the sequence of intermediate code considered earlier is given in Figure 8.1. In this example, the algorithm would proceed as follows, assuming four registers A, B, C and D were available:

1. Node n has six neighbours and may have to be spilled. It is marked as such and stacked, the graph is reduced by removing this node and its associated edges.

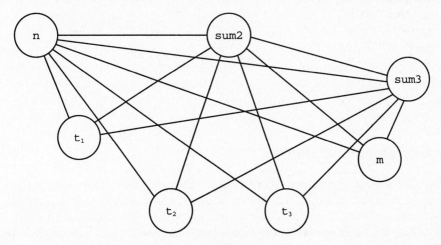

Figure 8.1

2. Node *sum2* has five neighbours (node *n* has been removed from the graph) and may have to be spilled. It is marked as such and stacked, the graph is reduced by removing this node and its associated edges.
3. Node *sum3* has four neighbours and may have to be spilled. It is marked as such and stacked, the graph is reduced by removing this node and its associated edges.
4. Node t_1 has no neighbours. It is stacked and the graph is reduced by removing this node.
5. Node t_2 has no neighbours. It is stacked and the graph is reduced by removing this node.
6. Node *m* has no neighbours. It is stacked and the graph is reduced by removing this node.
7. Node t_3 has no neighbours. It is the only node remaining and is coloured 'A'.
8. Node *m* is unstacked (along with the edges with which it was stacked). It has no neighbours and is also coloured 'A'.
9. Node t_2 is unstacked. It has no neighbours and is also coloured 'A'.
10. Node t_1 is unstacked. It has no neighbours and is also coloured 'A'.
11. Node *sum3* is unstacked. It has four neighbours all coloured 'A' so it may be coloured 'B'.
12. Node *sum2* is unstacked. It has five neighbours, four coloured 'A' and one coloured 'B', so it may be coloured 'C'.
13. Node *n* is unstacked. It has six neighbours four coloured 'A', one coloured 'B' and one coloured 'C' so it may be coloured 'D'.

The allocation has been successfully performed, the final allocation being consistent with the one suggested earlier.

Variable	Register
n	D
sum2	C
sum3	B
t_1	A
m	A
t_2	A
t_3	A

8.4 Code optimisation

The aim of code optimisation is to produce efficient object code, in terms of space and execution time. The degree of optimisation desired will depend on the circumstances. On occasions, it may be unimportant, for example if programs have short run times, modest space requirements and are likely to be short lived – student programs are often of this type. For programs that have long run times or substantial space requirements, and are likely to have long lifetimes, the need for optimisation may be considerable. The cost of optimisation is mainly in terms of compilation time, some optimisations being rather expensive in terms of compilation time, while others are relatively cheap. It is usually worth performing the cheaper types of optimisation, though it is not always worth performing the more expensive ones.

Some compilers may be capable of operating in more than one mode, depending on the degree of optimisation that is to be performed. The Borland C/C++ compiler has an extensive range of optimisation options available. For example, the user can opt to generate either fast *or* compact code. Some early Pl/1 compilers performed extensive code optimisation by means of a very large number of (optional passes) over the source code (up to about 30), consuming a correspondingly large amount of compilation time. In an environment in which good diagnostic information is a priority, it is often best to turn off all optimisations in order to avoid possible confusion arising from misleading messages!

The optimal optimiser – one that will produce optimal run-time code for all possible inputs – is not achievable. Its production is equivalent to the solution of the Halting Problem for Turing Machines, which of course is unsolvable. In fact many 'good' optimisers will produce *less* optimal code for a few (possibly rather contrived) inputs! Of course, it is essential that optimisations do not alter the meaning of the code, and sometimes extensive code analysis is required in order to ensure this. Such analysis is, largely, based on data-flow analysis, which we will consider in more detail in this section. We will also look at various semantics-preserving code transformations.

Optimisations may be:

- either *local* and based on relatively straightforward analysis and code transformations; or
- *global* and based on relatively complex analysis and code transformations.

We first consider local optimisations that tend to be based on analysis of a small number of consecutive instructions. They are invariably cheap to perform and can be extremely effective, especially when they are performed within inner loops of programs that account for a great deal of execution time. The following are examples of well-known types of local optimisations:

- constant folding;
- strength reduction;
- elimination of unnecessary instructions.

Constant folding consists of performing arithmetic operations at compile time that might otherwise be performed at run time. For example, the sequence

```
limit = 10
index = limit - 1
```

might be replaced by

```
limit = 10
index = 9
```

An example of *strength reduction* would be to replace multiplication or division involving a power of two, by appropriate shift instructions.

Examples of the *elimination of unnecessary instructions* would be to remove LOAD into register instructions, where the register already contained the required value; and STORE from register instructions where the memory address involved already contained the value in the register.

These types of optimisations applied to straight line code without any loops or branches might not be considered as optimisations at all, but merely as good practice, as far as code generation is concerned.

Analysis of control and data flow leads to further, more ambitious, optimisations such as:

- dead-code elimination;
- common subexpression elimination;
- loop optimisations.

Dead-code elimination consists of removing code that cannot be executed during *any* execution of the program. Such code may, for example, have been required in an earlier version of the program, but has become redundant because of subsequent revisions. It is possible, of course, that the fact that the code is not reachable is an indication of a fault in the program, but this is not something the compiler would be able to detect. Data-flow analysis is required in order to spot dead code. *Liveness analysis* may show that there is a three-address instruction of the form:

```
x = a + b
```

where x is not live on leaving the instruction. Such an instruction is clearly redundant and should be removed, reducing the size of the code. Dead-code elimination is thus a space optimisation, whereas most of the other optimisations that we discuss are run-time optimisations.

Common sub-expression elimination involves identifying those values on the right sides of three-address instructions that have already been evaluated and need not be re-evaluated. Such identification may (even must) also be based on data-flow analysis, but requires more information than merely the liveness of variables. The assignment of a value to a variable:

```
a = b + c
```

is referred to as a definition of the variable a and we say that this definition of a *reaches* some other instruction:

```
d = b + c
```

if data-flow analysis shows that neither *b* nor *c* can have changed in the interim. If this is the case, the above instruction may be replaced by:

```
d = a
```

thus avoiding the second evaluation of *b+c*.

It is useful to introduce the idea of *availability* in this context. If an expression is computed on every control-flow path to a statement, and none of its operands has been defined on any of these paths, then the expression is *available* at the statement, and does not need to be recomputed. It is not difficult to generalise the data-flow equations shown earlier to keep track of *available* expressions. Care has to be taken to consider the possibilities of aliases – different names for the same variable. The use of aliases may make a change to one variable affect the value of an, apparently different, variable. Aliases may occur in a number of ways:

- parameters called by reference in languages such as Pascal, where the corresponding actual and formal parameters are aliases for each other;
- assignment of addresses;
- use of the same actual parameter for two formal parameters.

An example of the latter case would be the procedure call in Pascal

comp (x,x)

corresponding to the procedure declaration

procedure comp (var p,q);

in which *p* and *q* are aliases for each other.

Alias analysis can identify *possible* aliases and suppress unsafe optimisations. In strictly typed languages, it can be assumed that variables of different types cannot be aliases of each other, thus potentially increasing the safe optimisations that may be performed.

Loop optimisations tend to be performed on source code or a representation closely related to it, and the range of such optimisations is extensive. For example in the following code, *a* * *b* is evaluated in every iteration of the loop:

```
int v[10];
void f(void)
{
    int i,x,y,z;
    for (i = 0; i < 10; i++)
        v[i] = a * b;
}
```

It could be optimised to produce the following:

```
int v[10];
void f(void)
{
    int i,x,y,z,t1;
    t1 = a * b;
    for (i = 0; i < 10; i++)
        v[i] = t1;
}
```

Other types of optimisation involving loops include;

- replacement of tail recursion with iteration;
- removal of unnecessary array bound checks;
- loop unrolling (replacing a loop by a piece of sequential code);

and many others. While we have not attempted to provide a comprehensive account of the full range of possible code optimisation, the examples given should provide a good idea of the possibilities. Compilers vary greatly in the extent to which they attempt to optimise code, from merely producing good (or occasionally not so good) code together with a few local optimisations, to performing extensive global optimisation across functions and procedures.

8.5 Code-generator generators

The idea of a code-generator generator that will produce a code generator given

- a description of an intermediate code and
- a description of the machine code that has to be generated

is an attractive one. The use of such a tool, along with a lexical analyser generator and a parser generator, would go a long way towards automating compiler production.

The matching of intermediate code to object code templates can be seen as a parsing problem. The prefix representation (operator, operand, operand) of a syntax tree, for example, could be defined by a context-free grammar, which could contain actions to emit object code. The grammar involved is typically highly ambiguous, and means have to be found of resolving the many shift–reduce and reduce–reduce conflicts likely to occur. These may be resolved with the aid of *cost information* concerning the cost (at run time) of generating the alternative sequences of code. For RISCs, the number of alternatives is usually not too large, but for CISCs the number of alternatives may be so large that the time taken to consider them all may be combinatorially explosive.

In the absence of cost information, it is usually preferable to generate code in as few steps as possible. This means that a *shift action* is preferred to a *reduce action* in a shift–reduce conflict, and the longer of two or more reductions is preferred in a reduce–reduce conflict. This approach tends to generate 'powerful', as opposed to 'less powerful', machine instructions. For example, it tends to generate the instructions with the more sophisticated addressing modes.

In addition to the obvious advantages already mentioned, code-generator generators also provide a relatively simple approach to porting code generators. However, there are a number of 'difficulties' associated with them, and they are not widely used. These include:

- the grammars involved can be very large;
- the speed of code generation tends to be rather slow because of parsing table manipulations;
- instructions with side effects (e.g. autoincrement instructions) are not well suited to the approach.

8.6 Summary

In this chapter we have:

- described how intermediate code, such as three-address code, P-code and bytecode, is produced for a selection of language features;
- discussed how the features of CISC and RISC architectures affect code generation;
- described code generation issues such as *instruction selection* and *register allocation*;
- described simple code optimisation techniques;
- introduced the notion of *code-generator generators*.

Further reading

Most of the textbooks that have been mentioned so far cover code generation including Aho, Sethi and Ullman (1985), Fischer and Leblanc (1988), Loudon (1997), Appel (1997) and Ullmann (1994). P-code for Pascal is described in Nori *et al.* (1981). The Java Virtual Machine is described in Lindholm and Yellin (1996), and in Meyer and Downing (1997) who provide a bytecode assembler with the text.

Both Aho, Sethi and Ullman, and Appel give extensive coverage to code optimisation. Grammar-based code-generator generators were first introduced by Glanville and Graham (1978).

Exercises

8.1 Produce three-address code for each of the following expressions:

(a) $a + b + c$
(b) $(a + b)*(c + d)*(e + f)$
(c) $x*y*z + -p*q$

8.2 Outline the arguments in favour of compiling first into intermediate code, rather than straight into machine code.

8.3 What are the relative advantages of using P-code and three-address code as intermediate codes?

8.4 What are the relative advantages of translating versus interpreting P-code?

8.5 Suggest a reason why the Java Virtual Machine does not support the type Boolean.

8.6 What advantages do

(a) CISC architectures
(b) RISC architectures

offer to the compiler writer?

8.7 State the areas in which each of the variables in the following sequence of code is *live*. Assume only p is live once the sequence has been executed:

```
1) a = c + d;
2) m = 2 *a;
3) n = a + m;
4) k = m + n;
5) p = c * k *3;
```

8.8 Which variables are live on entering the sequence of code in exercise 8.7?

8.9 Consider the piece of C code:

```
n = 0;
sum2 = 0;
while (n < 10)
{n = n + 1;
m = 2*n;
sum2 = sum2 + m;
}
```

Suggest how it might be optimised.

8.10 Give an example of how an 'optimisation' may *increase* the execution time of a program.

Solutions to exercises

Chapter 1

1.1 Adjacent languages in different Ts at the same vertical level should be identical. Source and object languages for Ts at the same vertical level should be the same (see Figure 1.5).

1.2 No, there would be no context information available to make the distinction.

1.3 See Figure S.1.

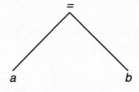

Figure S.1

1.4 Count the number of characters in the source code.
Count the number of symbols in the source code.
Count the number of functions and procedures in the source code.

1.5 Lexical analysis.

1.6 Semantic analysis.

1.7 Global storage.

1.8 Short time to completion.
Re-use of existing components from other projects.

1.9 Probability of the compiler failing on a given compilation.

1.10 For – compatibility with Lex and YACC.
Against – poor type-checking and other 'insecurities'.

Chapter 2

2.1 (a) Each string of the language consists of a sequence of zero or more *a*s.
(b) Each string of the language consists of a sequence of one or more *a*s, followed by one or more *b*s.

(c) Each string of the language consists of a sequence of zero or more xs, followed by the *same* number of ys, followed by the *same* number of zs.

(d) each string of the language consists of a sequence of zero or more xs, one or more ys and the same number of zs as there were xs.

(e) Each string of the language consists of a sequence of zero or more xs followed by zero or more ys followed by zero or more zs.

2.2 (a) Zero or more xs, followed by zero or more ys.

(b) x followed by zero or more xs, followed by y, followed by zero or more ys.

(c) x or y, zero or more times.

(d) a or b, followed by zero or more occurrences of a, followed by zero or more occurrences of b.

(e) a or b, zero or more times.

2.3 (a) Since it is right linear, not (b) since the productions are a *mixture* of left linear and right linear, not (c) since the first production is neither left nor right linear, not (d) since neither of the productions is of an appropriate form.

2.4 (a) Generates a regular language since the grammar is regular.

(b) Replacing the last production by

$$Y \rightarrow yY$$

makes the grammar regular so the language generated is regular.

(c) The language generated is regular, since an example of a regular grammar generating the same language is the one with the following productions:

$$S \rightarrow aA$$
$$A \rightarrow aA$$
$$A \rightarrow b$$
$$A \rightarrow bB$$
$$B \rightarrow b$$
$$B \rightarrow bB$$

(d) The language generated is not regular so it has no regular grammar.

2.5 A rightmost derivation is

$$S \Rightarrow S + x \Rightarrow S + x + x \Rightarrow S + x + x + x \Rightarrow x + x + x + x$$

The derivation is unique since at each stage there is a simple rule to determine which production to use. If the application of production 2 will complete the derivation use it, otherwise use production 1. No other strategy will generate the required string.

2.6 First rightmost derivation:

> *statement* ⇒ **if** *expr* **then** *statement* **else** *statement*
> ⇒ **if** *expr* **then** *statement* **else** *other*
> ⇒ **if** *expr* **then if** *expr* **then** *statement* **else** *other*
> ⇒ **if** *expr* **then if** *expr* **then** *other* **else** *other*

Second rightmost derivation:

> *statement* ⇒ **if** *expr* **then** *statement*
> ⇒ **if** *expr* **then if** *expr* **then** *statement* **else** *statement*
> ⇒ **if** *expr* **then if** *expr* **then** *statement* **else** *other*
> ⇒ **if** *expr* **then if** *expr* **then** *other* **else** *other*

First leftmost derivation:

> *statement* ⇒ **if** *expr* **then** *statement* **else** *statement*
> ⇒ **if** *expr* **then if** *expr* **then** *statement* **else** *statement*
> ⇒ **if** *expr* **then if** *expr* **then** *other* **else** *statement*
> ⇒ **if** *expr* **then if** *expr* **then** *other* **else** *other*

Second leftmost derivation:

> *statement* ⇒ **if** *expr* **then** *statement*
> ⇒ **if** *expr* **then if** *expr* **then** *statement* **else** *statement*
> ⇒ **if** *expr* **then if** *expr* **then** *other* **else** *statement*
> ⇒ **if** *expr* **then if** *expr* **then** *other* **else** *other*

Also

> *statement* ⇒ *unmatched*
> ⇒ **if** *expr* **then** *statement*
> ⇒ **if** *expr* **then** *matched*
> ⇒ **if** *expr* **then if** *expr* **then** *matched* **else** *matched*
> ⇒ **if** *expr* **then if** *expr* **then** *other* **else** *matched*
> ⇒ **if** *expr* **then if** *expr* **then** *other* **else** *other*

2.7 $G = (\{0, 1\}, \{S\}, P, S\})$

where *P* are

$S \rightarrow 0S \mid 1S \mid \varepsilon$

2.8   Leftmost derivation:

> *PROGRAM* ⇒ **begin** *DECS; STATS* **end**
> ⇒ **begin** *d; DECS; STATS* **end**
> ⇒ **begin** *d; d; STATS* **end**
> ⇒ **begin** *d; d; s; STATS* **end**
> ⇒ **begin** *d; d; s; s* **end**

Rightmost derivation:

> *PROGRAM* ⇒ **begin** *DECS; STATS* **end**
> ⇒ **begin** *DECS; s; STATS* **end**
> ⇒ **begin** *DECS; s; s* **end**
> ⇒ **begin** *d; DECS; s; s* **end**
> ⇒ **begin** *d; d; s; s* **end**

2.9   **(a)**   *letter (letter | digit |)(letter | digit |)(letter | digit |)(letter | digit |)*
(letter | digit |)

  (b)   *G = ({letter, digit}, {S, R, T, U, V, W}, P, S}*

where *P* are

> *S* → *letter | letter R*
> *R* → *letter T | digit T | letter | digit*
> *T* → *letter U | digit U | letter | digit*
> *U* → *letter V | digit V | letter | digit*
> *V* → *letter W | digit W | letter | digit*
> *W* → *letter | digit*

2.10   In C there is no *then* but the usual rule applies namely that the *else* belongs to the nearest preceding *if* which on reading from left to right does not already have an *else* associated with it. Most languages are the same. A counter-example is ALGOL 60 where the combination *then if* was illegal. However, the effect of the combination could be achieved by using a compound statement.

Chapter 3

3.1   Lexical analysis is relatively slow because it involves reading the source code character by character rather than symbol by symbol.

3.2   The values of constants are not required by the parser as such, only by the code generator. The parser only needs to know that the symbol is a constant and does not require its value.

3.3 A finite automaton to recognise a FORTRAN identifier is shown in Figure S.2

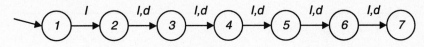

Figure S.2

All the states are final states except the first one. The transition from the first state to the second one is on reading a letter, and all the other transitions are on reading a letter or a digit.

3.4 **(a)** See Figure S.3. State *2* is the final state.

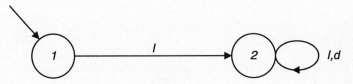

Figure S.3

(b) See Figure S.4. State *3* is the final state.

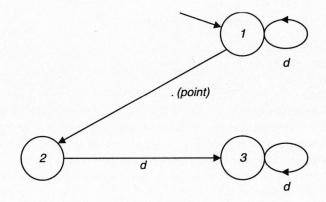

Figure S.4

(c) See Figure S.5. State 4 is the final state.

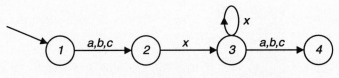

Figure S.5

3.5 In each case only the productions are given. S is the sentence symbol.

(a) $S \rightarrow lT \mid l$
$T \rightarrow lT \mid dT \mid l \mid d$

(b) $S \rightarrow dS \mid .T$
$T \rightarrow dT \mid d$

(c) $S \rightarrow aT \mid bT \mid cT$
$T \rightarrow xT \mid xU$
$U \rightarrow a \mid b \mid c$

3.6 See Figure S.6. States 4 and 7 are final states.

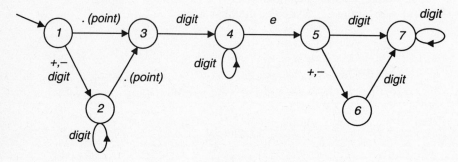

Figure S.6

The C code to implement the automaton is

```
int real()
{int state;
char in;
state = 1;
in = getchar();
while(isdigit(in) || issign(in) || in =='.' || in == 'e')
{switch (state) {
case 1: if (isdigit (in) || issign (in))
        state = 2;
        else if (in == '.')
        state = 3;
        else error();
        break;
case 2: if (isdigit(in))
        state = 2;
        else if (in == '.')
        state = 3;
        else error();
        break;
```

```
case 3: if (isdigit(in))
            state = 4;
        else error();
        break;
case 4: if (isdigit(in))
            state = 4;
        else if (in == 'e')
            state = 5;
        else error();
        break;
case 5: if (isdigit(in))
            state = 7;
        else if (issign(in))
            state = 6;
        else error();
        break;
case 6: if (isdigit(in))
            state = 7;
        else error();
        break;
case 7: if (isdigit(in))
            state = 7;
        else error();
        break;
    }
    in = getchar();
    }
    return(state == 4 | | state == 7);
}
```

3.7 R is the sentence symbol and the productions are

$R \rightarrow + A \,|- A\,|\, digit\ A\,|.\ P$
$A \rightarrow digit\ A\,|.\ P$
$P \rightarrow digit\ Q\,|\, digit$
$Q \rightarrow eE\,|\, digit\ Q\,|\, digit$
$E \rightarrow + F\,|- F\,|\, digit\ G\,|\, digit$
$G \rightarrow digit\ G\,|\, digit$

3.8   Finite automaton (Figure S.7). State *1* is the start and the final state. Reading *1* changes the state, reading *0* leaves the state the same.
Regular expression:

$(0^* 10^* 10^*)^*$

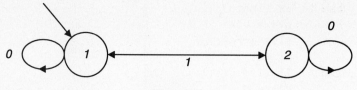

Figure S.7

Lex input

```
valid  (0*10*10*)*
```

3.9 Lexical faults correspond to an illegal character or an illegal character sequence. Recovery is to skip characters until a match is found.

3.10 Co-routines could be used. Avoids possible (but highly unlikely) heavy use of recursion, but perhaps is less intuitive.

Chapter 4

4.1 The grammar with productions

$$S \rightarrow S + x$$
$$S \rightarrow x$$

since it contains left recursion.

4.2 **(a)** Since there will be more than one leftmost derivation for some sentence of the language, the director symbol sets for some non-terminal must be disjoint, allowing it to be replaced in more than one way at some stage of the derivation.

(b) See section 4.3.

4.3 The productions only are given, in each case:

(a) $S \rightarrow xSy$
$S \rightarrow a$

(b) $S \rightarrow xSW \,|\, a$
$W \rightarrow y \,|\, z$

(c) $S \rightarrow R \,|\, T$
$R \rightarrow xRy$
$R \rightarrow a$
$T \rightarrow zTy$
$T \rightarrow a$

4.4 Advantages – suggest left association (evaluation from left to right), less need to store intermediate results.

Disadvantages – not suitable for LL parsing, including recursive descent.

4.5 **(a)** The last one.
(b) The first one.

4.6 The productions are (*S* is the sentence symbol in each case):

(a) $S \rightarrow 0S11 \mid a$
(b) $S \rightarrow 0S \mid 1T \mid \varepsilon$
$T \rightarrow 0S \mid \varepsilon$
(c) $S \rightarrow 1T \mid 0U \mid \varepsilon$
$T \rightarrow 0S \mid 1UU$
$U \rightarrow 1S \mid 0TT$

4.7 No, since

$$DS(S \rightarrow AB) = \{x, m\}$$
$$DS(S \rightarrow PQx) = \{x, p, q\}$$

which are not disjoint.

4.8 Strings in the language consist either of

- a string of zero or more *p*s followed by a string of zero or more *q*s followed by the symbol *x*; or
- the string *xy* or the string *m*, followed by a string of one or more *b*s.

4.9

S	→ *EXP*
EXP	→ *TERM MORETERMS*
MORETERMS	→ + *TERM MORETERMS*
	|− *TERM MORETERMS*
	|ε
TERM	→ *FACT MOREFACT*
MOREFACT	→ *FACT MOREFACT
	|/ *FACT MOREFACT*
	|ε
FACT	→ − *FACT*
FACT	→ (*EXP*)
FACT	→ *VAR*
VAR	→ *a* | *b* | *c* | *d* | *e*

4.10

S	→ *EXP*
EXP	→ *TERM MORETERMS*
MORETERMS	→ + <A1> *TERM* <A2> *MORETERMS*
	|− <A1> *TERM* <A2> *MORETERMS*
	|ε
TERM	→ *FACT MOREFACT*

$$MOREFACT \rightarrow *<A1> FACT <A2> MOREFACT$$
$$|/<A1> FACT <A2> MOREFACT$$
$$|\varepsilon$$
$$FACT \rightarrow -<A1> FACT <A2>$$
$$FACT \rightarrow (EXP)$$
$$FACT \rightarrow VAR <A3>$$
$$VAR \rightarrow a|b|c|d|e$$

Chapter 5

5.1 Basically because each production does not require to be recognised until it has been fully formed on the stack, rather than from a single terminal symbol alone.

5.2 *Shift–reduce conflict* – both a shift and a reduce action appear possible at a particular point in a parse.
Reduce–reduce conflict – reduction by more than one production seems possible at a particular point in a parse.

5.3 For a grammar to be ambiguous there must exist a sentence which can be derived in more than one (rightmost) way. Thus during a rightmost derivation there must be more than one action possible at some stage, thus there must be a shift–reduce or a reduce–reduce conflict in the LR parse table. Therefore the grammar cannot be LR(1).

5.4 Because the contents of the symbol stack do not affect the progress of the parse at any stage.

5.5 If the grammar is annotated as shown below, the corresponding SLR(1) parse table is shown in Table S.1.

1. $S \rightarrow {}_1 a_2 x_3 F_4$
2. $F \rightarrow {}_{3,6,5} J_6 F_7$

Table S.1

State	S	F	J	,	a	x	⊥
1					S2		
2						S3	
3		S4		S5			R3
4							R1
5			S6		S8	S10	
6		S7		S5			R3
7							R2
8						S9	
9				R4			R4
10				R5			R5

3. $|_{3,6}\varepsilon_{3,6}$
4. $J \rightarrow {}_5 a_8 x_9$
5. $|_5 x_{10}$

5.6 The grammar cannot be LR(1) since there is no way of detecting the 'middle' of a sentence (when production 3 or 4 should be applied) based on the history of the parse so far and a single symbol of lookahead.

5.7 If the grammar is annotated as shown below, there is clearly a shift–reduce conflict in state *8* that a single symbol of lookahead does not resolve – a lookahead of : can indicate a shift or a reduce! However two symbols of lookahead resolve the conflict since := indicates a reduce and anything else a shift. Therefore the grammar is LR(2). The problem can be dealt with at lexical analysis by treating the sequence := as a single symbol.

$$S \rightarrow {}_{1,6} V_2 :_3 = {}_4 E_5$$
$$S \rightarrow {}_{1,6} L_6 S_7$$
$$L \rightarrow {}_{1,6} I_8 :_9$$
$$V \rightarrow {}_{1,6} I_8$$

5.8 No solution given – depends on local environment.

5.9 For – provides a uniform approach to error recovery.

Against – does not take advantage of the fact that recovery from context-sensitive errors is often possible without affecting the parser actions at all.

5.10 The grammar at the end of section 5.8, used to illustrate reduce–reduce conflicts, would do.

Chapter 6

6.1 For C:

- consistent number of array indices;
- consistent number of function parameters;
- scope rules;
- type compatibility in assignments, etc.

6.2 No, since compound statements are not usually nested to any significant depth.

6.3 No, since this convention only distinguishes integers from reals and, in any case, may be overridden.

6.4 Information has to be inserted in the symbol table in a pass *prior* to the one which uses the information.

6.5 In Pascal recursive types may only be used in connection with pointers, and a pointer type must be defined immediately before the type to which it points.

6.6

- Data abstraction and encapsulation.
- Polymorphism.
- Inheritance.

6.7 Allows inheritance of different types of methods from different sources. Makes programs complex from users' and implementers' point of view.

Chapter 7

7.1 *For* – makes addressing simpler.
Against – requires more space.

7.2 One possibility would be to use a one-dimensional character array, together with a table, each row of which consists of

- a pointer into the array corresponding to the start of a constant;
- an integer corresponding to the number of characters in the constant.

7.3 The heap could be used, but is not entirely appropriate since the instant at which the space may be reused *is* predictable at compile time. Alternatively, the dynamic part of the stack could be used, in which case would need to allow the array to expand and contract during program execution. This, in turn, could involve moving other values on the dynamic stack!

7.4 Yes.

7.5 It requires one fewer pointer to be followed in accessing array elements – see section 7.4.

7.6 Care must be taken to avoid overwriting values as values are being moved.

7.7 The programmer should not have to worry about freeing storage. In addition, he/she cannot be trusted to do so correctly!

7.8 The fixed, and predictable, overhead of reference counters is much to be preferred in a real-time environment.

Chapter 8

8.1 (a)

```
t₁ = a + b
t₂ = t₁ + c
```

(b)

```
t₁ = a + b
t₂ = c + d
t₃ = t₁ * t₂
t₄ = e + f
t₅ = t₃ * t₄
```

(c)

```
t₁ = x * y
t₂ = t₁ * z
t₃ = -p
t₄ = t₃ * q
t₅ = t₂ + t₄
```

8.2 Separation of language dependent and language independent aspects of the compiler; ease of portability; economy of effort in implementing a number of languages; etc.

8.3 Three-address code is not language specific, P-code is language specific. P-code is stack based – an advantage or a limitation!

8.4 Interpretation – aid to portability, good support for diagnostics. Translation – more efficient.

8.5 It helps to limit the number of instruction types.

8.6 CISCs have powerful instructions designed for implementing high-level languages.
RISCs have many registers and a simpler instruction set.

8.7

Variable	Instructions
a	1–3
c	1–5
d	1
m	2–4
n	3–4
k	4–5
p	5–

8.8 c, d.

8.9 Replace the code with:

```
m = 0;
sum2 = 0;
while (m < 20)
{m = m + 2;
sum2 = sum2 + m;
}
```

8.10 Removing a statement from a loop will increase the execution time of the program, if the loop is executed zero times.

Glossary

Abstract syntax tree A tree-like structure used to represent the essential aspects of program structure (punctuation, brackets, etc. are usually omitted from the representation).

Address Location in memory.

Alphabet A finite set of symbols.

Ambiguous grammar A grammar for which there is more than one leftmost derivation (or parse tree or rightmost derivation) for at least one sentence that it generates.

Ambiguous language A language that cannot be generated by any unambiguous grammar.

Analyser The part of the compiler that analyses the source code.

Analysis stage The stage of compilation principally concerned with analysis of the source code.

Attribute grammar A context-free grammar enhanced by attribute rules, usually used to restrict the sentences which may be generated by the grammar.

Axiom See Sentence symbol.

Axiomatic semantics A type of semantics definition based on predicate calculus, in which the effects of the computation are described in terms of relationships between the values of variables before and after particular operations have taken place.

Back end (of a compiler) Those parts of the compiler closest to the machine.

Bottom-up parsing The parsing method that proceeds by reducing sentences of a language to the sentence symbol of a grammar generating it.

Bytecode An intermediate language normally used in Java implementations.

Characteristic finite state machine A finite automaton representation of a bottom-up parsing table.

Chomsky hierarchy of grammars/languages A classification of grammars and languages based on the types of productions used in the grammar.

Clean grammar A grammar with no productions that are either redundant or cannot be used in any derivation of a string of terminals.

Code optimisation Code improvement in terms of its size or execution time.

Compaction phase (of garbage collection) The process of moving all the heap storage still required to one end of the available space.

Compilation process The conversion of source code, normally written in a high-level language into semantically equivalent machine code or other representation close to machine code.

Compiler A piece of software that performs the compilation process.

Compiler-compiler A piece of software for building compilers automatically.

Compile-time addresse. What is known at compile time concerning a variable's, or other value's, address (at run time).

Configuration in a grammar A position before, after or between symbols on the right side of a production of a grammar.

Context-free grammar A grammar, all of whose productions have a single symbol on the left side.

Context-free language A language that may be generated by a context-free grammar.

Context-sensitive grammar A grammar, for all of whose productions, the length of the left side (in terms of numbers of symbols) is no longer than that of the right side.

Context-sensitive language A language that may be generated by a context-sensitive grammar.

Data abstraction Characterisation of data in terms of the operations which may be performed on it, as opposed to its internal representation.

Data encapsulation Separation of the implementation details of functions, operators, etc. from their use.

Denotational semantics A type of semantics definition based on functional calculus.

Derivation A sequence of steps whereby a sentence of a language is derived from a grammar generating the language.

Deterministic parsing A parsing method which proceeds without ever having to undo any steps already taken.

Direct recursion The type of recursion in which the nonterminal on the left side of a production of a grammar also appears on the right side of the production.

Director symbol set The set of terminals that are consistent with the application of a particular production during top-down parsing.

Disambiguating rules Rules that resolve ambiguities in a grammar.

Driver program Part of the parser that is language independent.

Dynamic analysis (of software) Analysis of software through executing it.

Dynamic pointers Pointers (to the run-time stack) that reflect the call structure at run time.

Dynamic storage Storage, the requirements for which will change dynamically at run time.

Empty string The string of length zero.

Equivalent grammars Grammars that generate the same language.

Error recovery Actions that allow the parser to continue parsing after an invalid input has been read.

Finite automaton A finite set of states together with a set of transitions between states defined by input symbols.

Follower symbol A symbol which may follow a particular symbol in a sentential form.

Front end (of a compiler) Those parts of the compiler closest to the source code.

Function table Compile-time table containing information concerning the functions in a program.

Garbage collection The process whereby heap storage no longer accessible to a program is reclaimed.

Generate Produce through the application of productions of a grammar.

Global storage Storage which may have to be retained until the program terminates.

Grammar A system for producing the sentences of a language, comprising a quadruple (V_T, V_N, P, S) where V_T is an alphabet whose symbols are known as *terminal symbols*, V_N is an alphabet known as *nonterminal symbols* (or *nonterminals*), P is a set of *productions*, S is a particular nonterminal known as the *sentence symbol*.

Graph colouring problem The problem of colouring each node of a graph with single colour chosen from a finite set of colours, in such a way that the colours of two adjacent nodes are always distinct.

Implementation The act of producing a compiler or the compiler itself.

Implementation language The language in which the compiler is written.

Indirect recursion Recursion involving more than one production.

Inheritance (in object oriented languages) The mechanism whereby a class assumes features (e.g. methods) of a superclass.

Inherited attributes Attributes (of the symbols of an attribute grammar), the values of which are passed from the left sides to the corresponding right sides of the context-free productions.

Input symbol A symbol read, or to be read, by a compiler.

Instruction selection Part of the code generation phase in which particular object code instructions or sequences of object code instructions are selected for output by the compiler.

Integrated development environment A software environment for developing software and supporting activities.

Interference graph A graph in which the nodes represent variables, and arcs are drawn between variables which cannot use the same register.

Intermediate code Code produced by a compiler as an intermediate step towards the production of object code.

Interpreter A language translator which executes each object code instruction as it is produced.

Java Virtual Machine The virtual machine used in implementing Java.

Kleene star The * symbol used in regular expressions to denote zero or more occurrences of that which precedes it.

Label table A compile-time table containing information concerning the labels in a program.

Language A set of strings from some alphabet.

Left linear grammar A grammar, all of whose productions are of one or other of the forms

$$A \rightarrow Bc$$
$$A \rightarrow d$$

where A and B are nonterminals and c and d are terminals of the grammar.

Leftmost derivation A derivation in which the leftmost nonterminal in the sentential form is replaced at each step.

Left recursion The type of recursion in which the symbol on the left side of a production of a grammar may generate (through the application of a single or a set of productions) a string of symbols with itself in the leftmost position.

Lex A lexical analyser generator.

Lexer See Lexical analyser.

Lexical analyser The part of the compiler that performs lexical analysis.

Lexical analyser generator A piece of software which may be used to produce a lexical analyser.

Lexical analysis The phase of compilation whose principal purpose is to form language symbols from strings of characters.

Linearly bound automaton A Turing machine with a finite length of tape.

Liveness analysis Analysis of which variables are live at particular locations in a program.

Live variable A variable, at a particular location in a program, whose value may be required later in the program execution.

LL(1) grammar A grammar in which, for each nonterminal that appears on the left side of more than one production, the director symbol sets of all the productions in which the nonterminal appears on the left side are disjoint.

LL(k) grammar A generalisation of an LL(1) grammar in which the sets of director symbols become strings of length k.

LL(k) language A language that has an LL(k) grammar that generates it.

Lookahead symbol The next symbol to be read by a parser, at a particular stage of a parse.

LR(k) grammar A grammar that has the property that all left to right bottom-up parsing conflicts are capable of resolution based on a fixed amount of information concerning the parse so far, and a limited amount (k symbols at most) of lookahead.

LR(k) language is one that may be generated by an LR(k) grammar.

Machine code generation The production of machine code.

Machine independent code Code output by a compiler which is independent of any particular machine.

Machine independent code generation The production of machine independent code.

Marking phase of garbage collection The phase of garbage collection at which storage cells on the heap whose values must be retained, are identified and marked in some way.

Middle recursion Recursion in a grammar production which is neither left recursion or right recursion.

Multiple inheritance Inheritance involving more than one parent class.

Nonterminal symbol (or **nonterminal**) Symbol used by a grammar to generate sentences of language.

Object text or object code The final output of a compiler, usually code for an actual machine.

Operational semantics A type of semantics definition in which the operations in the language are described in terms of the actions of an abstract machine executing the program.

Optimisation of machine code Improvement of machine code with respect to space utilisation or execution time.

Optimisation of machine independent code Improvement of machine independent code with respect to space utilisation or execution time.

Parser See Syntax analyser.

Parser generator A piece of software that may be used to produce a parser.

Parse table (or **parsing table**) Language dependent table used to guide decisions taken by the parser.

Parsing problem The problem of finding a derivation (if one exists) of a particular sentence using a given grammar.

Pass Compiler component that involves reading the source code, or a representation of it, a single time.

P-code An intermediate language widely used for implementing Pascal.

Phase A logical component of a compiler.

Polymorphism The use of the same function or operator name with different meanings depending on the types of its parameters/operands.

Production (rule) of a grammar A rule that forms part of a grammar, and is used to specify how a substring of a sentential form may be replaced by another substring during the derivation of a sentence.

Push-down automaton A finite automaton together with a stack, the contents of which may affect, and be affected by, the transitions.

Recursion (in a context-free grammar) The property that a nonterminal may generate a string of symbols that contains itself.

Recursive descent The top-down parsing method based on writing a function or procedure in the implementation language, to check each nonterminal in the grammar.

Recursively enumerable grammar The most general type of grammar admitted by the definition of a grammar.

Recursively enumerable language A language that may be generated by a recursively enumerable grammar.

Reduce action (in bottom-up parsing) An action associated with replacing the right side of a production of a grammar with its left side.

Reduce–reduce conflict (in bottom-up parsing) A situation in which more than one reduce action appears possible.

Reference counter Counter used to keep track of the number of pointers pointing to a particular cell of heap storage.

Register allocation The allocation of machine registers to variables and temporaries during code generation.

Regular expression An expression representing a set of strings over an alphabet consisting of symbols from an alphabet and the alternation, Kleene star and juxtaposition operators only.

Regular grammar A right linear *or* a left linear grammar.

Regular language A language which may be generated by a regular grammar.

Right linear grammar A grammar, all of whose productions are of one or other of the forms

$A \rightarrow bC$
$A \rightarrow d$

where A and C are nonterminals and b and d are terminals of the grammar.

Rightmost derivation A derivation in which the rightmost nonterminal in the sentential form is replaced at each step.

Right recursion The type of recursion in which the symbol on the left side of a production of a grammar may generate (through the application of a single or a set of productions) a string of symbols with itself in the rightmost position.

Self-embedding Middle recursion in a grammar rule or set of grammar rules.

Semantic analysis Analysis of source text to identify its meaning/intended effect.

Semantics Definition of the meanings of the strings of a language.

Sentence of a language A string belonging to the language.

Sentence symbol (or axiom) of a grammar A nonterminal used at the start of each derivation of a sentence.

Sentential form Any sequence of symbols that can be derived, using the productions of a grammar, from the sentence symbol of the grammar.

Shift action (in bottom-up parsing) An action associated with accepting a terminal.

Shift–reduce conflict (in bottom-up parsing) A situation in which both a shift action and reduce action appear possible.

Single inheritance Inheritance involving a single parent class.

SLR(1) grammar A subset of LR(1) grammars in which all potential conflicts are resolved by considering lookahead symbols alone.

Source text or source code The initial input to a compiler, usually a program written in a high-level language.

Stack frame A section of the run-time stack associated with a single function or procedure.

Stage (of a compiler) Principal logical component of a compiler.

Starter symbol (in top-down parsing) A terminal symbol which appears at the start of a string of symbols, or, for a string starting with a nonterminal, a terminal which may appear at the start of a string generated by the nonterminal.

State stack The stack on which states are stored during bottom-up parsing.

Static analysis (of software) Analysis of software without executing it.

Static pointers Pointers (to the run-time stack) that reflect the static call structure of the source code.

Static semantics Those aspects of semantics that may be determined statically.

Static storage Storage space that has to be allocated for the duration of the program execution, the requirements for which are known at compile time.

Storage allocation The allocation of storage space for the values of variables, etc. for use at execution time.

Symbol stack The stack on which sequences of symbols are stored during bottom-up parsing.

Symbol table Table used at compile time to store scope, type and other information concerning variables, etc.

Syntax analyser (or **parser**) The part of the compiler that performs syntax analysis.

Syntax analyser generator (or **parser generator**) A piece of software which may be used to produce a syntax analyser (parser).

Syntax analysis The phase of compilation whose principal purpose is to identify the structure of a program.

Syntax (of a language) The set of strings in a language.

Syntax tree A tree-like structure used to represent program structure.

Synthesised attributes Attributes (of the symbols of an attribute grammar), the values of which are passed from the right sides to the corresponding left sides of the context-free productions.

Synthesiser The part of the compiler that builds the object code.

Synthesis stage The stage of compilation principally concerned with building the object code.

T-diagram A type of diagram used to show the three languages (source, object and implementation) involved in a compiler.

Terminal symbol (or terminal) A symbol which forms part of grammar and may appear in the sentences generated by it.

Three-address code A type of intermediate code described in section 8.2.

Top-down parsing The parsing method that proceeds by generating sentences of a language from the sentence symbol of a grammar generating it.

Turing machine An automaton comprising states, transitions and a memory consisting of an infinite tape.

Type-0 grammar See Recursively enumerable grammar.

Type-1 grammar See Context-sensitive grammar.

Type-2 grammar See Context-free grammar.

Type-3 grammar See Regular grammar.

Type-0 language See Recursively enumerable language.

Type-1 language See Context-sensitive language.

Type-2 language See Context-free language.

Type-3 language See Regular language.

Type table A table used at compile time to hold information concerning the types in a program.

Unambiguous grammar A grammar from which no sentence can be generated which has more than one leftmost derivation (or parse tree or rightmost derivation).

Unclean grammar A grammar that is not clean.

Universal Intermediate Language (UIL) An intermediate language suitable for implementing a wide range of languages on a wide range of machines.

Virtual machine The target of a compiler implemented in software.

YACC Yet Another Compiler-Compiler (a parser generator).

References

Aho, A.V., Sethi and Ullman, J.D., 1985. *Compilers; Principles, Techniques and Tools*, Addison Wesley.

Aho, A.V., Hopcroft, J. and Ullman, J.D., 1974. *The Design and Analysis of Computer Algorithms*, Addison-Wesley.

Aho, A.V., Johnson, S.C., and Ullman, J.D., 1975. 'Deterministic parsing of ambiguous grammars', *Comm ACM*, vol. 18, pp. 441–452.

Appel, A.W., 1997. *Modern Compiler Implementation in C: Basic techniques*, Cambridge University Press.

Bennett, J.P., 1990. *Introduction to Compiling Techniques: A First Course using ANSI C, LEX and YACC*, The McGraw-Hill International Series in Software Engineering.

Chomsky, N., 1956. 'Three Models for the Description of Language', *IRE Transactions on Information Theory*, **IT-2:3**, pp. 113–124.

Cohen, J., 1981. 'Garbage Collection of Linked Data Structures'; *Computer Surveys*, vol. 13, no. 3, pp. 341–367.

DeRemer, F., 1971. 'Simple LR(k) grammars', *Comm ACM*, vol. 14, pp. 453–460.

Diller, A., 1988. *Compiling Functional Languages*, John Wiley and Sons, Ltd.

Fenton, N.E., Pfleeger, S.L. 1996. *Software Metrics: A Rigorous and Practical Approach*, International Thomson Computer Press.

Fischer, C.N., Leblanc, R.J., 1988. *Crafting a Compiler*, Benjamin Cummings.

Foster, J.M., 1968. 'A Syntax Improving Device', *Computer Journal*, vol. 11.

Glanville, R.S. and Graham Susan, L., 1978. 'A new method for compiler code generation', *Fifth Annual ACM Symposium on Principles of Programming Languages*.

Gries, D., 1971. *Compiler Construction for Digital Computers*; John Wiley and Sons.

Johnson, S.C., 1975. 'YACC – yet another compiler compiler', *Computing Science Technical Report 32*, AT&T Bell Laboratories, Murray Hill, N.J.

Jones, R. and Lins, R., 1996. *Garbage Collection: Algorithms for Automatic Dynamic Memory Management*, John Wiley and Sons, Chichester, England.

Kleene, S.C., 1956. 'Representation of events in nerve nets' in Shannon C. and McCarthy J., *Automata Studies*, Princeton University Press.

Knuth, D.E., 1965. 'On the translation of languages from left to right', *Information and Control*, vol. 8, pp. 607–639.

Knuth, D.E., 1968a. 'Semantics of Context-free languages', *Mathematical Systems Theory*, **2:2**, pp. 127–145.

Knuth, D.E., 1968b. *The Art of Computer Programming, volume 1, Fundamental Algorithms*, Addison Wesley.

Knuth, D.E., 1971. 'Topdown Syntax Analysis', *Acta Informatica*, vol. 1, pp. 79–110.

Lesk, M.E., 1975. 'Lex – a lexical analyser generator', *Computing Science Technical Report 39*, Bell Laboratories, NJ.

Levine, J.R., Mason, T. and Brown, D., 1992. *Lex and YACC* (2nd edn), O'Reilly and Associates.

Lindholm, T. and Yellin, F., 1996. *The Java Virtual Machine Specification*, Addison Wesley.

Loudon, K.C., 1997. *Compiler Construction: Principles and Practice*, PWS Publishing Ltd.

Lucas, P., 1961. 'The structure of formula translators', *Electronische Rechenanlagen*, vol. 3, pp. 159–166.

Meyer, J. and Downing, T., 1997. *Java Virtual Machine*, O'Reilly and Associates.

Naur, P., 1964. The Design of the GIER Algol Compiler, *Annual Review in Automatic Programmimg*, vol. 4, pp. 49–85.

Nori, K.V. et al., 1981. Pascal P implementation note, in Barron D.W., *Pascal and its Implementation*, J. Wiley.

Randell, B. and Russell, L.J., 1964. *Algol 60 Implementation*, Academic Press.

Schreiner, A.T. and Friedman, H.G., 1985. *Introduction to Compiler Construction with Unix*, Prentice Hall.

Stallman, R., 1994. Using and porting GNU CC, Gnu ftp distribution (prep.ai.mit.edu), Cambridge, MA, Free Software Foundation.

Terry, P.D., 1997. *Compilers and Compiler Generators: an Introduction with C++*, International Thomson Computer Press.

Ullmann, J., 1994. *Compiling in Modula-2*, Prentice Hall.

Watt, D.A., 1977. 'An extended attribute grammar for Pascal', *Report number 11*, Department of Computing, University of Glasgow.

Watt, D.A., 1993. *Programming Language Processors*, Prentice Hall.

Welsh, J. and Hay, A., 1986. *A Model Implementation of Standard Pascal*, Prentice Hall International.

Welsh, J., Sneeringer, W.J. and Hoare, C.A.R., 1977. 'Ambiguities and insecurities in Pascal', *Software – Practice and Experience*, vol. 7, pp. 685–696.

Wilhelm, R. and Maurer, D., 1995. *Compiler Design*, Addison-Wesley.

Wirth, N., 1971. 'The design of a Pascal compiler', *Software Practice and Experience*, vol. 1, pp. 309–333.

Wirth, N., 1996. *Compiler Construction*, Addison-Wesley.

Index